T0252405

iPhone Game Development

Paul Zirkle and Joe Hogue

O'REILLY®

Beijing · Cambridge · Farnham · Köln · Sebastopol · Tokyo

iPhone Game Development
by Paul Zirkle and Joe Hogue

Copyright © 2010 Paul Zirkle and Joe Hogue. All rights reserved.
Printed in the United States of America.

Published by O'Reilly Media, Inc., 1005 Gravenstein Highway North, Sebastopol, CA 95472.

O'Reilly books may be purchased for educational, business, or sales promotional use. Online editions are also available for most titles (*http://my.safaribooksonline.com*). For more information, contact our corporate/institutional sales department: 800-998-9938 or *corporate@oreilly.com*.

Editor: Andy Oram		**Indexer:** Lucie Haskins
Production Editor: Loranah Dimant		**Cover Designer:** Karen Montgomery
Copyeditor: Audrey Doyle		**Interior Designer:** David Futato
Proofreader: Loranah Dimant		**Illustrator:** Robert Romano

Printing History:
November 2009:   First Edition.

ISBN: 978-0-596-15985-6

[LSI]   [2011-12-16]

1323161259

Table of Contents

Preface

If you're reading this Preface, you might be trying to decide whether this book is right for you. So, we'll explain what we intend to cover and who we expect will get the most out of reading the book. But we'll start with why you should even listen to us.

The Authors

We're two programmers who have been buddies in the Los Angeles area for a long time and have been making mobile games since 2003. Between the two of us we have developed and ported close to a hundred titles for cell phones, including *Ninja Gaiden*, *Castlevania: Order of Shadows*, *Dance Dance Revolution: Mobius*, and *Contra 4*, among many, many others. Paul currently works for Konami, and occasionally gives lectures about game programming at USC. Joe works at EA and recently published a game for the iPhone. Paul wrote most of the theory, while Joe cooked up some great example projects.

Our Goal

We expect there is—scratch that—we *know* there is a lot of interest in the iPhone as a new game platform. The high-end hardware promises plenty of power and memory for graphics and content, while the unique touch screen and gyroscope interface pose an interesting challenge that encourages innovative game designs. Add to that the open market of the iTunes App Store, which promises easy entry for independent developers as well as accurate revenue tracking for serious publishers, and it's no surprise that the iPhone is making a huge splash in the mobile space.

Our goal was to write a book that can put iPhone game development in the reach of any programmer out there, in a format that suits both beginning and advanced game programmers.

This book is not a course on Objective-C, though it will contain a primer. This book is not an exhaustive study of the iPhone SDK, as we will use only the functionality needed to make our games. This book is not a five-year course on game programming technology. However, this book *is* the source for all you need to know not only to build the example games we have provided but also to build your own.

By the end of the book, you will have learned all of the core concepts of creating a game engine, and how to apply it to the iPhone. You will learn enough Objective-C to utilize the iPhone SDK to make a 2D game. You will have been introduced to OpenGL ES on the iPhone for making 3D games. And finally, you will be familiar with the certification process so that making the last plunge into the App Store is much less scary.

Prerequisites

To get the most out of this book, you will need to have some programming knowledge. The iPhone uses Objective-C, but most people are more familiar with C/C++ or Java, so the Objective-C primer in Chapter 1 will help familiarize you with the basics.

You will also need a Mac. The iPhone Software Development Kit (SDK) is available only for OS X, so a trip to the Apple store may be in your future if you are serious about developing for the iPhone. Fortunately, the base model Mac Mini has plenty of power to develop for the iPhone, and you can use your existing monitor and keyboard setup. Meanwhile, once you have a Mac, the Xcode Integrated Development Environment (IDE) is free. But we're getting ahead of ourselves.

The third requirement is not 100% necessary, but strongly recommended: an iPhone or iPod Touch. Although we use the term *iPhone* throughout the book, games made for the iPhone will also work on iPod Touch. Some people will undoubtedly try to create an iPhone game using only the iPhone Simulator. It may be possible to do this, and even get it placed into the App Store, but we strongly recommend that you develop and test on the device itself. After all, what good is a game you can't play yourself?

Beyond those three requirements, everything else you need you can either download or learn. We are working on useful classes and examples at *https://sourceforge.net/ projects/iphonegamebook/*, where you will also find the source code for all examples.

Audience

As we mentioned earlier, we expect you to have some basic programming knowledge. That aside, all kinds of programmers are interested in the iPhone. Developers of all levels are going to be reading up to try their skill.

You might not have any game programming experience and will need some basic theory on game engines and user-interface design. Or perhaps you have plenty of experience making video games on other platforms and just need to become familiar with the iPhone SDK and build process, along with some touch-screen concepts. You may also be interested in advanced topics, such as how to write portable code for cross-platform games and what middleware solutions currently exist. Either way, this book has got you covered.

Organization of This Book

Chapter 1, *Introduction to the iPhone*, gets you set up to build interfaces and write code in Objective-C, including logistics such as setting up a developer account with Apple.

Chapter 2, *Game Engine Anatomy*, introduces the elements of game logic and good design that will let you write a maintainable and enjoyable game application.

Chapter 3, *The Framework*, shows the code that will wrap your particular game implementation as well as critical classes we wrote to supplement the features provided by the Apple SDK.

Chapter 4, *2D Game Engine*, creates a complete four-level game based on the framework in Chapter 3. We start with 2D because both the game tasks and the coding complexity are much easier in 2D than in 3D. Basic movement, visual and audio effects, movement through game levels, and other elements of game programming are covered.

Chapter 5, *3D Games*, explains the more sophisticated tasks required to write a 3D game. Although the chapter uses the OpenGL library, its goal is not to explain 3D basics or OpenGL, but to give you the unique skills required to use them in game programming.

Chapter 6, *Considerations for Game Design*, wraps up the book with some large-scale considerations for advanced developers, and pointers to more resources, including useful libraries and middleware.

Appendix, *References*, points to useful sources of information, libraries, and products.

Conventions Used in This Book

The following typographical conventions are used in this book:

Italic
> Indicates new terms, URLs, filenames, and file extensions

`Constant width`
> Indicates variables, method names, and other code elements, as well as the contents of files

`Constant width bold`
> Highlights new code in an example

`Constant width italic`
> Shows text that should be replaced with user-supplied values

This icon signifies a tip, suggestion, or general note.

 This icon indicates a warning or caution.

Using Code Examples

This book is here to help you get your job done. In general, you may use the code in this book in your programs and documentation. You do not need to contact us for permission unless you're reproducing a significant portion of the code. For example, writing a program that uses several chunks of code from this book does not require permission. Selling or distributing a CD-ROM of examples from O'Reilly books *does* require permission. Answering a question by citing this book and quoting example code does not require permission. Incorporating a significant amount of example code from this book into your product's documentation *does* require permission.

We appreciate, but do not require, attribution. An attribution usually includes the title, author, publisher, and ISBN. For example: "*iPhone Game Development* by Paul Zirkle and Joe Hogue. Copyright 2010 Paul Zirkle and Joe Hogue, 978-0-596-15985-6."

If you feel your use of code examples falls outside fair use or the permission given here, feel free to contact us at *permissions@oreilly.com*.

We'd Like to Hear from You

Every example in this book has been tested, but occasionally you may encounter problems. Mistakes and oversights can occur and we will gratefully receive details of any that you find, as well as any suggestions you would like to make for future editions. You can contact the authors and editors at:

O'Reilly Media, Inc.
1005 Gravenstein Highway North
Sebastopol, CA 95472
800-998-9938 (in the United States or Canada)
707-829-0515 (international or local)
707-829-0104 (fax)

We have a web page for this book, where we list errata, examples, and any additional information. You can access this page at:

http://www.oreilly.com/catalog/9780596159856

To comment or ask technical questions about this book, send email to the following, quoting the book's ISBN number (9780596159856):

bookquestions@oreilly.com

For more information about our books, conferences, Resource Centers, and the O'Reilly Network, see our website at:

http://www.oreilly.com

Safari® Books Online

 Safari Books Online is an on-demand digital library that lets you easily search over 7,500 technology and creative reference books and videos to find the answers you need quickly.

With a subscription, you can read any page and watch any video from our library online. Read books on your cell phone and mobile devices. Access new titles before they are available for print, and get exclusive access to manuscripts in development and post feedback for the authors. Copy and paste code samples, organize your favorites, download chapters, bookmark key sections, create notes, print out pages, and benefit from tons of other time-saving features.

O'Reilly Media has uploaded this book to the Safari Books Online service. To have full digital access to this book and others on similar topics from O'Reilly and other publishers, sign up for free at *http://my.safaribooksonline.com*.

Acknowledgments

Thanks to Andy Oram, Marlowe Shaeffer, Isabel Kunkle, and the rest of the crew at O'Reilly. Special thanks to Erin Reynolds, for game art. Thanks to Brad O'Hearne, Jonathan Hohle, and Trina Gregory for technical reviews of this book. And thanks to all of the readers who left comments on Rough Cuts.

Paul would also like to thank his family, Amanda Joy and William "Nizor" Eiten.

CHAPTER 1

Introduction to the iPhone

The iPhone is one of the most distinctive game platforms currently available. The touch screen, integration with iTunes, programming in Objective-C, low development cost, and ease of publishing all make for a very strange but promising new development opportunity. As the newest kid on the block, the iPhone instantly captured a noticeable portion of the mobile phone market and inspired a wave of copycat devices by makers such as Motorola, Samsung, and LG.

As a programmer, you might not be impressed with sales figures and market shares, but you should be interested in the viability of the iPhone as a whole. If no one owns an iPhone, no one will buy the games you make for it. The good news is that even in the face of the 2009 economic downturn, iPhones continued to sell.

To get started with the iPhone, you'll need to get a free Apple developer account. Next you'll download the iPhone SDK on your Mac, which also contains the Xcode IDE and Interface Builder tool for laying out screens. (Apple doesn't provide a toolkit for Windows or any other non-Mac platform.) And because the iPhone API requires you to write in Objective-C, you will need to read a primer on the language if you do not already understand it. This chapter takes you step by step through all of these tasks.

Apple Developer Account and Downloading the SDK

The first step in setting up your iPhone development environment is to register an Apple developer account. Signing up for an account is free and gives you access to Apple's online documentation, tutorial videos, and the SDK download:

1. Go to *http://developer.apple.com/iphone/*.
2. Click the Register link, and then click Start Now. Choose the option to create a new Apple ID, or to log in using an Apple ID from an iTunes or App Store account.
3. Once you have registered, you can log in to the iPhone Dev Center.
4. Apple may already have emailed you a link to download the free SDK, or you may choose to download the SDK using the link from the website. Note that you should

not download Xcode separately because it is included within the SDK download package (and the version of Xcode that comes with the SDK may be newer than what is otherwise available).

5. Once downloaded, install the SDK, which will make Xcode and Interface Builder accessible to you in the */Developer/Applications* folder on your hard drive (you can also activate Spotlight and search for Xcode and Interface Builder to launch either application quickly).

The free developer account will allow you to build applications and run them in a simulator on your Mac. However, to load your application onto a phone, you will also need to sign up for the paid developer program. This requires a small annual fee, so even if you are a private developer, it won't hurt your wallet too much:

1. Go to *http://developer.apple.com/iphone/program/apply.html*.

2. You will have two options: Standard Program and Enterprise Program. If you are writing games for the general public, you probably do not want the Enterprise Program. If you read closely, you will notice the Enterprise Program is actually for creating applications that only you and your company will use internally. If you plan to create games that will be sold via the App Store, rest assured that the Standard Program is the correct choice for you.

3. Select Enroll Now and log in if necessary.

4. You now have another choice: enroll as an individual or as a company. If you choose Individual, you will not be able to add other programmers or quality assurance members to your account, which is necessary to distribute your application to others during the development and testing process. However, if you select Company, you will be required to provide detailed information about your company.

5. Continue through the website, selecting the appropriate information, until you arrive at a screen that says "Thank you for submitting your enrollment." Now you must wait for an email from Apple (which may take on the order of a month to arrive).

 Signing up for the paid developer program will also give you access to beta releases of future versions of the iPhone OS and SDK, but only during the times at which Apple chooses to make them available.

It is good to get your paid developer account enrollment going as soon as possible so that it will be available when you actually need it.

Application Bundles

When you build an application using Xcode, the end result is called an *application bundle*. In Mac OS X and the iPhone, an application bundle is a special type of directory that holds an executable file and the resources needed to run it. This includes an icon to represent the application, files with special information about the application, and any images or sounds the application uses.

 In the Finder, an application bundle simply appears as its application icon; right-click or Ctrl-click on it and select View Package Contents from the menu to see what's inside.

Although you can't do this on the iPhone, you can find iPhone applications in the iPhone Simulator. If you have the iPhone SDK installed, you can use Spotlight to search for the *MobileSafari.app* file. Show this file in the Finder (don't try to run it on your Mac), and view its package contents (some of which appears in the following list).

A typical iPhone application bundle might have the following structure:

Executable
>(Required.) This is the compiled code executable; it will typically have the same name as your application. In *MobileSafari.app*, this is the file named *MobileSafari*.

Info.plist
>(Required.) This is a collection of properties, in key-value pair form, that specifies important information about your application. Notable properties listed here are the display name of your application, the version number, and a unique ID number. These files use a binary format that can't be read in a text editor, but you can use the Property List Editor located in */Developer/Applications/Utilities* to view them.

icon.png
>(Required.) This is a 57 × 57 pixel icon used to represent your application on the iPhone's home screen. Glossy button effects will be added on top of this image automatically, so it should be flat-colored.

Various resources
>(Optional.) All common resource files, such as images, sounds, and binary data, used by your application will be placed in the same folder as the executable. The only subfolders present in an iPhone application bundle are for localized resources.

Localization folders
>(Optional.) If your application supports multiple languages, you may add subfolders to the bundle, which contain resources that cater to individual languages. The folder names will have a language name or an ISO language abbreviation followed by ".lproj"; for example, *English.lproj, French.lproj, German.lproj,* and *uk.lproj* would each contain resources specific to English, French, German, and UK English languages, respectively.

Settings.bundle
>(Optional.) You will create this file if you want your application to provide user preference options in the Settings application that comes with the iPhone.

Icon-Settings.png
(Optional.) If you added a *Settings.bundle* file, this image is used to represent the application in the Settings application. The image should be 29 × 29 pixels. However, if you do not add this image, the *Icon.png* image will be scaled and used automatically.

MainWindow.nib
(Optional.) Created by the Interface Builder application, *MainWindow.nib* contains code and resources necessary to draw your application as it starts up. More *.nib* files can be loaded after this one, but it will always be the first in memory.

Default.png
(Optional.) This image is displayed as the application is loading the *MainWindow.nib* file. It should be full screen, which is 480 × 320 pixels on the iPhone. If this image is close to what the user will see when the application is finished loading, the load process will appear to take less time.

iTunesArtwork
(Optional.) If you are distributing the application outside the App Store, this artwork is used to display your application when loading onto a handset using iTunes. More on this later.

As you will see in the next section, when you're creating your application, Xcode and Interface Builder will create most of these files for you.

Xcode and Interface Builder

If you are unfamiliar with Xcode, you may be reluctant to learn a new IDE at first. However, the way iPhone development works, you pretty much have to. Fortunately, once you get used to it, you'll see that Xcode is pretty good at what it does. It has all the features you would expect from an industry-standard IDE: it jumps to the line of compile errors, auto-completes complicated API methods, and has integrated SDK references.

And it gets better: Xcode supports on-device debugging, a full-featured iPhone Simulator, useful project wizards, refactoring tools, and even direct integration with Subversion revision control repositories.

An Xcode project contains all the code, resources, certificates, and configurations you need to create an iPhone application. To get acquainted with the environment, open your Xcode IDE and follow these steps to create a typical "Hello World" application:

1. Open Xcode.
2. Select File→New Project.
3. In the dialog that opens, select iPhone OS, then View-Based Application (see Figure 1-1), and click Choose.
4. Name the project "HelloWorld" and click Save.

5. At this point, you can build and run (click the Build and Go icon in the toolbar). The HelloWorld application shows only a blank gray screen when run in the Simulator, as shown in Figure 1-2.

Figure 1-1. Selecting View-Based Application

Not very interesting yet, is it? Before we go on to make this a proper "Hello World" application, here is a quick rundown of the files that were generated when you created the project:

HelloWorldAppDelegate.m, HelloWorldAppDelegate.h
The class held in these files can be considered the main code entry point of the application. The *app delegate* controls the main window and main View Controller, and is responsible for setting them up for display.

HelloWorldViewController.m, HelloWorldViewController.h
This class in these files holds the main view, and is responsible for showing the horribly uninteresting gray screen. We will be editing it to say "Hello World" soon.

Figure 1-2. Empty application in the Simulator

MainWindow.xib

> This Interface Builder file results in a *.nib* file that is placed in your application bundle when the project is compiled. When loaded, it creates the app delegate, and loads the main window and View Controller.

HelloWorldViewController.xib

> This file lays out the design for the `HelloWorldViewController`'s view.

 NIB stands for NeXTSTEP Interface Builder, and XIB stands for Xcode Interface Builder. NIB files are dense compiled binary files; XIB files are human-readable XML files. As we mentioned earlier, Xcode compiles XIB files into NIB files. The XIB format was created specifically to solve issues with merging NIB files in projects under source control, since you can diff XML files more easily than binary files.

Now we need to draw the "Hello World" text. We can go about this in several ways:

- Add a Cocoa `UILabel` by writing code directly in *HelloWorldViewController.m*.
- Add a Cocoa `UILabel` in Interface Builder to *HelloWorldViewController.xib*.
- Define a subclass of `UIView`, and use a Quartz font rendering in `drawRect`.
- Create a texture-mapped font in OpenGL ES to render with.

Let's start with the first method: adding a `UILabel` by writing code in *HelloWorldView-Controller.m*. A stub method named `viewDidLoad` is already inside *HelloWorldView-Controller.m*, which is a good place to add our code. This method will be called after *.nib* file loading is done, but before rendering begins:

1. Replace the `viewDidLoad` function in *HelloWorldViewController.m* with the following (this function is commented out by default, so be sure to remove the /* that precedes it and the */ that follows it):

```
- (void) viewDidLoad {
    [super viewDidLoad];
    //draw "Hello World" using Cocoa UIKit.
    //grab the screen dimensions
    int w = self.view.frame.size.width;
    int h = self.view.frame.size.height;

    //create a text label: the size 100,50 here is arbitrary
    // but it must be large enough to fit the "Hello World" text.
    UILabel* label = [[UILabel alloc] initWithFrame:CGRectMake(0, 0, 100, 50)];
    //put the label at the center of the screen
    label.center = CGPointMake(w/2, h/2);
    //align the text to the center of the label (default is left)
    label.textAlignment = UITextAlignmentCenter;
    //don't draw the label's background (default is white)
    label.backgroundColor = [UIColor clearColor];
    label.text = @"Hello world!";
    //add label to our view, so that it can be rendered
    [self.view addSubview:label];
    //since we alloc'd label in this method we need to release label here
    [label release];
}
```

2. Build and run the project (if you haven't quit the Simulator from its previous run, you'll be prompted to stop it). The app should now display your text (see Figure 1-3).

Figure 1-3. "Hello world!" text shown

Now let's go over the second method, adding a `UILabel` to *HelloWorldViewControl-ler.xib* using Interface Builder. You must undo your changes if you followed the preceding example:

1. Open the *HelloWorldViewController.xib* file in Interface Builder by double-clicking it from the list of project files in Xcode.
2. Double-click the View object to begin editing it (Figure 1-4).

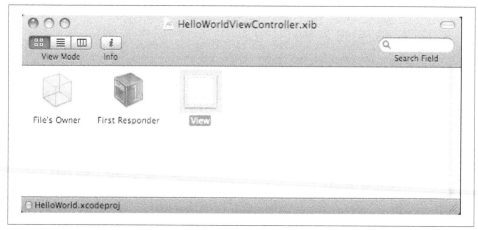

Figure 1-4. Double-clicking the View object to edit the file

3. Find the Label object in the Library panel (open the panel by selecting Tools→Library Panel, if it is not already open). See Figure 1-5.
4. Drag the label into the View editing window, as shown in Figure 1-6.
5. Double-click the new label and edit the text to say "Hello World". You can also edit it from the Attributes Inspector (Tools→Attributes Inspector).
6. In the Label Size Inspector (Tools→Size Inspector), click both of the Placement buttons to center the label horizontally and vertically, as shown in Figure 1-7.
7. Save the *.xib* file and return to Xcode. Building the application will update the *.nib* file, which will cause the changes to appear when the application is run, as shown in Figure 1-8.
8. When the *.nib* file is loaded, it creates and displays the `UILabel`. If our code needs access to read or modify the created label, we can link it to an `IBOutlet` in our code. In *HelloWorldViewController.h*, replace the stub definition of `HelloWorldViewCon troller` with the following:

```
@interface HelloWorldViewController : UIViewController {
    IBOutlet UILabel* myLabel;
}
```

An IBOutlet is a code tag that enables Interface Builder to recognize possible handles in code that can be linked to.

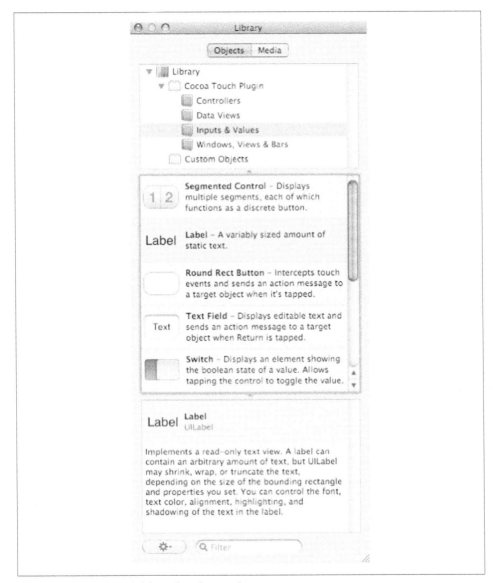

Figure 1-5. Selecting Label from the Objects Library

9. To link the *.nib*'s label to the outlet, open *HelloWorldViewController.xib* in Interface Builder and open the Connections Inspector (Tools→Connections Inspector). Then, click to select the label, drag the label's New Referencing Outlet to the File's Owner object, release, and click on the "myLabel" text that shows up in the

Figure 1-6. Adding a new label to the view

pop-up menu (see Figures 1-9 through 1-11). Because we set the Referencing Outlet, the two objects will be linked together when the *.nib* is loaded. Specifically, when *HelloWorldViewController.nib* is loaded in the application, it will know to set the variable myLabel to point at the UILabel we just linked to.

10. Save *HelloWorldViewController.xib* and quit Interface Builder.

Now our code has access to the label through myLabel. This linking process is used frequently in Interface Builder to specify outlets, actions, delegates, and data sources. Any interaction between visible elements of the interface and your code is made via Interface Builder links.

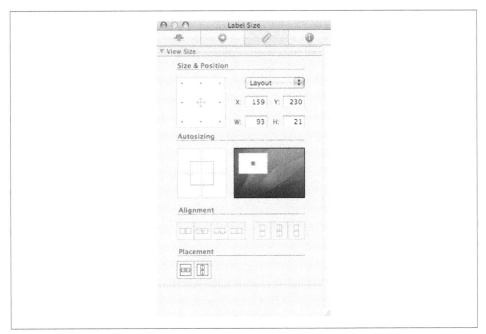

Figure 1-7. Modifying the Label object properties

Figure 1-8. "Hello World!" text with Label object

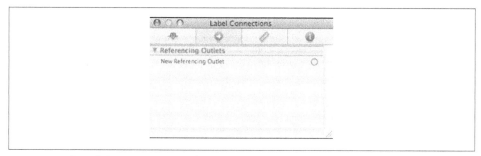

Figure 1-9. The Label Connections window

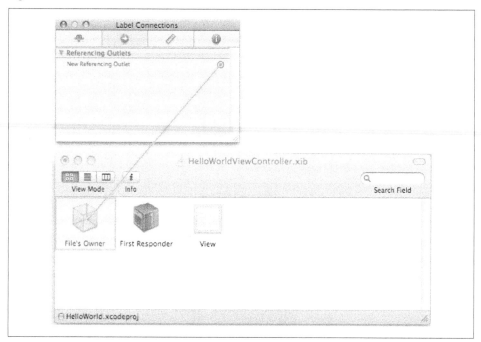

Figure 1-10. Clicking and dragging from New Referencing Outlet to File's Owner

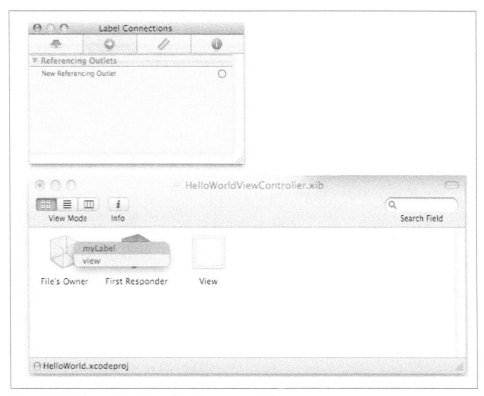

Figure 1-11. Selecting "myLabel" from the pop-up window

Views and Controllers

The UIView class represents a View object in the iPhone SDK. Views are visible rectangular portions of the screen that handle drawing and animation, event handling, and subview management. If you look at the iPod application that comes with your iPhone, you'll see that the navigation bar at the top, the tab bar at the bottom, and the content area in the middle are three separate views.

When creating a view-based application in the New Project Wizard, start with a single View Controller and a single View. You may want more Views as your application becomes more complex. For example, you may have one View for your game, another for a Main menu, one for a Settings screen, and another for an online High Score screen.

If your Views share a lot of the same code, it makes sense to add those Views to the same View Controller, along with the shared code. In the preceding example, we may want to put the Main menu and the Settings in the same View Controller, but put the main Game state and High Score screen each in their own View Controller. Nothing is stopping us from putting them all in one View Controller, or using a different View Controller for each one; it's purely an organizational consideration.

Adding a new View and View Controller to an existing window

Follow these steps to add a new View and View Controller to an existing window:

1. In Xcode, create a new class that extends `UIViewController`. We are calling ours `TestViewController`.

2. Create a new XIB file by selecting File→New File and choosing View XIB from the User Interfaces section, as shown in Figure 1-12.

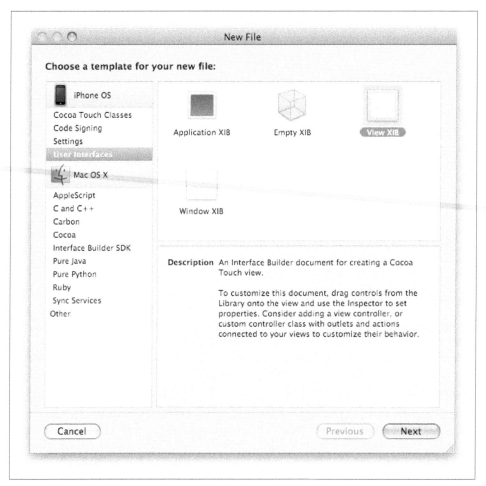

Figure 1-12. Adding a new View XIB file

3. In Interface Builder, select the File's Owner icon. In the Identity Inspector, set the Class Identity to TestViewController. If the Identity Inspector window is not open, you can access it from Tools→Identity Inspector. See Figure 1-13.

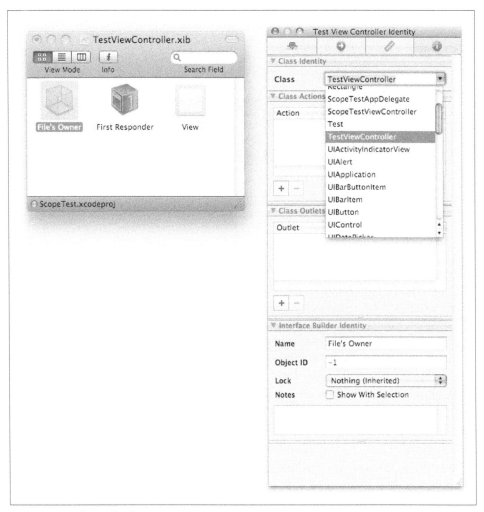

Figure 1-13. Editing the class name

4. Set the View's Referencing Outlet to the File's Owner view, the same way we did in the Hello World example earlier (Figure 1-14).

5. Add a `TestViewController` instance to your code and label it as an `IBOutlet`. We are putting it in the app delegate class, `TestAppDelegate`. In *TestAppDelegate.h*, the new code will look like this:

```
IBOutlet TestViewController* testViewController;
```

6. Edit your main window's XIB file and add a `ViewController` object by dragging it from the Library window into the *MainWindow.xib* window. You can find the ViewController object in the Library under Library→Cocoa Touch Plugin→Controllers, as shown in Figures 1-15 and 1-16.

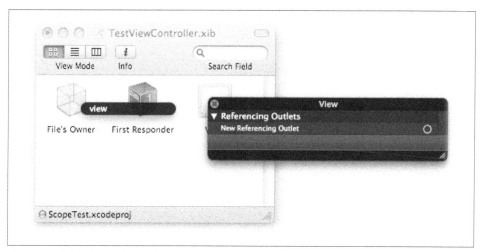

Figure 1-14. Linking to the File's Owner object

7. Edit this object to change the name of the class and the NIB to load to "TestView-Controller". Do this by selecting the `ViewController` object in the *Main-Window.xib* window and editing the class name in the Identity Inspector window. Next, select the Attributes button in the same window to switch it from the Identity Inspector to the Attributes Inspector. Finally, edit the NIB name in the Attributes Inspector (Figures 1-17 and 1-18).

8. Link this object's Referencing Outlet to the `IBOutlet` in `TestAppDelegate` that we created earlier: `testViewController`. See Figure 1-19.

9. Use the following code to add the `View` object to the `Window` object before it can be displayed:

```
[window addSubview:testViewController.view];
```

10. Once the `View` object has been added to the `Window` object, activate it by calling:

```
[window bringSubviewToFront: testViewController.view];
```

Figure 1-15. Adding a View Controller from the Library

Figure 1-16. Modifying the ViewController object

Note that only one View can be active at any time. Calling bringSubviewToFront will remove the currently active View from the responder chain. It will not show up on the foreground or receive input events until you call bringSubviewToFront on it again.

Adding a new View to an existing View Controller

Follow these steps to add a new View to an existing View Controller:

1. Open the View Controller's *.h* file in Xcode and add an IBOutlet UIView pointer for the new View. Ours is named secondView. The code will look like this:

   ```
   IBOutlet UIView* secondView;
   ```

2. In Interface Builder, open the View Controller's XIB file window and add a UIView object from the Library. You can find UIView under Library→Cocoa Touch Plugin→Windows, Views & Bars, as shown in Figure 1-20.

3. Set the UIView's Referencing Outlet to the IBOutlet you created earlier, secondView.

4. For organizational purposes, you may wish to name the UIView object in the View Controller's XIB file window.

5. To switch to the new View, somewhere in the View Controller, call this:

   ```
   self.view = secondView;
   ```

Since we are overwriting the View Controller's view property here, we will want to make sure we have another reference to the old View in case we want to switch back to it. We typically put each UIView into its own IBOutlet, and additionally assign the initial startup UIView into the view property. You can have more than one Reference Outlet for any UIView, so the initial View will have outlets named initialView and view.

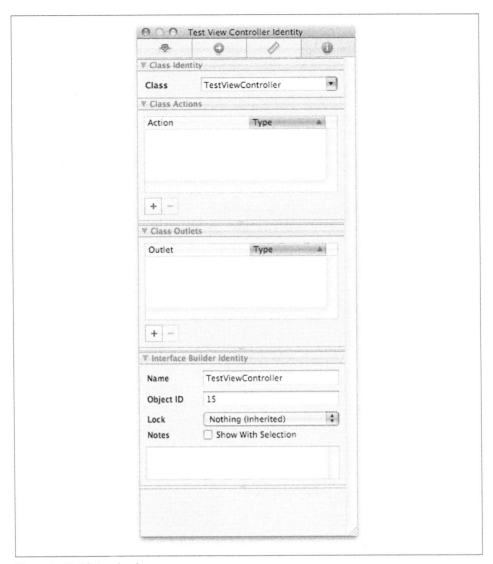

Figure 1-17. Editing the class name

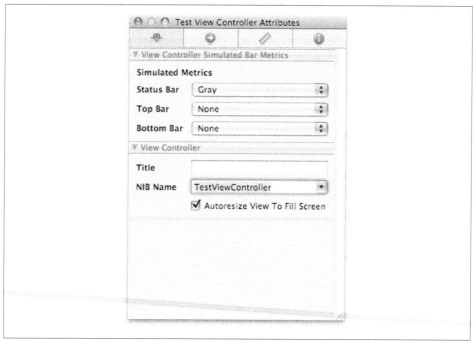

Figure 1-18. Editing the NIB name

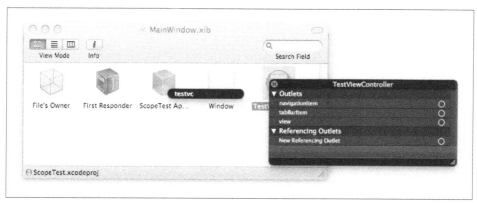

Figure 1-19. Linking to TestViewController

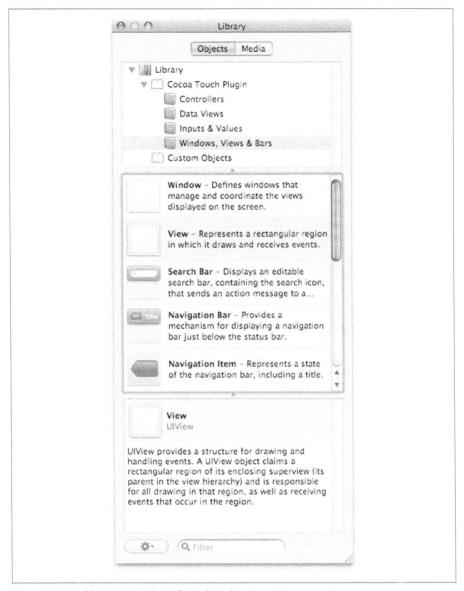

Figure 1-20. Adding a View object from the Library

Proxy objects

Objects inside the NIB have access to properties inside the File's Owner class. To access properties outside the NIB, you need to use `Proxy` objects. The `Proxy` has an associated class name and proxy name, but it does not create an instance of the associated class. You have to pass in a `Proxy` instance yourself when initializing the NIB file:

```
//Instead of auto-loading the view controller from the main window NIB,
// load it manually so that we can set up the proxy object.
viewController = [[HelloWorldViewController alloc] init];
//We want viewController to be able to access IBActions in
// HelloWorldViewController and in HelloWorldAppDelegate.
// The File's Owner will be the View Controller,
// and the Proxy named AppDelegate will be the app delegate [self].
NSDictionary*    proxies = [NSDictionary
                    dictionaryWithObject:self forKey:@"AppDelegate"];
                    //link proxy object name to app delegate instance
NSDictionary*    options = [NSDictionary
                    dictionaryWithObject:proxies
                    forKey:UINibProxiedObjectsKey];
                    //set up options with our proxy
[[NSBundle mainBundle] loadNibNamed:@"HelloWorldViewController"
                    owner:viewController options:options];
```

Loading Devices

Assuming you have finished the process of signing up for the paid developer program, you are now authorized to load applications such as the "Hello World" example onto an iPhone using Xcode. However, you have to jump through a couple more hoops before you can do this.

Since the iPhone is a secured platform, a lot of bookkeeping is required before you can execute your code on the device. You have to sign builds, Apple has to trust your signature, and the device you are loading has to be provisioned for self-signed applications.

You manage signatures, certificates, and provisioning profiles through the online Program Portal on Apple's website. Once you are a paid developer, you can find it at *http://developer.apple.com/iphone/manage/overview/index.action*.

The portal has step-by-step guides for each section—generating Certificate Signing Requests (CSRs), creating a distribution profile, adding a device ID, and so on. However, this can be a complex process, so we will go over the general concepts.

Certificates and Profiles

To publish your application to a phone or to the App Store, you need two signed profiles. One is a developer profile, which you use while developing and testing your app. The other is a distribution profile, which you use when sending your finished application off to the App Store to be published. In a corporate setting, the lead programmer might keep track of the developer profile, whereas the production manager might keep track of the distribution profile.

To create these profiles, you need to generate a certificate that has a public and private key. Apple has to sign the certificate for it to be valid, so first you must use Keychain Access on your Mac to create what is called a Certificate Submission Request, which gets sent to Apple's developer program. When Apple has reviewed and approved your request, you can download the certificate from the Apple Developer Portal website.

Once you have the signed certificate, you will need an Application Identifier (App ID), a Unique Device Identifier (UDID), and the WWDR certificate.

App ID

The App ID is generated on the Developer Portal to be used in a profile and in your application bundle. An App ID looks like this: com.*YourGameCo*.*YourAwesomeGameName*. This is called reverse domain notation, and Java and C# programmers may be familiar with it as the format that package names use in those languages.

If you will be making multiple applications, you can use a wildcard format so that the same developer can use one App ID for multiple applications. A wildcard App ID looks like this: com.*YourGameCo*.*.

When listed in the Developer Portal, the ID may have 10 alphanumeric characters appended to the front. These are for Apple's internal use and you can ignore them.

After creating an App ID on the Developer Portal, you must open the *Info.plist* file in your application bundle and replace the default value of the bundle identifier key with your App ID. If you used a wildcard when creating the App ID on the Portal, you should also replace the asterisk (*) with the name of your game when updating the *Info.plist* file.

UDID

The UDID is a 40-character hex string that you can obtain from the iPhone device you wish to load by attaching it to your Mac and running iTunes or the Xcode Organizer window.

 The UDID is used only for the developer profile and is not useful for the distribution profile.

WWDR certificate

Apple's World Wide Developer Relations (WWDR) certificate is available from Apple at *http://developer.apple.com/certificationauthority/AppleWWDRCA.cer*. Download and install the certificate so that you can use it to certify builds. The WWDR certificate links your development certificate to Apple, completing the trust chain for your application.

Installing the profile

Once you have these three items, you can download a provisioning profile from the Developer Portal. This file will have a *.mobileprovision* file extension. Once you download this file, double-click it to install the profile. It should load into Xcode's Organizer and show up there when you connect your iPhone to your computer. Make sure the profile is listed in the device's installed profiles.

Keep in mind that an application is limited to the devices listed in its developer profile.

Xcode Configuration

Once you have all the certificates, keys, and profiles installed, you are ready to set up Xcode to compile an application that will run on your iPhone.

Set the code signing profile in Project→Edit Project Settings→Build→Code Signing Identity→Any iPhone OS Device. See Figure 1-21.

If your provisioning profile does not show up in the drop-down list, you are missing some part of the certificate chain:

- Private key
- Signing certificate
- WWDR certificate
- Provisioning profile

Change the bundle identifier to match the App ID name in the provisioning profile. Select the Build Clean menu option after any *Info.plist* changes; otherwise, the changes will not be reflected in the build (see Figure 1-22).

Set Xcode to build for the device, as shown in Figure 1-23.

If everything goes smoothly, you should be able to build and run the application on the device. Xcode will install your app on the device during the build process.

If something goes wrong, you won't see any helpful error messages; you will see "ApplicationVerificationFailed," which could mean anything went wrong. Here is a list of some common issues that could be the source of an error:

The bundle identifier contains typos or whitespace
    The bundle identifier must match the App ID. You must select Build→Clean after modifying the bundle identifier.

Part of the certificate chain is missing
    The WWDR certificate is easy to miss.

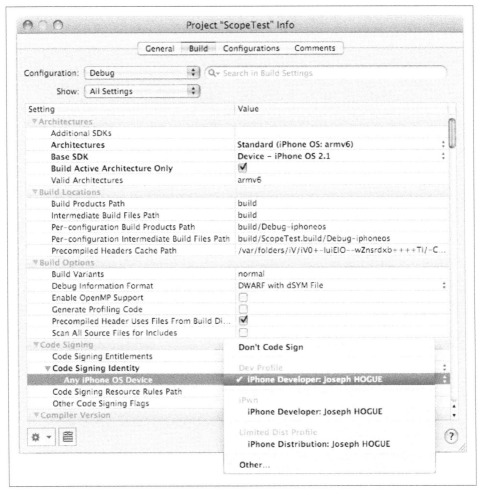

Figure 1-21. Setting the code signing profile

Your certificate has expired

> If everything has been working fine and you suddenly encounter a problem as you get closer to your deadline, you may have an expired certificate.

Sometimes just rebooting the iPhone and reconnecting it will get things back on track.

Objective-C Primer

The iPhone API uses the Objective-C language. Objective-C is an application of principles from Smalltalk to the C language. The idea was to combine the power of the C language, which is an industry standard, with the object-oriented programming approach of the Smalltalk language. The result is a language that might be confusing at first, but it makes sense once you understand a few concepts.

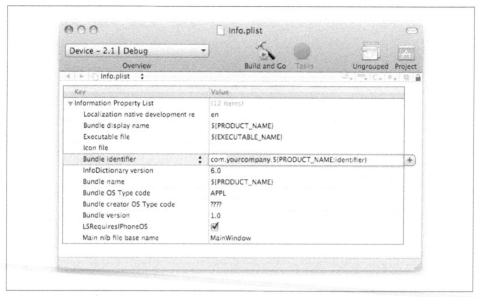

Figure 1-22. Editing the App ID in Info.plist

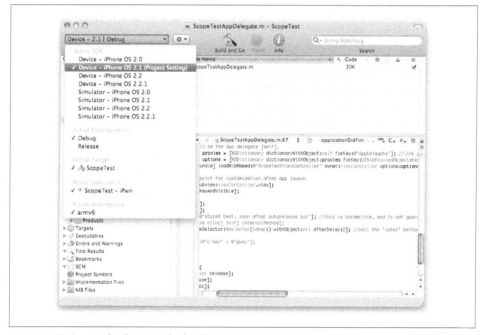

Figure 1-23. Setting the device as the build target

The first thing to know is that Objective-C is a strict superset of C. Anything that you can write in C you can compile using the Objective-C compiler. C-style structs, function calls, memory allocation, and pointers are all available. However, in addition to all of the normal C language syntax, Objective-C adds some of its own features as well, such as thread synchronization, try-catch blocks, and garbage collection. The primary improvement provided (and the reason for the language) is an object-oriented structure.

Classes

Classes in Objective-C are conceptually very similar to Java and C++ classes. A *class* is an object that contains data, called *member variables*, and functions, called *methods*. Just like in Java and C++, classes are usually defined before they can be used (although in Objective-C, they can also be created at runtime). You define a class using the @interface keyword. Similar to C++, Objective-C classes should be defined in an *.h* file, while their implementations should be separated into an *.m* file. Also as with C++, you may use the @public or @private keyword to denote the level of syntax protection of the following lines. Objective-C is different from C++ or Java, however, in that it defines its methods outside the curly braces of the class. The methods are associated to the previous class and terminated by an @end keyword.

The following code creates a class named Animal:

```
@interface Animal
{
    // Member Variables go here
@private
    int foo;
}
    // class Methods go here, outside the braces
    - (int) bar: (double) input1;
@end
```

Notice the interesting way methods are defined: they begin with a - for normal functions (or a + for class methods, which we will discuss shortly), followed by the return type of the function in parentheses and the name of the function. If the function has parameters, each is written with a parameter description followed by a colon, the parameter type in parentheses, and the parameter name (except for the first parameter, which uses the function name instead of a parameter name).

Here is the same class in C++; note the semicolon required at the end:

```
class Animal
{
    // Member Variables and Methods go here
private:
    int foo;
public:
    int bar( double input1 );
};
```

Once more for Java:

```
class Animal
{
    // Member Variables and Methods go here
    private int foo;
    public int bar( double input1 ) {}
}
```

All three languages can use // for single-line comments.

And just as in Java and C++, classes can *extend* or *inherit* other classes. A common base class that almost all Objective-C classes inherit from is NSObject, which we will explain later. The syntax for inheritance is similar to C++, except that public and private keywords are not used in front of the parent class:

```
@interface Animal : NSObject
{

}
    //Objective-C inheritance
@end

class Animal : public NSObject
{
    //C++ inheritance
};

class Animal extends NSObject
{
    //Java inheritance
}
```

It is important to note that just like Java Objective-C cannot inherit from multiple classes. Say you want to create a class Animal that inherits NSObject, but also inherits a class GameEventListener, which allows it to respond to special events in your game. In C++, you could define GameEventListener as an abstract base class and inherit from both. However, in Java, you would have to define GameEventListener as an interface class, and in Objective-C, you would define it as @protocol. A protocol in Objective-C is similar to an abstract base class in C++, except that it must be absolutely virtual. It cannot have any member variables or method implementations. Just like interfaces in Java, a class in Objective-C may implement as many protocols as necessary.

Here is the implementation in C++:

```
class GameEventListener
{
    // Member Variables, Methods and Virtual Methods go here
private:
    bool active;
public:
    bool isListening(); //returns true if active is true
    virtual void handleEvent( int event ) = 0;
};
```

```
class Animal : public NSObject, public GameEventListener
{
    // Member Variables and Methods, and Override Methods go here
    // any pure virtual functions from GameEventListener must be implemented
private:
    int foo;

public:
    int bar( double input1 );
    void handleEvent( int event );
    // isListening() already implemented, no need to override
};
```

Here is the same implementation in Java:

```
interface GameEventListener
{
    // interfaces may not contain Member Variables
    // Method definitions go here, they cannot be implemented yet
    public bool isListening( );
    public void handleEvent( int event );
}

class Animal extends NSObject implements GameEventListener
{
    // Member Variables, Methods and Override Methods go here
    private int foo;
    private bool active; //must be defined here

    public int bar( double input1 ) {}
    public bool isListening( ) {}
    public void handleEvent( int event ) {}
}
```

The Java interface class is called a protocol class in Objective-C, so we define it using @protocol:

```
@protocol GameEventListener
    // protocols may not contain Member Variables, no curly braces
    // Method definitions go here, they cannot be implemented yet
    - (BOOL) isListening;
    - (void) handleEvent: (int) event;
@end

@interface Animal : NSObject <GameEventListener>
{
    // Member Variables go here
@private
    int foo;
    BOOL active;
}


    // Methods and Override Methods go here
    - (int) bar: (double) input1;
```

```
    - (BOOL) isListening;
    - (void) handleEvent: (int) event;
@end
```

 Programmers who are experienced in using template classes in C++ or generics in Java may get confused here. Although the syntax for using protocols in Objective-C looks like the syntax for templates in C++ and generics in Java, it is not the same thing.

As we mentioned earlier, function implementations are separated into .*m* files. The C++ implementation of the example would look like this:

```
bool GameEventListener::isListening()
{
    return active;
}

void Animal::bar( double input1 )
{
    //do something with input1
}

void Animal::handleEvent( int event )
{
    //do something with event
}
```

And the Objective-C implementation would look like this:

```
@implementation Animal

@synthesize foo;

- (void) bar: (double) input1
{
    //do something with input 1
}

- (BOOL) isListening
{
    return self.active;
}

- (void) handleEvent: (int) event
{
    //do something with event
}

@end
```

Instantiation

Once you have defined a class, you will want to create an instance of it.

In both C++ and Java, the instance would look like this:

```
Animal* beaver = new Animal();
```

While Objective-C would use this:

```
Animal* beaver = [Animal alloc];
```

Messaging

The use of those brackets around the call to alloc is known as *messaging*, one of the interesting features of Objective-C. It is basically the way you call functions on Objective-C objects. Although the syntax may be new, the concept is the same as a function call in C++ or Java. The preceding example calls the new function on the Animal class, which will return a newly allocated instance of that class.

Predictably, you could now call functions on that object, like so:

```
BOOL listening = [beaver isListening];
```

In C++, the preceding code would look like this:

```
bool listening = beaver->isListening();
```

And in Java, it would look like this:

```
boolean listening = beaver.isListening();
```

Sending parameters is also possible. Parameters are separated by colons:

```
[beaver handleEvent: EVT_EXAMPLE ];
```

In C++, the preceding code would look like this:

```
beaver->handleEvent( EVT_EXAMPLE );
```

And again in Java:

```
beaver.handleEvent( EVT_EXAMPLE );
```

One of the additions of messaging is keywords. Each parameter after the first is preceded by a keyword. If the Animal class also had a function called findFood that expected an amount of food to find and a flag to indicate only vegetables were allowed, you might see this:

```
[beaver findFood: 50 vegetablesOnly: true];
```

The same function in C++ would look like this:

```
beaver->findFood(50, true);
```

Although this makes function calls use more room on the screen, it also attempts to make reading them easier. You do not need to look up the function definition or rely on an IDE's code completion feature to understand the nature of the values passed in.

You can also nest messages by inserting another set of brackets where a parameter would go. If the Animal class had a function BOOL -isVegetarian, you might see this:

```
[beaver findFood: 50 vegetablesOnly: [beaver isVegetarian]];
```

In C++, it would look like this:

```
beaver->findFood(50, beaver->isVegetarian());
```

 The Objective-C equivalent to a *const* or *factory* method in C++ or Java is to use + in front of the method name in the @interface section. This allows you to call the function on the class itself without the need for an instance of the class.

For example:

```
@interface Animal
    + (BOOL) canAnimalsTalk;
@end
```

can be called this way:

```
[Animal canAnimalsTalk];
```

These are called class methods in Objective-C, since they are called directly on the class itself instead of an instance of the class. Functions declared this way cannot make use of the class's member variables.

Member Variables

Objective-C provides a number of ways to access class member variables. The first way uses messaging, where the name of the function is the same as the name of the member variable being accessed. This is called an *accessor* function, and it would be similar to writing get and set functions in C++ or Java. The functions are created automatically when you use the @synthesize keyword in the @implementation section of the class and @property when defining it in the *.h* file.

The usage syntax looks like this:

```
int example = [beaver foo]; //returns the value of int foo

[beaver setFoo:10]; //sets the value of int foo to 10
```

Notice that the name of the automatically generated setter method is set followed by the variable's name with the first character in uppercase. You can also use dot notation for the same purpose, like so:

```
int example = beaver.foo; //returns the value of int foo

beaver.foo = 10; //sets the value of int foo to 10
```

Just like the this keyword in C++ and Java, the self keyword is available inside Objective-C class methods.

Memory Management

Since Objective-C is a superset of C, all of the rules regarding malloc and free still apply. On the iPhone, there is no Garbage Collector that takes care of all objects for you, like the one in Java does, so it is possible to have memory leaks if allocated memory is not properly deallocated.

However, Objective-C does implement a reference counter inside the base class NSObject. Therefore, any class that inherits from NSObject (and most will) has the same reference counting functionality built-in. Specifically, the copy, new, retain, release, autorelease, and alloc methods provided by NSObject are what get the job done.

Whenever an NSObject subclass instance is created using the alloc method or any function with new or copy at the beginning of its name, it will be created with a reference count of 1. You can use the retain function to increment the value by one, and the release and autorelease functions to decrement the value by one. Once the reference value has reached 0, the object will be removed from memory.

If you call retain on an object, you will leak memory if you do not also call release or autorelease on that object because the reference count will never reach 0.

Constructors and Destructors

Like C++, Objective-C classes support the concept of constructor and destructor functions, but with some slight variation. When an object is allocated, the programmer must call the initialization function manually. By default, initialization functions are named init.

The following code is typical of Objective-C:

```
Animal* beaver = [[Animal alloc] init];
```

When an Objective-C class is destroyed from memory, its dealloc function will be called, similar to a destructor. If you overload the dealloc function in your class, you must also call the dealloc method of the superclass or it may leak memory:

```
-(void) dealloc {
    //perform destructor code here
    [super dealloc];
}
```

Interface Builder Integration

Because Objective-C and Interface Builder are used together for iPhone apps, two macros have been included to allow you to link Objective-C code to Interface Builder views: IBOutlet and IBAction.

By putting IBOutlet in front of UI variables and IBAction in front of class methods, you allow Interface Builder to know what variables and functions your code has made available for its use:

```
@interface myWindow
{
IBOutlet UIImageView *backgroundImage;
IBOutlet UIWindow *window;
IBOutlet UISwitch*soundToggle;
}
- (IBAction) playgame;
- (IBAction) toggleSound:(id) sender;
- (IBAction) handleEvent:(id) sender forEvent:(UIEvent*) event;
@end
```

At compile time, IBAction is replaced with void, and IBOutlet is simply removed. They are used only to determine which methods and variables show up in Interface Builder and have no runtime effect.

Mixed C++ and Objective-C

Because Objective-C is a superset of the C language, you can write portions of your code entirely in C. But the Objective-C compiler also allows you to use C++ in your projects. It is possible to use C, C++, and Objective-C syntax in the same file. Files that contain C++ implementations should use the extension *.mm* instead of *.m*.

Conclusion

This chapter provided you with a basic understanding of the Objective-C language and the procedures necessary to write, compile, and run code on the iPhone. We encourage you to read as many tutorials as necessary to round out your knowledge of the language and API. Documents at *http://developer.apple.com* are particularly helpful, and access is free with your Apple developer account.

However, games can be very complicated applications, and without an understanding of the theory behind game programming, game development will be a very challenging task. If you are new to game programming, reading the next chapter thoroughly before attempting to create your game will benefit you greatly.

CHAPTER 2

Game Engine Anatomy

To solve the large problem of how to create a game on the iPhone, we first need to solve a series of smaller problems such as how to display graphics and play sounds. These are problems associated with building parts of a game engine. And just like the human body, each part of a game engine is different but vital. Thus begins our chapter on game engine anatomy. We will discuss each major part of a game engine, including the application framework, state machine, graphics engine, physics engine, audio engine, player input, and game logic.

Writing a serious game is a big task that involves a lot of code. It is important to design that code in an organized fashion from the start, rather than adding bits and pieces over time. When building a house, an architect creates blueprints for the whole house, which the contractors then build. However, many programmers who are new to game programming build one part of the "house" from a tutorial, and add each "room" piece by piece as they learn. It's no surprise when the end result is bad.

Figure 2-1 shows the structure of a game engine that works well for most games. By understanding all of the parts of a game engine and how they work together, we can design the whole game at the start, and build our application the "Right Way." In the following sections, we'll cover each part of Figure 2-1:

- Application framework
- Game state manager
- Graphics engine

Application Framework

The application framework consists of code necessary to get an application started, including creating an instance of the application and initializing the rest of the subsystems. Our code first creates a Framework class when our application starts and, in turn, will be in charge of creating and destroying the state machine, graphics engine, and

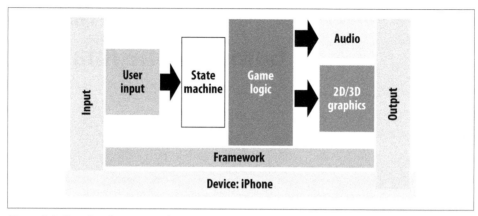

Figure 2-1. Functional structure of a game engine

audio engine. If our game is complex enough to require a physics engine, the framework will manage that as well.

The framework should take care of the peculiarities of the platform we are working on, including handling any system events (such as Shut Down or Sleep), and managing the loading and unloading of resources so that the rest of the code can focus only on the game.

Main Loop

The framework will provide the main loop that is the driving force behind any interactive program; on each iteration of the loop, the program will check for and handle incoming events, run updates on the game logic, and draw to the screen as necessary (see Figure 2-2).

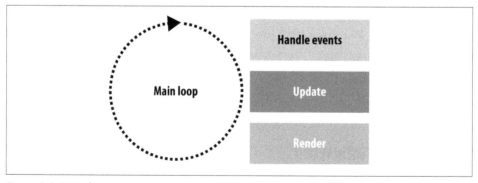

Figure 2-2. Main loop sequence

Exactly how the main loop is implemented depends on the system you are using. For a basic console application, it could be as simple as a while loop that calls each function:

```
    while( !finished ) {
        handle_events();
        update();
        render();
        sleep(20);
    }
```

Notice the sleep function here. It puts the code to sleep for some small period each loop so that it does not form a solid loop that would constantly suck up all of the time on the CPU.

Some systems don't want user code to write loops like that at all; instead, they use a callback system that forces the programmer to release the CPU regularly. This way, when the application starts, the programmer registers some functions to be called back during each loop:

```
    void main(void) {
        OS_register_event_handler( myEventHandler );
        OS_register_update_function( myUpdate );
        OS_register_render_function( myRender );
    }
```

Once the program starts, those functions are called periodically, as needed. The iPhone is closest to this last example, which you will see in the next chapter and in the examples provided with the iPhone SDK.

Legacy C and C++ Code

If you have a C/C++ code base you want to port to the iPhone, or want to keep the option of reusable code from an iPhone application on other platforms such as Windows Mobile or Android, Objective-C presents a challenge to porting. The good news is that you can write C++ code that runs directly on the iPhone. However, you will have to write Objective-C to use certain portions of the iPhone SDK. The framework is the perfect place to wrap those interfaces in C++ classes so that the rest of your code can be written in pure C++.

If you or your company is dedicated to launching cross-platform titles, we strongly suggest developing engines with similar features and interfaces on each of the platforms. After you isolate your game-specific code this way, it is an easy task to copy code from one project to another and make minor adjustments to get it up and running. With a little care, this technique even works when switching between C++ and Java!

Game State Manager

A serious video game offers more than just a theater of action holding the game: it has a Main menu that allows the player to set options and start a new game or continue a previous one; a Credits screen that shows the names of all the hardworking people who helped make the game; and if your game doesn't come with a user manual, perhaps a Help section that gives the player a clue about what he's supposed to be doing.

Each of these is a *game state* and represents a separate part of the application code. For instance, the functions and navigation invoked by a player in the Main menu are quite different from those invoked by a player in the Credits screen, so the program logic is a lot different, too. Specifically, in the Main menu, you will likely be drawing a title image and some kind of menu, and listening for player input to select one of the menu options. When you are in the Credits screen, you will be drawing the names of all the people who worked on the game, while listening for player input that will cause your current game state to change from the Credits screen back to the Main menu. And finally, in the Game Play state, you will be rendering the actual game and listening for the player's input to interact with the game logic.

Each of these game states is responsible for handling player input, rendering to the screen, and providing any application logic that is specific to that state. You might recognize these tasks from our earlier discussion about the main loop, and that's because they are exactly the same tasks. However, each state implements them in its own way, which is why we have to keep them separate. You don't want to have to search through the Main menu code to make a change to the Game Play event handler.

State Machine

The Game State Manager is a state machine, which means it keeps track of the current game state. When the application starts, the state machine creates the basic state information. It goes on to create information required by each state and to destroy temporary information when the application leaves a state.

A large number of different objects have state that is maintained by the state machine. One obvious state is the screen the player is on (Main menu, Game Theater, etc.). But if you have an enemy artificial intelligence (AI) agent on the screen that can be in a "sleeping," "attacking," or "dead" state, a state machine can be used to keep track of those states as well.

What is the right architecture for a Game State Manager? Let's take a look at some state machines and decide which design pattern best fits our needs.

There are many ways to implement a state machine, the most basic of which is a simple `switch` statement:

```
class StateManager {
    void main_loop() {
        switch(myState) {
        case STATE_01:
            state01_handle_event();
            state01_update();
            state01_render;
            break;
        case STATE_02:
            state02_handle_event();
            state02_update();
            state02_render;
```

```
        break;
    case STATE_03:
        state03_handle_event();
        state03_update();
        state03_render;
        break;
    }
  }
};
```

All that is necessary to switch states is to change the value of the myState variable and return to the start of the loop. However, as you can see, the more states we add, the larger that code block gets. Furthermore, we typically have entire blocks of tasks we need to perform predictably when entering or leaving a state: initialize state-specific variables, load new resources (such as images), and deallocate resources used by the previous state. In a simple switch statement, we'd have to add that block to each case and make sure not to forget a step.

This is fine for simple tasks, but something as complex as our Game State Manager needs a better solution. The next best way to implement a state machine is to use function pointers:

```
class StateManager {
    //the function pointer:
    void (*m_stateHandleEventFPTR) (void);
    void (*m_stateUpdateFPTR)(void);
    void (*m_stateRenderFPTR)(void);


    void main_loop() {
        stateHandleEventFPTR();
        m_stateUpdateFPTR();
        m_stateRenderFPTR();
    }

    void change_state(  void (*newHandleEventFPTR)(void),
                        void (*newUpdateFPTR)(void),
                        void (*newRenderFPTR)(void)
    ) {
        m_stateHandleEventFPTR = newHandleEventFPTR;
        m_stateUpdateFPTR = newUpdateFPTR;
        m_stateRenderFPTR = newRenderFPTR
    }
};
```

Now the main loop is very small and simple, even if we handle many game states. However, this solution still does not help us initialize and deallocate states. Because each game state has not only code but also unique resources, it is appropriate to think of game states as attributes of an *object*. So, next we will look at an object-oriented programming (OOP) approach.

We start by creating a class to represent our game states:

```
class GameState
{
    GameState();          //constructor
    virtual ~GameState();    //destructor

    virtual void Handle_Event();
    virtual void Update();
    virtual void Render();
};
```

Next, we change our state manager to use that class:

```
class StateManager {
    GameState* m_state;

    void main_loop() {
        m_state->Handle_Event();
        m_state->Update();
        m_state->Render();
    }

    void change_state( GameState* newState ) {
        delete m_state;
        m_state = newState;
    }
};
```

Finally, we create a specific instance of our game state:

```
class State_MainMenu : public GameState
{
    int m_currMenuOption;

    State_MainMenu();
    ~State_MainMenu();

    void Handle_Event();
    void Update();
    void Render();
};
```

When it is represented by a class, each game state can store its unique variables inside that class. It can also allocate any resources it needs in its constructor and deallocate them in its destructor.

Furthermore, this system keeps our code nicely organized because we have to put the code for each state in separate files. If you are looking for the Main menu code, all you have to do is open the State_MainMenu class and there it is. And the OOP solution makes this code easy to reuse.

This seems to best fit our needs, so we will use the OOP solution for our Game State Manager.

Graphics Engine

The graphics engine is in charge of visual output. This includes drawing graphical user interface (GUI) objects for the player to interact with, animating 2D sprites or 3D models, and rendering backgrounds and special effects.

Although the techniques used to render 2D and 3D graphics may be different, they evolve from the same set of graphics tasks. These include texturing and animation, in increasing order of complexity.

Texturing

Texturing is central to the display of graphics. In 2D, a flat image is displayed pixel by pixel to the screen, while in 3D, a collection of triangles (also called a *mesh*) undergoes some mathematical magic to produce a flat image, which is then also displayed on the screen. From there on, everything else gets more complicated.

Pixels, textures, and images

When drawing to the screen, the basic unit of measurement is a *pixel*. Each pixel can be broken into Red, Green, and Blue color values, along with an Alpha value for transparency that we'll discuss shortly.

A *texture* is a collection of data about how to render a group of pixels. It contains color data for each pixel to be drawn.

An *image* is a high-level concept and is not directly related to a particular set of pixels or textures. When a human sees a group of pixels, her brain puts them together to form an image; e.g., if the pixels are in the right order, she might see an image of a giraffe.

It is important to keep these concepts separate. A texture might contain pixels that form the image of a giraffe. It might contain enough pixels to form multiple images of a giraffe, or it may contain only some of the pixels required to render an image of a giraffe. The texture itself is just a collection of pixels, and does not inherently understand that it contains an image.

Transparency

At any one time, your game will likely have several if not many objects rendering textures to the screen, and some of them will overlap one another. The question is, how do you know which pixel of which object should be rendered?

If the texture on top (being drawn after the other texture) at each location is completely opaque, its pixels will be displayed. However, for game objects, which have nonrectangular shapes and partially transparent objects, the result might be a combination of the two textures.

The most commonly used form of blending in 2D graphics is full transparency. Let's say we want to draw an image of a koala (Figure 2-3) on top of a background of eucalyptus trees (Figure 2-4). The image of the koala is stored in a rectangular texture in memory, but we don't want to draw the whole rectangle; we want to draw only the pixels of the texture that shows the koala. For each pixel in the texture, we need to know whether the pixel should or should not be drawn.

Figure 2-3. Koala source texture

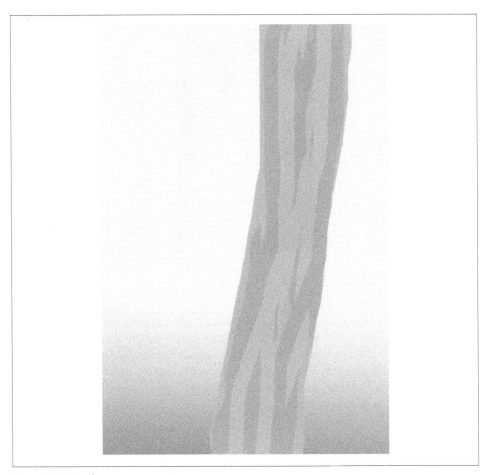

Figure 2-4. Eucalyptus source texture

Some graphical systems accomplish this by adding a mask. Imagine that we have another texture in memory that is the same size as the koala texture; however, it contains only black and white pixels. Each white pixel in this mask texture represents a pixel in the original koala texture that should be drawn, and each black pixel represents a pixel that should not be drawn. If we have this mask texture present when we are drawing our koala to the screen, we can check the value of each pixel in the koala texture against each pixel in the mask texture and draw only the appropriate pixels to the screen. If each pixel allows a range of values instead of just a binary white/black value, it can support partial transparency (see Figure 2-5).

However, this would require us to store and load two separate textures for each image. Some texture formats incorporate transparency right into the texture by adding a visibility value to the pixel in addition to the Red, Green, and Blue color values. This is called the *Alpha* value.

Figure 2-5. Koala mask texture

Texture blending

The memory devoted in textures to Alpha values is large enough for each pixel to have a range. Typically, an Alpha value occupies a whole byte of a pixel, allowing a value from 0 to 255. Interesting visual effects can be achieved by blending together the color values of two pixels. This effect is usually used for partial transparency, such as objects that are partially or fully see-through (see Figure 2-6).

Figure 2-6. Partially transparent green rectangle

We can use the Alpha value for each pixel to determine how it should be blended. If the range of a pixel color value is 0–255, the range of the Alpha value would also be 0–255. Although 0 for a Red color value means that no red would be used when drawing that pixel, a 0 for an Alpha value would mean the pixel would not be drawn at all. Meanwhile, a value of 128 for Red would indicate that half of the maximum Red value should be used when drawing the pixel, and a value of 128 for Alpha would indicate that half of that pixel's color value should be used when blending with another pixel.

It becomes very important to properly sort the drawing order of objects when blending is used. Because each blended render operation can only blend the source with the destination, items that are drawn first will not be blended with objects drawn after

---

them. Although this is easy to manage in 2D graphics, it can become complicated very quickly in 3D graphics.

To correctly sort meshes for texture blending in 3D graphics, you have to sort objects before rendering them. The objects must be drawn in order, starting with the object that is farthest from the camera and ending with the one that is closest to it.

Fortunately, the OpenGL ES implementation on the iPhone was specifically designed to handle this problem. This makes it much easier to sort geometric objects and obtain the right composite texture.

Rotation

In 2D graphics, most textures are rendered directly to their destinations without rotation. This is because standard hardware does not have functionality for rotations, so the rotations must be calculated in software, which is a slow process and often results in a poor-quality image.

Commonly, game developers will avoid this by prerendering their objects at several different rotations and simply drawing the image that corresponds to the correct rotation.

In 3D graphics, rotation is calculated similarly to the way lighting is, as part of the rendering process on the hardware.

If you are developing a 2D application that requires a large number of objects to be rotated, you might consider using a 3D engine and merely setting up an orthogonal camera so that the scene still looks 2D.

On the iPhone, this is not necessary. Quartz 2D, the 2D Graphics API on the iPhone, has a nice rotational system already in place so that rotations are not expensive; you can continue developing your game in pure 2D as planned.

Clipping

For reasons that we will explain in the next section, another important aspect of texturing is clipping. Although the examples we have used so far have been drawing entire source textures onto destination textures, it often becomes important to draw only part of the source to a limited section of the destination.

For instance, if your source contains multiple images in one texture file, cropping allows you to render only the portions of each source texture that contains the image you wish to draw.

Clipping also allows you to limit drawing access to a subsection of the destination texture. This helps you render objects in 3D through *texture mapping*, which spreads a texture over a mesh of triangles that can be an arbitrary shape. For instance, a texture could represent clothing or the pelt of an animal and could undulate in a supple 3D fashion as the character underneath it moves. The texture in this case is usually called a *skin*.

 The first 3D games used 2D sprites mapped to very simple rectangle meshes. These meshes were called *billboards*, and they always faced directly toward the camera when rendered. However, because their position and scale were based on 3D projection, they acted like 3D objects.

Billboards are still useful in today's games, mostly in the form of particle systems in which hundreds of small billboards are generated and move together in a semirandom fashion. Because the geometry is so simple, it is easy to render many of these objects at once.

Animation

By rendering a consecutive sequence of images, we can convince the player that he is watching a moving object, even though all he's doing is staring at the same pixels as they rapidly change color. This is the concept of animation. Two-dimensional animation has remained pretty simple, whereas 3D animation is more sophisticated because it usually involves more objects and more motion.

In addition to discussing animation techniques, this section also covers the main types of optimizations that enable our graphics engine to efficiently and reliably perform complex graphics tasks that would be impossible to do with a naive approach. Some of the major optimization techniques include culling, texture sorting, smart texture file usage, resource management, and level-of-detail rendering.

Two-dimensional animation: Sprites

In 2D graphics, if we wanted to render a horse in full gallop, we could do so by first creating an image of the horse in each pose that we will be rendering to the screen. Each image is called a *frame*, and when each frame is rendered one after the other, the horse is animated (see Figure 2-7). This is quite similar to the way film creates the illusion of animation, by presenting successive frames that differ just in the parts that are meant to move.

To keep these frames together, they are put into the same texture, called a *sprite*. Using the cropping method we described in the previous section, only the section containing the current frame is rendered to the screen.

Depending on how fast you want the animation to play, and how many frames of the animation are provided, you may render each frame multiple times before moving on to the next one in the sequence. In fact, you can create many effects by controlling the order and speed of the rendered frames.

Figure 2-7. Stanford's horse in motion

Three-dimensional animation: Models

Instead of maintaining a complete image to be rendered on each redraw, as in 2D sprites, 3D animation actually calculates the effects of movement geometrically. As we described earlier, all 3D objects comprise a group of one or more triangles, called a *mesh*. There are several ways to animate a mesh, and the technology has evolved along with game development and graphics hardware. The basic idea behind these techniques is called *keyframing*.

Keyframes are slightly different from the frames we discussed for 2D animation. Two-dimensional animation requires every single frame to be created by an artist and stored in a texture. However, in 3D, if we store only the most distinctive frames (the key-frames), we can re-create the other frames mathematically.

The first games that used animated meshes actually stored multiple copies of the mesh, each in a different keyframe position. For instance, if we were rendering the horse in 3D, there would be a separate mesh for each keyframe listed earlier in the sprite. At time(1), the first frame would be drawn as is; at time(2), the second frame would be drawn as is.

Between major keyframes, a technique called *interpolation* would be used. Since we know that the first and second frames have the same number of triangles but with slightly different positions, we can calculate a third "temporary" mesh that combines the two based on the current animation time. So, at time(1.5), the temporary mesh would look like it was exactly halfway between the first and second keyframe meshes. And at time(1.8), it would almost completely resemble the second frame.

For obvious reasons, this is very inefficient. This is acceptable for meshes with a small number of triangles and a small number of keyframes; however, modern graphics require high-resolution models with detailed animation. Fortunately, there is a better way to store the keyframe data.

The technique is called *skeletal animation*, or *bone rigging*. If you consider the horse example, you will note that most of the triangles move together in groups, such as the head group, the tail group, and four separate leg groups. If you were to say that each group had a "bone" associated with it, you could consider that together all of the bones form a skeleton.

A skeleton is a group of bones that can be applied to a mesh. An animation is formed when a series of skeletons in different positions is shown in succession. Each frame of the animation uses the same mesh, but with the bones moved slightly from their previous position to indicate motion.

By storing the mesh in one position, but applying one of the keyframe skeletons to it, we can create a temporary mesh to render to the screen. By interpolating between two skeleton keyframes, we can create the same animation effect at a fraction of the cost.

 Another advantage of bone rigging over storing a mesh for each keyframe is animation blending. Say we have one animation of our horse trotting forward and a different animation of the horse standing still but shaking his head and tail. If we combined the body and legs of the first animation with the head and tail of the second animation, we would get a horse trotting forward while shaking its head and tail; a complex animation built from two simple animations.

If we were to try to do this with the old technique of one mesh per keyframe, we would have to interpolate between four separate meshes. With bone rigging, we can blend the keyframes together at the bone level very easily and then apply that skeleton to the mesh as usual.

Animation controllers

An animation controller object is useful to abstract the low-level tasks of choosing what frame to render, how long to render it, and which new frame to substitute afterward. It is the glue that bridges the game logic and the graphics engine wherever animation is concerned.

At the top level, the game logic is worried only about setting an object to something like the "Run" animation, and possibly what speed it should be running at in units per second. The Controller object knows which sequence of frames corresponds to the "Run" animation, and how fast they should be played, so the game logic doesn't have to know.

Particle systems

Another useful object, similar to the Controller, is the Particle System Manager. A particle system is used when drawing special effects that have highly fragmented elements, such as fire, cloud particles, or sparkle trails. Although each object in the particle system has very limited detail and animation, their combined motions can produce very entertaining visual effects.

Culling

The best way to increase the number of times you can draw to the screen per second is to reduce the amount of drawing done on each iteration. Your scene might contain hundreds or even thousands of objects at the same time, but if you have to draw only a few of them, you can still render the scene quickly.

Culling is the removal of unnecessary objects from the drawing path. You can perform culling on many levels simultaneously. For instance, at a high level, you may consider that a user in a room with a closed door cannot see any of the objects in the next room, so you do not even have to try to draw any of those objects.

At a low level, 3D graphics engines will often try to remove portions of the meshes you ask them to draw. Consider that at any given time approximately half of a mesh's geometry is the *back* side—facing way from the camera. The camera cannot see that geometry, so it will be overdrawn by the *front* side of the mesh. Therefore, all triangles that are facing away from the camera can safely be ignored when rendering each mesh; this is called *back-face culling*.

Texture sorting

Each time an object is rendered to the screen, the graphics hardware has to load the source texture into its local memory. This is part of what is called *context switching*.

If three images are going to be drawn to the screen and two of them share the same source texture, there are two ways to handle the texture sorting: the efficient method draws the two images that share the same texture in sequence and requires only one context switch, whereas the inefficient method requires two context switches. You don't want the third image to be drawn in between the two that share a texture.

Sorting your rendering process by objects that share the same texture will reduce the number of unnecessary context switches, resulting in faster rendering.

Texture files

Planning out your texture organization at the start will help you sort your textures in an optimal manner. For instance, let's say you are going to be drawing level geometry, a player avatar, and several types of creatures throughout your game.

If the first two levels are grassy areas and the next is a desert, you might keep all of the tree, grass, bush, rock, and flower images used to render the first two levels together, and keep the sand images used by the third level in a separate texture. Similarly, you will want to keep all of the images used to render the player avatar in one texture.

If all of the creatures are used in all of the levels, it may be optimal to keep them all together in one texture. However, if the first level has howler monkeys and flying squirrels, but the second level has only wood rats and a Surinam toad, you may wish to keep the first two animals together in one texture, and the second two together in a separate texture.

Resource management

Most video games render only a small portion of their total graphical content at any one time. It is very inefficient to have all of those textures loaded into memory at the same time.

Fortunately, game design usually dictates which resources are visible at different segments of the game. By keeping necessary textures loaded while unloading unused textures, you can make the most efficient use of the limited amount of memory available.

Using the last example from the previous section, when the game engine loads the first level, your resource management code would make sure the texture with the howler monkeys and flying squirrels was loaded into memory. When progressing to the next level, it would unload that texture because it is known to be unused for the second level.

Textures can also be managed dynamically. For instance, if you have room for five textures in memory, and the current level is using only two textures, while the next level is going to use only one, it is not necessary to unload either of the first two. Furthermore, if the third level uses the same textures as the first, it does not have to load any textures into memory because its texture is already prepared. This system would remove unnecessary textures only when it ran out of room to allocate new ones.

Level of detail

Another optimization technique, particular to 3D graphics, is level of detail. Consider an object that is far away from the camera, such as on the horizon; because it is so far away, it looks very small and most of the detail of the shape is lost. You could easily draw the same object at that size with a much simpler mesh, or even a billboard.

Level of detail will do exactly that, by keeping simplified copies of objects in memory. Your graphics engine can determine which copy to use based on the object's distance from the camera.

Physics Engine

A *physics engine* is the part of a game engine that deals with distance, movement, and other aspects of game physics. Not all game engines will require a physics engine; however, *all* graphics-based games have physics code at some level.

Don't believe us? Take tic-tac-toe, for example. A very simple game, yes; however, even this game has physics. When the user selects a square in which to place a mark, we have to check whether that square is available. If it is, we have to place the mark and check whether the user has won the game. This is an example of the two most basic tasks of the physics engine: detection and resolution.

Collision detection versus collision resolution

It is very important to keep these two aspects separate in your mind. In game code, detection is independent of resolution. Not every object in your game will collide with every other object in the same way (or at all). Furthermore, not every collision that has been detected will be resolved in the same way.

For example, let's propose a pretend game: the *O'Reilly Wildlife Adventure*. In this top-down adventure game, the player's avatar has unwittingly found his way onto the wrong side of the fence at the O'Reilly Wildlife Preserve and is now trying to avoid the odd (and sometimes dangerous) animals while making his way to safety.

Several physical interactions can happen in this game:

1. Player-world collision
2. Animal-world collision
3. Player-animal collision
4. Player-goal collision

The first type, player-world collision, is very simple. We check the bounding area of the player against the walls in our level. If the player is colliding with one of the walls, we offset his avatar to a place where he and the wall will no longer collide.

The second interaction is slightly more complicated. We use the same collision detection method: check the bounding area of the animal against the walls in our level. However, our resolution needs to be different because the animal is controlled by the computer—not by a player. When we resolved case 1, we simply stopped the player from moving into a wall. It was up to the player to realize he was hitting a wall and to decide to change direction.

If we were to do the same thing for case 2, the AI would not realize it was hitting walls and would continue to walk blindly into them. Instead, we resolve the situation by first moving the animal to an offset where it no longer collides with the walls, and then notifying the AI that an animal has collided with a wall. This will allow the game logic that controls that animal to cause it to change directions.

In case 3, we first detect the collision by checking the player's bounding area against the animal's bounding area. Once we have determined they are colliding, a number of different outcomes might occur. If the animal is a tarsier, it might run away. If the animal is an asp or a lion, it might attack the player. A camel would probably ignore the player. And if the animal is a grasshopper, it might get squished!

Finally, case 4 is a new situation. The goal is different from the world, player, and animal scenarios, because it does not have a graphical representation. It is an invisible trigger area that sends an event when the player steps into it. Fortunately, even though it doesn't have a graphical representation, it still has a physical representation. So again, all we have to do is test the player's bounding area against the goal's bounding area. If we determine that the player has triggered the goal, we notify the game logic, which will then change to the "You Win!" game state.

Two-dimensional collision detection

Two-dimensional collision detection is a relatively simple process. Most of it can be summed up in the following set of detection routines: rectangle-to-rectangle, point-in-rectangle, circle-to-rectangle, point-in-circle, and circle-to-circle. (It might also be necessary to check line segments, but that can usually be avoided.)

Since these routines will be used many times per second, it is very important to make them as efficient as possible. To do this, we will perform a series of cheap tests to prove that two objects *did not* collide before determining that the objects *did* collide:

```
bool cd_rectangleToRectangle( Rect r1, Rect r2)
{
    //can't be colliding because R1 is too far left of R2
    if( r1.x + r1.width < r2.x ) return FALSE;
    //can't be colliding because R1 is too far right of R2
    if( r1.x > r2.x + r2.width ) return FALSE;
    //can't be colliding because R1 is too far below R2
    if( r1.y + r1.width < r2.y ) return FALSE;
    //can't be colliding because R1 is too far above R2
    if( r1.y < r2.y + r2.width ) return FALSE;

    //if we get here, the two rects MUST be colliding
    return TRUE;
}
```

Even though this will result in more code being run in the case that objects do collide, most of the time objects are not in collision with each other; we optimize for the case that happens most often (objects not in collision) because it's much more efficient.

High-Speed Collision Detection

Physics detection works best between two similarly sized objects moving at slow speeds. High-velocity objects require special consideration. Consider a pinball game: a very small ball moves at high speeds and bounces off many different objects. Because the pinball is moving so fast, simply checking whether it collides with a bumper is not enough (see Figure 2-8).

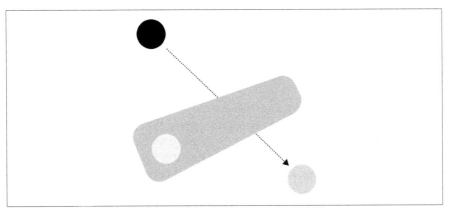

Figure 2-8. Pinball versus bumper

At time 1, the ball is to the left of the bumper, but by time 2, the ball has enough speed to move clear through the bumper, and a circle-rectangle collision check would fail because the ball and the bumper are not touching. Instead of checking collision between the ball and the bumper, the collision detection code should check the *path* of the ball. In this way, the pinball's collision with the bumper will be properly detected no matter how large its velocity (see Figure 2-9).

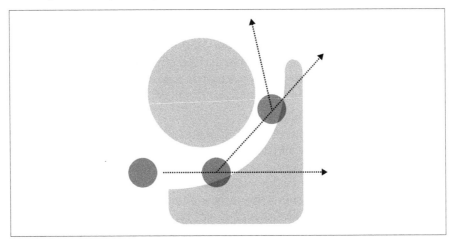

Figure 2-9. Multiple collisions in one step

But we're not done yet. If we performed only one check, the ball's velocity could be so large that even after bouncing off one bumper it still has enough speed to pierce another bumper. To accurately simulate the pinball's motion (and avoid having it shoot through your bumpers), it is necessary to perform multiple collision detection steps on the pinball until its full velocity has been calculated for that entire game loop.

Before we continue, let's focus for a moment on a very important concept: *the graphical representation of a game object is separate from its physical representation*. Computers can supply only a limited amount of calculating power per second, and it's hard to perform very detailed physical simulations in real time. Because of this, game physics code has a long and proud tradition of being only as accurate as it needs to be to let the game feel right to the player.

For example, in our proposed game, the player's avatar is going to collide with a rhinoceros. (Obviously, the player was either not paying much attention, or he was busy running away from an angry mama tiger.) The player, being a human, has many appendages animating forward and backward as he runs. The rhino, being a rhino, has a similar number of appendages, as well as a decidedly unfriendly looking horn poking out of its head.

Although the graphical representation of the player needs to show where the player's arms and legs are as he is animated running across the screen, do we really need to know where they are in the physics representation? Do we really need to check the avatar's two arms and two legs, as well as a head and a torso for collision against the rhino's head, torso, four legs, and horn? (And don't forget about that vicious tail!) Of course not, since our game is top-down, a simple rectangle bounding the player versus a simple rectangle bounding the rhino is all we need.

Three-dimensional collision detection

Collision detection in 3D can be a lot more difficult than in 2D. You must be familiar with some 3D math, such as linear algebra. And if the math requirement weren't enough, 3D games tend to have much more detailed physical worlds. Fortunately, you can still rely on approximation techniques to help reduce the number of calculations you'll while still being as accurate as necessary to make the game "feel" right to the player.

As we discussed earlier, an object's graphical representation is different from its physical representation. However, sometimes we want to make sure the difference is as small as possible. Consider a first-person shooter game. When the player fires a bullet at another player's head, we want to know not only whether the bullet hit the player, but also whether it scored a head shot. Obviously, a simple bounding box will not do. But we can't afford to check the bullet's path against every triangle in every player's avatar.

We use the same technique in 3D collision detection as we did in 2D collision detection: perform a series of cheap failure tests before performing the more expensive and accurate test. For the bullet example, we would first test to see whether the bullet path intersected each player's bounding boxes. If it didn't hit any of them, we exit our collision check. For the boxes it did hit, we determine which is closest to the projectile's starting point and then do a more detailed check against every triangle in that player's mesh. This is the physics version of the level-of-detail concept in graphics optimization. If the check on the closest player failed, we would do the detailed test on the next player whose bounding box was hit in the first check. In this way, we can efficiently and accurately determine even a complex case in which a bullet flies between the legs of one player to hit another player behind him.

Additional 3D Optimizations

Three-dimensional physics scenes tend to get very complicated very fast. Another optimization that physics engines borrow from graphics code is culling. Although level-of-detail optimization can help speed up our collision detection tests for complex objects, our physics code will be faster if we have fewer objects to test in the first place. By using detailed knowledge of the physical scene, culling reduces the total number of objects we have to check.

The Binary Space Partition or BSP tree is one such method that is commonly used for indoor scenes. By slicing the level into a binary tree of geometry nodes we can separate large portions of the level that are not visible to each other. For example, let's say we have a building consisting of three rooms, where Room A opens into Rooms B and C, but Rooms B and C do not open into each other (see Figure 2-10).

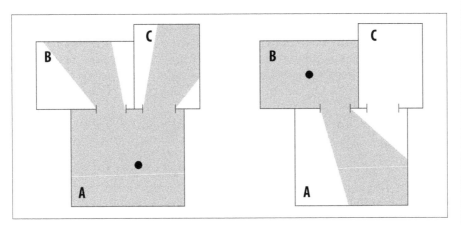

Figure 2-10. Room visibility

When a player fires a bullet from Room A, we may have to check geometry in Rooms A, B, and C for collision. However, if the player fires from Room B, we know for certain that we have to check geometry only in rooms A and B, saving us from having to check any geometry in Room C.

Collision resolution

Once a collision has been detected, it's time to perform collision resolution. The first thing to consider is what "low-level" or "high-level" actions must take place. Low-level actions are those that the physics code can resolve, such as adjusting a player's position so that he is just above the ground instead of falling into it. High-level actions are signals that get sent out to the game logic section of the game engine; these signals let the game logic know things such as when an animal has run into a wall or whether a player has reached the "goal" trigger area.

Some collision responses will require multiple high- and low-level responses at the same time. For instance, when a pinball hits a bumper, it should bounce off the bumper appropriately (low level) but also send a signal to the game logic that will animate the bumper, produce a sound, and increase the user's score (high level).

When testing the results of low-level collision resolution code, pay special attention to detail. One of the most visceral elements of game "feel" is the physics code. Does the avatar respond quickly to player input? Does the car in a racing game accurately model a realistic suspension and transmission? Does the whole screen shake when someone fires the "big gun"?

Ultimately, it is the designer's job to declare when the game play feels right. But it is the programmer's job to make that happen. Don't be afraid to write special cases to get the right results.

For example, one common technique is to flag objects that are at rest. When an object has made contact with geometry considered to be the "ground," you can set a "grounded" flag on that object to "true." When the grounded flag is true, the object is considered at rest and you do not need to apply gravity to the object or test its collision with the world. This not only saves you from having to run collision detection on a large number of stationary objects, but it also avoids the possible jittering of objects that can happen in some physics simulations when objects bounce back and forth on the ground.

Audio Engine

Audio is often a neglected dimension of game development, which is perplexing when you consider that audio makes up one-third of the human senses used to play video games. Using the right sounds at the right time can greatly increase the value of game play with very little effort on the part of the programmer.

Basic audio features include loading and unloading a sound sample; playing sound; and stopping, pausing, resuming, and looping. Typically, all sounds can play at the same volume, but you may wish to allow users to change the master volume level for all sounds to suit their preferences.

Games that require 3D sound, also known as *positional audio*, can use the iPhone's OpenAL library.

Sound samples

Before you can play a sound, you need to load a sound sample from a file or a memory buffer. The iPhone API supports AAC and MP3 formats for high-quality sounds, as well as PCM and IMA4 for smaller samples and a number of other less common formats.

Playing sound

Once you've loaded a sound sample, your API provides functions to start and stop playback of the sample. Most APIs also provide pause and resume functionality, and some allow you to seek to a position in the sample. More advanced features are available, but typically these are all a game developer will need.

 Sometimes you can load multiple sounds more efficiently by putting them into one sound sample and seeking to the start of each sound that needs to play. Although this reduces the overhead of loading several samples, it allows you to play only one of these sounds at a time.

Multichannel sound

Because sound playback is hardware dependent, the number of sounds you can play at one time is limited. Each sound playing at the same time is using one *channel*. On the iPhone, all MP3 and AAC samples use the same hardware channel, and only one is available; however, multiple channels are available for PCM and IMA4.

This means that at any one time only one MP3/AAC-formatted sample can be playing, but multiple PCM/IMA4 samples can play simultaneously (and at the same time as an MP3 or AAC).

Music versus SFX

Most sounds used in games fall into two categories: ambient sound (typically background music) and sound effects (SFX). Sometimes environmental or ambient sounds are used instead of music, but they share the same characteristics.

Music typically involves one relatively long sample that may loop after playing, or it may immediately proceed to another music sample. Typically, only one music sample is playing at any given time, which makes the MP3/AAC format limitation a nonissue.

Sound effects are much shorter and may require many different types of samples to be playing in an overlapping fashion. The PCM/IMA4 sample formats work well for this purpose.

Because a limited number of channels is available to PCM/IMA4, if your game can result in many SFX samples trying to play at the same time, some of them may not play. It might become important to assign priorities to SFX samples to ensure that certain sounds play when audio channels are scarce.

For instance, let's say the player's avatar from our earlier example walks into a room full of angry rhinos. Each rhino will play an "angry snort" sample, possibly followed by a "charging" sample, and the player avatar will want to produce a "shrill cry" sample. We should give the player's avatar sound effects a higher priority than others so that his shrill cry is not drowned out by the sound of charging rhinos.

Fortunately, the current iPhone supports at least 32 sample channels, so it is highly unlikely that you will have to prioritize samples on that platform.

Output devices and interruptions

The iPhone supports internal speakers and headphones as output devices. It is recommended that the device use only one at a time. When the player inserts headphones into her iPhone, the audio should switch over to the headphones automatically.

Because the iPhone is a mobile device, it is possible for the headphones to accidentally fall off as the player is walking about. A good design choice is to pause the game when headphones are removed to allow the user time to find the plug and reattach the headphones. Optionally, you may wish to stop sound during the pause state for this reason.

Most importantly, consider audio from the player's perspective. Playing your game is not the only reason players use their iPhone, so don't let the game become annoying by allowing it to take priority, or players will turn it off.

Player Input

The player input portion of the game engine is focused on receiving "low-level" events from the operating system, and translating them into "high-level" events that the game logic code can use. For PC games, the low-level events could be mouse and keyboard input. For console games, they could be generated by the controller's joysticks, triggers, and buttons. In our case, the iPhone will handle touch and gyroscope events.

Touch events

Touch-screen interfaces require an approach to interface design that's fundamentally different from the approach found in most mobile, console, and PC platforms. For starters, there tends to be much more latency between the moment the user touches the screen and the moment your application receives an event (although the iPhone does a good job of keeping that latency as short as possible). However, the real problem is that whenever the user performs a touch, he is forced to cover part of the screen with his finger, effectively reducing the visibility of the game.

You can mitigate the problem by providing a graphical button for the user to click (thus returning to the old button-click system, but at the cost of screen space) or by using clever metaphors. For instance, if the player clicks a space in the game world, you could have the player's avatar walk in that direction, thereby reducing the need for continuous player input by making the game smarter.

Although user interface design falls under the responsibility of the designer, it's the programmer's job to let the designer know what the target platform can and can't do. The iPhone supports the following touch events:

- Touch start
- Touch moved
- Touch end
- Touch canceled

You may wonder what could trigger the "canceled" event. When some event suspends your application between the "start" and "end" of a touch event, the program receives the canceled event to let you know you won't be receiving the rest of the events (such as "touch end").

To handle multiple touches, the UIEvent object sent to your application can contain a list of multiple UITouch objects. If one finger is touching the screen, you will receive only one UITouch object; if two fingers are touching the screen, you will receive two UITouch objects, and so on. Furthermore, the iPhone keeps track of up to five simultaneous tap events (a TouchStart followed quickly by a TouchEnd) that are or have happened recently.

Unfortunately, using these events to determine when the player is trying to single-tap, double-tap, or perform swipe or pinch motions can get complicated. It isn't difficult to do; it's just not obvious at first. Take the following example:

```
Time 0:   TouchStart - numTaps(0) numTouches(1) Touches { (40,40) }
Time 100: TouchEnd  - numTaps (1) numTouches(1) Touches { (40,40) }
    Handle single-tap..
```

So far, the user has touched the screen once, so your code might perform the action that corresponds with a single tap. But wait!

```
Time 0:   TouchStart - numTaps(0) numTouches(1) Touches { (40,40) }
Time 100: TouchEnd  - numTaps (1) numTouches(1) Touches { (40,40) }
    Handled single-tap.. INCORRECTLY
Time 200: TouchStart - numTaps (1) numTouches(1) Touches { (40,40) }
Time 300: TouchEnd  - numTaps (2) numTouches(1) Touches { (40,40) }
    FAILED to handle double-tap
```

The player tapped the screen a second time. If your code had acted immediately on the TouchEnd event, it would have incorrectly responded to a single tap instead of the double tap the player was trying to perform.

How can we handle these events correctly for both cases? The solution is to defer the first TouchEnd event to a timed callback. When we receive the first TouchEnd, we set up a callback. If we receive a second TouchEnd before the callback is called, we know the player is double-tapping, and we can cancel the callback and act on the double tap. If we do receive the callback, we know the player never tapped a second time and we should handle a single tap.

Here are some examples showing those two cases:

```
Time 0:   TouchStart - numTaps(0) numTouches(1) Touches { (40,40) }
Time 100: TouchEnd   - numTaps (1) numTouches(1) Touches { (40,40) }
    Initiate callback timer
Time 200: TouchStart - numTaps (1) numTouches(1) Touches { (40,40) }
Time 300: TouchEnd   - numTaps (2) numTouches(1) Touches { (40,40) }
    Handle double-tap, cancel callback
```

This time, the player has double-tapped and the code handled it correctly:

```
Time 0:   TouchStart - numTaps(0) numTouches(1) Touches { (40,40) }
Time 100: TouchEnd   - numTaps (1) numTouches(1) Touches { (40,40) }
    Initiate callback timer
Time 500: Callback recieved
    Handle single-tap
```

And now, the player has single-tapped and the code handled it correctly as well.

Note that you do not have to jump through these hoops for interfaces that expect only single taps.

Detecting actions such as swipes is even more involved, but a little bit more obvious. The code has to store a start point and an end point for the touch, and then evaluate whether the line the user made was up, down, left, or right, and whether she swiped her finger fast enough.

Resolving into high-level events

Once you have determined the physical action the player is performing, your code must convert that action into something the game logic component can use. Exactly how you do that depends on the context of your game, but there are a few typical patterns:

- If the player is trying to control an avatar, there is usually a continual interaction between the player and the game. It is often necessary to store a representation of the current player input. For example, if the input device were a joystick, you might keep track of its current position in the x- and y-axes and then modify the player avatar's momentum during the main loop. The level of interaction expected between the player and his avatar is usually so tightly coupled that the physical state of the controller represents a high-level model of the state of the avatar: when the joystick is held "forward," the avatar is moving forward, and when the "jump" button is pressed, the avatar is jumping.

- If the player is interacting with the game world itself, a more indirect approach is necessary. For example, if the player must touch an object in the game world, the code would have to translate the player's touch position from screen coordinates to world coordinates to determine what the player actually touched. That might be as simple as inverting the y-axis and subtracting a 2D camera offset, or as difficult as performing a camera-ray collision detection within a 3D scene.

- Finally, the user might be trying to perform an action that indirectly affects game play, such as pausing or interacting with the GUI. In this case, a simple message or function can be triggered to notify the game logic of what to do.

Game Logic

Game logic is the part of the game engine that makes your game unique. The logic keeps track of the player state, takes care of the AI agents, determines when goals are met, and generally enforces all of the rules of the game. It will be different for each game because essentially, it *is* the game. Given two similar games, the graphics engine and physics engine might have slight discrepancies, but the game logic code will show the most difference.

The game logic works closely with the physics engine, and in small games where there is no separate physics engine code, it may be responsible for whatever physics the game has. However, for games that do warrant a physics engine, it is important to keep the two separate. The best way to do this is to have them communicate by having the physics engine send the game logic "high-level" game events.

High-level events

As much as possible, the game logic code should be concerned with only these high-level problems. It does not care when the player touched the screen, what order to draw to the screen, or whether two rectangles are intersecting. It does care about when the player wants to "move forward," when new game objects should be created or removed, and what to do when two objects are "hitting" each other.

To maintain this conceptual distance, the parts of code that deal with low-level concepts (such as player input and the physics engine) should create high-level messages to send to the game logic code to be processed. This will not only help keep code separate and modular, but it will also aid in debugging. By logging the high-level messages that are being passed around, you can determine whether the cause of a bug is incorrect processing of the message (a problem in the game logic code) or a failure to send the message at the right time (a problem with the "low-level" code).

A very basic technique for sending high-level messages is to write a string and send that. For instance, let's say the player has pressed the up arrow key and that it should move his avatar forward:

```
void onPlayerInput( Input inputEvt ) {
    if(inputEvt.type == IE_KEY && inputEvt.value == KEY_UP ) {
        g_myApp->sendGameLogicMessage( "player move forward" );
    }
}
```

Although this is very easy to read as a programmer, it is not very efficient for the computer. It requires much more memory and processing than is necessary. Instead, we should take a hint from the player input method itself; rather than using a string, it uses an object with a "type" and a "value." Because the number of possible events is structured and finite, we can use integers and enumerations to specify the event information we want to send in our messages.

First, we have to set up an enumeration to specify exactly what those events could be:

```
enumeration eGameLogicMessage_Types {
    GLMT_PLAYER_INPUT,
    GLMT_PROJECTILE_WEAPON,
    GLMT_GOAL_REACHED,
};
```

Next, we set up enumerations to specify values for the events:

```
enumeration eGameLogicMesage_Values {
    GLMV_PLAYER_FORWARD,
    GLMV_PLAYER_BACKWARD,
    GLMV_PLAYER_LEFT,
    GLMV_PLAYER_RIGHT,

    GLMV_ROCKET_FIRED,
    GLMV_ROCKET_HIT,
};
```

Now, we define an object to hold our message data:

```
struct sGameLogicMessage {
    short type;
    short value;
} Message;
```

And now, we can use an object to send our message from the previous example:

```
void onPlayerInput( Input inputEvt ) {
    if(inputEvt.type == IE_KEY && inputEvt.value == KEY_UP ) {
        Message msg;
        msg.type = GLMT_PLAYER_INPUT;
        msg.value = GLMV_PLAYER_FORWARD;
        g_myApp->sendGameLogicMessage( msg );
    }
}
```

This may seem like more work, but it runs much more efficiently. The first (bad) example uses 20 bytes to send the message (20 characters at one byte each; don't forget the null terminator). The second example uses only four bytes for the same message! But more importantly, when the sendGameLogicMessage() function tries to handle the message, it has to go through only two `switch` statements to find the right response, instead of having to parse the data from a string, which is very slow.

Artificial intelligence

Another of the game logic's duties is to manage the AI agents. Two types of games typically use an AI system: one matches a player against a computer opponent, whereas the other models a system containing semiautonomous entities within the game world itself. In both situations, AI agents receive input and provide output that controls the actions of objects in the game world.

In the first type of game, the AI is called an *expert system*. It is expected to emulate the actions of a human who understands the rules of the game and employ strategies of various difficulties to challenge the player. The AI typically has inputs and outputs similar to those of the player, to closely reproduce human behavior. Because humans are much better at processing complex information than current real-time AI agents, the input for an expert system sometimes provides more information than the player receives to make the AI system seem more intelligent.

For instance, if it is a real-time strategy (RTS) game in which a "fog of war" is used to limit the human player's view, the AI opponent might be able to see all units everywhere. Although this can allow you to easily increase the ability for the AI to compete against a more intelligent human, if the advantage becomes too large, it may seem like the AI is cheating. Remember, the point of the game is to be fun for the players, not to let your AI defeat them.

In the second type of game, there may be many AI agents, each individually much less intelligent. In some cases, the agents will be directly opposing the player, whereas in others, they might be neutral, and in yet others, you may have a combination of both.

Some agents may be entirely dumb, offering very specific, limited behavior that doesn't pay any attention to what's happening in the game world. One example may be an enemy that merely walks back and forth in one hallway. Others may be slightly dumb, with only one input and one output, such as a door that allows the player to open and close it. And yet others may be very complex, and even coordinate their behavior in groups. Choosing appropriate inputs for AI agents will allow you to simulate "awareness" and increase their realism.

No matter how simple the AI agent is, a state machine will typically have to be employed. For instance, the entirely dumb object in the first example would have to keep track of which direction it was walking. The slightly dumb object would have to keep track of whether it was open or closed. More complex objects could track states between "neutral" and "aggressive" behaviors, such as patrolling, confronting, and attacking.

Path Finding

Depending on your game's design, it may be important for your agents to decide where to move and how to get there. When the domain they have to move across involves obstacles, finding their way requires planning a route in advance instead of just moving directly toward their goal. This is called *path finding* and can be very CPU-intensive. If this is necessary for your game, consider precomputing common travel routes to include with that level's data for the AI logic to use.

Transparent suspend and resume

It is important to treat game play as a simulation within the main game state. Do not confuse real-world time with game time. If the player decides to take a break, your game should pause to allow him to do so. The game should then be able to resume smoothly, as though nothing had happened. Because the iPhone is a mobile device, saving and resuming state becomes even more important.

Only one application is allowed to run on the iPhone at a time, and users expect those applications to load very quickly. At the same time, they expect to be able to resume what they were doing after switching between applications. That means being able to save the state of your game to the device, and later resume it as quickly as possible. For a game, the task requires saving the current level and reloading it so that the player can continue playing immediately upon restarting the application. You need to choose which data to save and find a compact, consistent format in which to write it to disk; this structured data saving is called *serialization*.

Depending on the type of game, this could be more difficult than it sounds. For a puzzle type of game, you would only have to keep track of which level the player is on and what the current state of the board looks like. However, for an action game, you might have to store the position of every object in the level in addition to the state of the player's avatar. At a certain point, this becomes unmanageable, especially when it's expected to happen quickly. For situations such as this, you can take a number of steps at the game design level to ensure success.

First, you should decide exactly what is necessary to save the state. The position of every little flame in a fire particle system isn't important, but the position of that particle system in the larger game might be. The state of each enemy in the game might not be important—if they can be spawned from the level data. Taking this idea further, the exact position and state of the player's avatar might not be necessary, if you can simply start him at a "check point."

Serialization Options

There are many ways to serialize game data. You could create a format for storing the position and states of entities and write the data to a file in that format. However, this requires processing the data, creating and using a buffer as the game state is examined, and then reading in that format and re-creating those objects later.

There is another viable solution that trades efficiency of file space usage for speed. Rather than parsing the game objects and creating a specially formatted file, you can "freeze" the actual structures in memory to a file. Then, upon resuming, you would load that file directly back into memory and use those objects immediately as they are.

Of course, most cases are not quite as simple as this. For one, you have no control over the memory address location of the data; therefore, any pointers to memory addresses would be invalid. Furthermore, some resources (such as images and sounds) are managed by the OS and cannot be frozen.

Instead, a hybrid approach is useful. By keeping game logic objects segmented into "freezable" and "unfreezable" data, you can partially freeze those objects. When resuming the application, load those parts directly back into memory and then re-create the "unfreezable" portions.

For instance, the player avatar could store his position, hit points, and animation state in a "freezable" object, but let the image used for the avatar's sprite be destroyed. When that object is loaded back into memory, the game logic re-creates the sprite image and attaches the two together.

Frame-based versus time-based logic

Frame-based logic updates game objects based on changes to individual frames. Time-based logic, which is more complex but more closely associated to the actual state of the game, updates game objects based on the time that has transpired.

Programmers who are new to game development often make the mistake of combining frame- and time-based logic. The difference is subtle in definition, but it can cause very noticeable bugs if not handled appropriately.

For example, let's take the case of player movement. Novice programmers might write something such as this:

```
void onPlayerInput( Input inputEvent ) {
    if(inputEvt.type == IE_KEY && inputEvt.value == KEY_UP) {
        //apply movement based on the user input
        playerAvatar.y += movementSpeed;
    }
}
```

Every time the player presses a key, the avatar moves forward a set amount. This is frame-based logic because the change in movement can potentially happen with every new frame. Actually, in the current example, it will happen once per input event, which might be more or less than an iteration of the main loop. The visual impact of the move will be noticed only on the next iteration of the main loop, so any intermediate avatar movements will be wasted calculations. Let's make the following improvement:

```
void onPlayerInput( Input inputEvent ) {
    if(inputEvt.type == IE_KEY && inputEvt.value == KEY_UP) {
        //save the input state, but don't apply it
        playerAvatar.joystick = KEY_UP;
    }
    if(inputEvt.type == IE_KEY_RELEASE) {
        playerAvatar.joystick = 0;
    }
}

void Update() {
    //update the player avatar
    if( playerAvatar.joystick == KEY_UP ) {
        playerAvatar.y += movementSpeed;
    }
}
```

Now we know that the movement speed will be applied exactly once per game loop while the key is being held down. However, this is still frame-based logic.

The problem with frame-based logic is that frames do not always happen at the same time interval. If, during a game loop, the rendering or game logic takes longer to complete than normal, it could push back the next loop. So, sometimes you will have 60 frames per second (fps), and other times, you might have only 30 fps. Because the movement is being applied per frame, sometimes you will move only half as fast as other times.

You can represent movement properly by using time-based logic instead. By keeping track of the time since the last update frame, you can apply a portion of the movement speed. In this way, you can specify a movement speed based on units per second, and no matter what the current frame rate is, the avatar's movement will always be the same:

```
void Update( long currTime ) {
    long updateDT = currTime - lastUpdateTime;

    //update the player avatar
    if( playerAvatar.joystick == KEY_UP ) {
        //since currTime is in milliseconds, we have to divide by 1000
        // to get the correct speed in seconds.
        playerAvatar.y += (movementSpeed * updateDT)/1000;
    }

    lastUpdateTime = currTime;
}
```

In this example, the same amount of movement speed would be applied whether we had 2 fps or 60 fps. Time-based logic takes a little extra code to set up, but it allows you to be accurate regardless of temporary lag.

It is certainly possible to develop a game using frame-based logic. The important thing is to avoid mixing the two. For instance, if your graphics code uses time-based logic to animate the player avatar's sprite moving forward, but the game logic code uses frame-based logic to move the avatar forward in the game world, the walking animation is not going to sync up with the distance the player has traveled.

For some applications, time-based logic is a requirement. Networked multiplayer games, for instance, require synchronization between two clients. So, it's absolutely necessary to use time-based logic to ensure that both clients render the same movement rate for all objects. Developers working on 3D games will notice that most physics APIs also use time-based logic for their simulations.

If you can get away with frame-based logic, do so. But thinking in terms of time-based logic will help you in the long run.

Game logic organization

The core function of game logic code is to manage the rules and progress of the Game Play state. Depending on your game design, this can mean just about anything. However, there are a few typical patterns based on the type of game you are making.

Game logic typically is not associated with a particular class. Instead, it starts by being manifested in the Game State object. When the main game state is initialized, it will load and initialize the resources necessary for the current level, such as a list of hints and words to find in a crossword puzzle, graphics data for player avatars, and physics data for the area the player is currently in. During a game loop, the game logic will receive user input, run the physics simulation, and handle any resulting collision resolution messages, simulate AI action, and enforce game rules. Finally, when the application needs to end the main game state, it will release any game-specific resources and possibly save the state to the hard drive.

Depending on the complexity of your game, you may find it convenient to split up the game logic further. For instance, if you are developing an adventure game, you most likely have a world with environment data (ground, buildings, rivers, trees, etc.), entities that can move or interact (player avatars, enemies, nonplayer characters, switches, obstacles, etc.), and perhaps some kind of user interface for performing special actions and displaying vital information. Each feature entails a large amount of code, and although they work together to make the game what it is, you can separate them to keep the workload modular.

You might create a class called Level Manager to handle the world environment, including loading and unloading the physics and graphics data necessary to display the world, as well as calling the physics engine to test collisions between entities and the world. You could create another class, or series of classes, to handle the entities that exist in the world. Each class signals the loading and unloading of the physics and graphics necessary to render those objects, and contains the AI to control them.

And finally, you would likely create another separate class to handle the in-game user interface, allowing you to keep the code for all three concepts separate.

This architecture works with any type of game, adventure or not. First, evaluate the major features of your design and then group the features in a way that keeps similar functionality and data together.

Conclusion

You should now have a basic understanding of some of the tasks that must be completed when making a game engine, which will help in the next chapter as we describe the creation of these elements in preparation for our game.

CHAPTER 3

The Framework

In this chapter, we'll start creating a game application by building up the application framework. This will contain code necessary to get your application started, by initializing subsystems and starting the main loop. It will also form a layer between the iPhone OS and your game, providing resource management and abstracting complicated APIs such as graphics and sound. In essence, the framework should take care of as many common tasks as possible, so developers on new projects can immediately begin to implement game-specific code with as little work as necessary.

For our example game, the framework will consist of the following components:

The `GameState` and `GameStateManager` classes
> These are the base classes from which each major application state will inherit.

The `AppDelegate` class
> This is where the application begins and ends.

Event handling
> This will be handled separately by each game state class.

The Resource Manager
> We will create a singleton to provide resource loading and management, as well as functionality including textures, sounds, and user data.

The render engine
> This uses OpenGL ES to render textures in 2D format. Later we can expand on this to allow 3D graphics as well.

The sound engine
> This uses OpenAL and Audio Queue to play music and sound effects.

The data store
> This uses `NSUserDefaults` to store and load user preferences and game progression data in persistent memory.

Finally, in this chapter, we will create a skeleton project to show off the framework features. After preparing all of the framework components, we will have produced a reusable code base that will facilitate the creation of all kinds of exciting iPhone games.

Before you begin, please download the Chapter 3 examples at *https://sourceforge.net/projects/iphonegamebook/files/*.

Game State Management

Unfortunately for us, the iPhone is not centered on games. Instead, its focus is on utility and productivity applications such as web browsers, email clients, and music players. This is evident in the iPhone SDK, where its core APIs are mainly focused on GUI interaction and expect an event-callback scenario for processing data. This is not to say that games on the iPhone are at all inferior: it just takes a few extra steps to get what we want from the SDK.

First, let's look at the UIView and UIViewController classes from the iPhone SDK. At first glance, they seem similar to our GameState and GameStateManager classes. The UIViewController is responsible for managing one or more UIViews, just as the GameStateManager handles multiple GameStates. The UIView is responsible for rendering graphics in drawRect and handling input events from the touch screen in touchesEnded, roles similar to the GameState class's Render and Handle_Event functions we discussed in the preceding chapter.

However, one small difference creates an important mismatch between UIView and GameState: UIView lacks an Update function. This serves to highlight an important difference in the purpose of the two classes: UIView is not meant to represent separate application states.

So, how should we coordinate the use of GameState and UIView? There are a number of configurations we could try:

- One UIViewController and one UIView for the entire application
- One UIViewController for all GameStateManagers and one UIView for each GameState
- One UIViewController for each GameStateManager and one UIView for each GameState

All of these configurations will work, so it doesn't matter which one you choose. We chose to go with the second configuration, for the following reasons.

To begin, there is no need for multiple UIViewControllers because for our purposes, they do not do much. The real design decision comes down to whether to have one UIView for each GameState or one for the entire application.

Because each UIView contains its own event handling function, you can easily keep the event handling code for each GameState separate under the second configuration. Also, because each UIView has its own set of drawing coordinates, if multiple GameStates are drawn to different portions of the screen at the same time (such as a "game play" state overlaid by a "pause menu" state), the render code for each state does not have to worry about the screen offset of the origin in the state's window. And finally, because OpenGL

ES code does not play nicely with Cocoa and Quartz rendering code, it is advantageous to have a separate UIView for the different types of rendering we will be doing (more on this later).

Implementation

Now we are going to begin the framework. We will start by creating a new project and adding classes to represent our GameState and GameStateManager:

1. Open Xcode and select File→New Project→View-Based Application.
2. Add two new classes named GameState and GameStateManager.
3. In *GameStateManager.h*, add the following function to GameStateManager:

   ```
   - (void) doStateChange: (Class) state;
   ```

   This will allow you to change game states simply by passing the Class type of the state you want the GameStateManager to create.
4. In *GameState.h*, change the GameState class to inherit from UIView instead of NSObject. Also add the member variable GameStateManager* m_pManager; and the following functions:

   ```
   -(id) initWithFrame:(CGRect)frame andManager:(GameStateManager*)pManager;
   -(void) Render;
   -(void) Update;
   ```
5. Open *ExampleViewController.m* and uncomment the loadView function there, but leave it empty.

The first thing we did was to create a new view-based application. This automatically creates a few classes for us, including a single UIViewController and an AppDelegate.

The GameStateManager class is very basic; it is supposed to be a base class and provides just the doStateChange function, which will be inherited and overridden.

The GameState class is slightly more interesting; it is also a base class, but since we chose to have a single UIView for each of our GameStates, we will actually inherit UIView in our GameState class! This means that every GameState object *is* a UIView. Because our class is a UIView, we need to be sure to call initWithFrame on the superclass, but we also want to receive a pointer to our GameStateManager, so we need to create a new constructor that will initWithFrame: andManager.

We also have the Render and Update functions we discussed in Chapter 2. You will notice we do not have a Handle_Event function; this is because the UIView comes with a function that does this already, named touchesEnded: withEvent.

The implementation of the new GameState class functions looks like this:

```
//GameState.m
-(id) initWithFrame:(CGRect)frame andManager:(GameStateManager*)pManager;
{
```

```
    if (self = [super initWithFrame:frame]) {
        // Initialization code
        m_pManager = pManager;
        self.userInteractionEnabled = true;
    }
.   return self;
}

-(void) Update
{

}

-(void) Render
{

}

-(void) drawRect:(CGRect)rect
{
}
```

The `Update` and `Render` functions are empty because they will be overloaded. The `init WithFrame` function will also be overloaded, but we want to make sure to set up the `UIView` and set our `GameStateManager` pointer so that classes that inherit `GameState` don't have to. The `drawRect` function is inherited from `UIView` and gets called to render new graphics when the View gets invalidated; here we rerouted it to our own `Render` function.

Finally, notice that we did not declare or implement the `touchesEnded` function. That is because it is already taken care of inside the `UIView` class, and any of our classes that inherit from `GameState` will also inherit the `UIView` class as well.

Now that we have created the base class, we should start our first real `GameState`. We will call it `gsMain`, defined in the *gsMain.m* and *gsMain.h* files in the *Classes* subdirectory of the application, and for now all the class will do is display some text. Although we define `touchesEnded` and a few related variables, we have no code yet for handling touches:

```
//gsMain.h
@interface gsTest : GameState {
//no new member declarations necessary
}
@end

//gsMain.m
@implementation gsMain

-(gsMain*) initWithFrame:(CGRect)frame andManager:(GameStateManager*)pManager
{
    if (self = [super initWithFrame:frame andManager:pManager]) {
        NSLog(@"gsTest init");
```

```
    }
    return self;
}

-(void) Render
{
    CGContextRef g = UIGraphicsGetCurrentContext();
    //fill background with gray
    CGContextSetFillColorWithColor(g, [UIColor greyColor].CGColor);
    CGContextFillRect(g, CGRectMake(0, 0, self.frame.size.width,
self.frame.size.height));
    //draw text in black
    CGContextSetFillColorWithColor(g, [UIColor blackColor].CGColor);

    [@"O'Reilly Rules!" drawAtPoint:CGPointMake(10.0,20.0)
            withFont:[UIFont systemFontOfSize:[UIFont systemFontSize]]];
}

-(void)touchesEnded:(NSSet*)touches withEvent:(UIEvent*)event
{
    UITouch* touch = [touches anyObject];
    NSUInteger numTaps = [touch tapCount];

    //todo: implement touch event code here

}
@end
```

The gsMain class inherits from GameState (which inherits from UIView). In the constructor, we make sure to call the GameState constructor (which calls the UIView constructor).

Removing the Status Bar

Because this game will want to take up as much of the screen as possible, we need to hide the status bar from view. This will also hide the green "touch to return to call" bar that shows up when running an application during an active phone call (which is nice because we don't have to worry about resizing our game due to the change in visible screen space):

1. In Xcode, double-click the *Info.plist* file in the left window.
2. Add a key named UIStatusBarHidden to *Info.plist*.
3. Right-click the value field and set the type to Boolean, and then check True.

The App Delegate

One of the classes Xcode created for us was AppDelegate. This is the first piece of code that gets loaded when our program is run, and the last to unload. We are going to modify this class to inherit from GameStateManager because it is going to manage all of the important GameStates in our game. Like the other classes, *GameStateManager.m* and *GameStateManager.h* are located in the *Classes* subdirectory. Begin by modifying the `Test_FrameworkAppDelegate` class:

```
//Test_FrameworkAppDelegate.h
#include "GameStateManager.h"

@interface Test_FrameworkAppDelegate : GameStateManager <UIApplicationDelegate>
```

When our application starts up, the `applicationDidFinishLaunching` function is called on our `AppDelegate` to let us start initializing our game. We need to do two things here: start our main loop code and create an instance of our first `GameState`.

Add the following code to your `AppDelegate` class (don't forget to add the appropriate header functions):

```
//Test_FrameworkAppDelegate.m
#include "Test_FrameworkAppDelegate.h"

- (void) applicationDidFinishLaunching:(UIApplication *)application
{
    //set up main loop
    [NSTimer scheduledTimerWithTimeInterval:0.033
            target:self
            selector:@selector(gameLoop:)
            userInfo:nil
            repeats:NO];

    //create instance of the first GameState
    [self doStateChange:[gsMain class]];
}

- (void) gameLoop: (id) sender
{
    [((GameState*)viewController.view) Update];
    [((GameState*)viewController.view) Render];

    [NSTimer scheduledTimerWithTimeInterval:0.033
            target:self
            selector:@selector(gameLoop:)
            userInfo:nil
            repeats:NO];
}

- (void) doStateChange: (Class) state
{
    if( viewController.view != nil ) {
        //remove view from window's subviews.
        [viewController.view removeFromSuperview];
        [viewController.view release]; //release gamestate
    }

    viewController.view = [[state alloc]
            initWithFrame:CGRectMake(0, 0, IPHONE_WIDTH, IPHONE_HEIGHT)
            andManager:self];
```

```
        //now set our view as visible
        [window addSubview:viewController.view];
        [window makeKeyAndVisible];
    }
```

First, the applicationDidFinishLaunching function starts a callback to our gameLoop function. Next, it changes to our first GameState, which will be gsMain.

Our gameLoop function is the main loop of our application. First it calls the Update function on the current GameState class and redraws the screen with the Render function. It finishes by setting up a new callback to continue the next cycle of the main loop.

The doStateChange function is inherited from our GameStateManager class. It accepts a class as a parameter; this should be a class that inherits from GameState because it will be instantiated and set as the current view. It begins by checking to see whether a previous state exists; if so, the state is removed from the window and released to avoid leaking any memory. Then it creates a new instance of the class that was passed in, being sure to send a pointer to our AppDelegate class in the addManager parameter. Finally, it sets the new GameState as our viewController's current UIView object and sets it as the window's active view.

Remember when we implemented ExampleViewController's loadView function but left it empty? That was so that when our application starts, it does not set up a UIView of its own from the *.nib* file.

Frames per Second

As an added exercise to make sure we understand the way the main loop works, we will add code to display the current frames per second (fps) in our gsMain class.

First, we will calculate the fps in our AppDelegate class so that we can provide the information to any of our GameStates that wants to know. Add the following variables to your @interface definition in *AppDelegate.h*:

```
        CFTimeInterval m_FPS_lastSecondStart;
        int m_FPS_framesThisSecond;
        int m_FPS;
```

Now open *AppDelegate.m* and add the following code to the start of the gameLoop function:

```
        double currTime = [[NSDate date] timeIntervalSince1970];
        m_FPS_framesThisSecond++;
        float timeThisSecond = currTime - m_FPS_lastSecondStart;
        if( timeThisSecond > 1.0f ) {
            m_FPS = m_FPS_framesThisSecond;
            m_FPS_framesThisSecond = 0;
            m_FPS_lastSecondStart = currTime;
        }
```

What is going on here? To start, we have a counter named m_FPS_framesThisSecond that will start at 0 every second and increment each time the game loop is run. Once we have passed one second, as determined by m_FPS_lastSecondStart, we store the value in m_FPS for use by our GameState, and reset the counter and start time.

The iPhone SDK treats time differently from most APIs. Unless you are an OS X developer, you may be used to getting the time in milliseconds as an unsigned 32-bit integer. However, OS X and the iPhone refer to time as a 64-bit double, and a value of 1.0 means one second; milliseconds are found behind the decimal place.

It takes a second (pun intended) to get used to, but once you understand the difference it's quite easy to work with. For instance, why did we use 0.033 as our sleep timer? One second divided by 30 frames = 1.0 / 30.0 = 0.033 seconds per frame. So, to have 30 fps, the standard refresh rate to produce smooth effects to the human eye, we need our game loop to run once every 0.033 seconds.

Now that we know our fps, we need to display it. There are plenty of ways we could pass the data from the GameStateHandler to the GameState; we will use a straightforward method and add a function to the AppDelegate with the signature - (int) getFramesPerSecond. The function just returns the value of m_FPS.

In our gsMain state, edit the Update function to add the following code:

```
int FPS = [((Test_FrameworkAppDelegate*)m_pManager) getFramesPerSecond];
NSString* strFPS = [NSString stringWithFormat:@"%d", FPS];
[strFPS drawAtPoint:CGPointMake(10.0,60.0) withFont:[UIFont
systemFontOfSize:[UIFont systemFontSize]]];
```

First, we retrieve the value of m_FPS from our GameStateHandler, which we know to be the AppDelegate class. Next, we format a string from the integer value, and then draw that string to the screen with a default system font.

Event Handling

Because our GameState class inherits from UIView, we can override its event handling functions for our purposes. To show this behavior, we will add to our example by creating a second GameState named gsTest. We will modify gsMain to change to the new state when the user double-taps the screen, and switch back again when she double-taps from gsTest:

```
//gsTest.h
@interface gsTest : GameState {
//no members necessary
}
@end
//gsTest.m
@class gsMain //forward declaration
@implementation gsTest

-(gsTest*) initWithFrame:(CGRect)frame andManager:(GameStateManager*)pManager
{
```

```
    if (self = [super initWithFrame:frame andManager:pManager]) {
        NSLog(@"gsTest init");
    }
    return self;
}

-(void) Render
{
    CGContextRef g = UIGraphicsGetCurrentContext();
    //fill background with blue
    CGContextSetFillColorWithColor(g, [UIColor blueColor].CGColor);
    CGContextFillRect(g,
        CGRectMake(0, 0, self.frame.size.width, self.frame.size.height));

    //draw text in black
    CGContextSetFillColorWithColor(g, [UIColor blackColor].CGColor);

    [@"it works!" drawAtPoint:CGPointMake(10.0,20.0)
                withFont:[UIFont systemFontOfSize:[UIFont systemFontSize]]];
}

-(void)touchesEnded:(NSSet*)touches withEvent:(UIEvent*)event
{
    UITouch* touch = [touches anyObject];
    NSUInteger numTaps = [touch tapCount];
    if( numTaps > 1 ) {
        [m_pManager doStateChange:[gsMain class]];
    }
}
}
@end
```

For the return to gsTest, we need to add the same touchesEnded function to our gsMain class, but making doStateChange call [gsTest class]. When compiled and run, the application should now respond to a double tap by switching to the gsTest state, and back to the gsMain state with another double tap.

What is going on here? To start, we take a UITouch object from the set of touches that gets passed into our touchesEnded function. Keep in mind that the user can be touching the screen with multiple fingers at the same time. To keep track of that, the iPhone keeps an array of UITouch objects, one for each finger, and sends that to each touch event handling function.

At this point, we don't really care how many fingers were used or which UITouch object we respond to, so we grab anyObject from the set. Next, we find out the number of taps this UITouch object has performed so far, and if that number is greater than one, we perform our desired action: a state change.

Handling touch events can get much more complicated, but this is all we need to get started.

The Resource Manager

To begin drawing images, playing music, and saving user preferences, we first need to be able to load textures and sound samples, and to read and write binary files. That is the first responsibility of the Resource Manager. The second responsibility is to unload resources when they are no longer needed, to make room for others.

First we must decide what formats to use for our textures and sound samples, and how we will distribute them with our application. Next, we will have to write code to load those resources when needed, and unload them when they are not being used.

Texture Format

For the texture format, the iPhone prefers PNG files. The PNG file format provides compressed textures with decent quality as well as the option of alpha blending for transparent pixels.

As we will discuss in the next chapter, we will be using OpenGL ES as our graphics API. To use a texture with OpenGL, we first have to load the texture file, uncompress it into a buffer, and use that buffer to generate a GL_TEXTURE_2D texture. To keep all of this simple so that we can stay focused on game programming, we are going to need a class to represent OpenGL textures, which we will name GLTexture.

A number of example applications distributed by Apple during the iPhone SDK Beta are no longer available, and one of them provided a class that acted as a simple 2D texture interface for OpenGL ES. We have tracked the class down and modified it for use in our framework.

In addition to providing GLTextures, we will also provide GLFonts to draw text using OpenGL. We will go into more detail about this in the section "The Render Engine" on page 80.

Sound Format

The native sound format for the iPhone is CAF, which stands for Core Audio Format. To get the best performance, all sound effects used should be *.caf* files. Meanwhile, music files tend to be much too large and should be stored using the compressed *.mp3* format instead.

We will need to use both OpenAL and Audio Queue APIs to handle these two formats. Fortunately, another piece of code is available from Apple that we have managed to incorporate into our framework to make handling sounds much easier.

The tool to convert a sound file to CAF format is called afconvert and is available on OS X from the command line, like so:

```
/usr/bin/afconvert -f caff -d LEI16 mySound.wav
mySound.caf
```

Deploying Resources

For your program to access these sound and image files, the files need to be a part of your application bundle. Adding resources to your application bundle is very easy. Simply drag the files you wish to include from the filesystem into the *Resources* folder in your Xcode project window. They will automatically be included in the bundle the next time you build your application.

Management

Now that we know what formats we are supporting, and some classes that make loading and using those formats simple, we want a class that will give us easy access to all of the resources in our bundle. We also want it to keep track of the ones we have already loaded into memory, as well as unload those resources when they are no longer in use.

We will begin by creating a class called ResourceManager that will keep track of our resources. It will have a single instance that is globally accessible so that it is easy to access all of our game code. All we need to do to add a texture to a class is call getTexture on the instance of our ResourceManager like so:

```
GLTexture* myTexture = [g_ResManager getTexture:@"myTexture.png"];
```

If the *myTexture.png* file is already loaded into memory, the ResourceManager class will simply hand it to us. If not, it will automatically load the image and then hand it over. Loading and playing sounds is just as easy:

```
[g_ResManager playSound:@"mySound.caf"];
```

This will automatically load the sound if it isn't already in memory, and then play it.

Now comes the question of when to unload resources. Optimally, only resources currently in use would be in memory at any one time so that we would not end up with memory allocated for a resource that is not in use. However, loading resources can be slow, so having to unload and reload a resource between each use can also be inefficient. More resources in memory means less CPU time wasted reloading them, but our memory is limited.

Fortunately, although games tend to use a large amount of resources, they also have an easy way to predict which groups of resources will be necessary during certain application states. Specifically, most game designs split game play among many distinct levels. As the game programmer, you know ahead of time which resources may be needed for each level and which are not. You can simply purge resources when leaving one level and load only the resources necessary for the next level.

To do this, we provide purge functions for each resource:

```
[g_ResManager purgeTextures];
[g_ResManager purgeSounds];
```

Simply call the purge functions to release resources when you know you don't need them, such as when you are changing GameStates.

 Resource management can be very complex. Consider a system that automatically releases old resources that have not been used recently to make room for new ones. This system would be beneficial in reducing the amount of redundant loading and unloading between state changes, as long as there was enough memory to go around.

In fact, this idea is very close to garbage collection, of which there are many types of implementations. However, it can be very hard to do well, and since it is unnecessary in our case, we will avoid the complexity in our framework.

The Render Engine

There are several APIs for drawing in the iPhone SDK, each useful for different purposes. Cocoa uses Objective-C and focuses on manipulating high-level GUI objects such as UIImage, UIColor, and UIFont. Quartz Core Graphics uses C and is great for drawing vector graphics such as lines, gradients, and shading, and for rendering PDF content. However, most games require a high-performance rendering API, which is why OpenGL ES is available.

OpenGL ES is a very low-level API focused on 3D rendering, so we are going to have to build up some code to bridge the gap between what we want to do—draw 2D animated sprites—and what OpenGL ES can do: render textures onto 3D geometry.

2D Graphics with a 3D API

At this point, you might be asking yourself: "How are we going to use OpenGL to draw 2D sprites? I thought OpenGL was for 3D!"

Without getting into the math, 2D is a subset of 3D. That means anything you can do in 2D you can also do in 3D. Specifically, imagine a table with a piece of paper on it. The table and the paper are 3D. However, if you point a camera straight down at the paper, the camera sees what looks like a 2D scene. That is essentially what you will be doing with your 2D game. Meanwhile, when you get to the 3D example, you can use the full power of OpenGL ES with very little additional work, since it's already set up.

Three-dimensional rendering concepts and code can become complicated and confusing very quickly, and this is not a book about OpenGL ES. For this chapter and the next, we will try to use as little OpenGL ES code as necessary, and this code will be available to you at *http://iphonegamebook.sourceforge.net/* so that we can focus on *what* is being done, rather than *how* it is being done.

Three things are required to perform basic rendering with OpenGL ES on the iPhone: a GLContext object, an OpenGL layer for that context to draw to, and the ability to load an image into memory and bind it for use as a GL_TEXTURE_2D texture.

We need only one GLContext for the life of our application, and it needs to be accessible by all game states that wish to render using OpenGL ES. Meanwhile, we will want a separate OpenGL layer for each game state that renders using OpenGL. Because, as we discussed earlier, our GameState class inherits from UIView, each GameState instance can use the layer provided by its UIView. By overriding the UIView function named layer Class, we can specify a custom type of layer for that View and create an OpenGL layer instead. And once we have set up the GLContext and OpenGL layer, we will be able to get textures from our ResourceManager.

GLESGameState

To encapsulate these ideas, we will create a new type of GameState class called GLESGameState. It will contain all of the code necessary to instantiate the GLContext instance and prepare OpenGL for rendering, as well as inherit from GameState and override the layerClass function.

The code we'll be writing is available in the example files as *GLESGameState.m*. If you are familiar with OpenGL, you will recognize much of this code; if not, don't worry about it. You don't need to know what you're doing with OpenGL in this section; you just need to know enough to plug the code into your application. We'll describe what we're doing and how to incorporate the code into an application in this section.

To begin, notice the global gles_context variable at the top, of type CAEAGLContext. This will be our GLContext, and we made it global so that any of our GLESGameState classes will be able to use it easily.

Next, take a look at the initialize function. In Objective-C, every class can have a function of this name, and it gets called exactly once (*not* once for each instance), before that class receives any other messages. This is perfect for initializing singleton class instances that don't depend on other resources. Our initialize function calls setup2D, which will prepare our OpenGL context to draw in a 2D fashion.

Now take a look at the layerClass method. The UIView class calls this method for each instance when it's created, to create its UILayer. Our GLESGameState class overrides the layerClass method of UIView to return a CAEAGLLayer class instead of a CALayer class so that our layer object will be the right type for OpenGL ES to draw to.

Finally, in our `initWithFrame` function, notice the call to `bindLayer`. This needs to happen every time we create a new `GLESGameState` so that we tell `GLContext` that a new OpenGL layer is available and that we should be rendering to it now. The heart of the function is the call to the `EAGLContext` function, `setCurrentContext`, which loads this instance's context into the global variable we defined for the current context, `gles_context`.

Once a `GLESGameState` is created, we are prepared to use OpenGL API calls to render to an OpenGL layer. All you need to do is create some `GLTextures` and draw with them in the `Render` function of your `GLESGameState`.

Textures

Now that we have a `GLContext` and an OpenGL layer, all we need to render an image to the screen is a `GL_TEXTURE_2D` texture. Unfortunately, OpenGL does not provide any code to open image files and load them into memory, a task that is filesystem dependent. Instead, we must rely on Quartz2D to load an image format into a buffer in memory, after which we can use OpenGL to create a `GL_TEXTURE_2D` texture from that buffer.

We have assembled this functionality in the `GLTexture` class, which is based on some examples provided by Apple. You do not need to be able to follow every line of the code; you only need to plug it into your application.

As you may recall, the `ResourceManager` class will load an image file and create a `GLTexture` object when we call the `getTexture` function. That function simply creates a `UIImage` into which to load the image file, which is then sent to the `initWithImage` function of `GLTexture`.

Once a `GLTexture` has been created, you can use it to draw to the screen in your `Render` function by calling any of its draw functions. The simplest method is to specify a point on the screen where the entire image will be drawn, like so:

```
GLTexture* myTexture = [g_ResManager getTexture:@"myTexture.png"];
[myTexture drawAtPoint:CGPointMake(150, 150)];
```

This will draw the center of your image 150 pixels from the left and 150 pixels from the bottom of the screen.

 The coordinate system for OpenGL starts with the origin (0,0) at the bottom left by default, where the Y value increases as you move up the screen. This is different from the way Quartz draws, with the origin at the top left and the Y value increasing as you move down the screen.

Of course, it may be necessary to draw textures in more complicated ways, such as with rotations, or to draw only a portion of your texture, which is why additional draw functions are also available.

Furthermore, it may be helpful to know more information about our textures, such as the height and width of the original image file. For instance, let's say we wanted to draw the previous example from the top left of the image instead of from the center. Given the original height and width, we could do this as follows:

```
GLTexture* myTexture = [g_ResManager getTexture:@"myTexture.png"];
[myTexture drawAtPoint:
    CGPointMake(150 - [myTexture contentSize].width/2,
                150 - [myTexture contentSize].height/2)];
```

Armed with these basic tools, we can proceed to more complex rendering tasks, such as fonts.

Tricks for Drawing Textures with OpenGL

Note the following tricks when drawing textures with OpenGL:

- All GL_TEXTURE_2D textures should be sized in powers of 2, which means that even if your image is 250 × 31, when you create the texture on hardware to store it you will be making a 256 × 32 pixel texture buffer. Your GLTexture class will round up the buffer size transparently, so you may not even realize it, but keep in mind that, for example, a 257 × 33 pixel image will actually end up occupying the space of a 512 × 64 image in memory.

- Transparent edges can "bleed" color when blended. Pay careful attention to the cropped image in the example state at the end of this section. You may see a tinge of red around the green pixels that should have been cropped. Make sure to edit the transparency of the pixels in source images correctly to avoid this.

 Each time you change the texture you are drawing with, OpenGL has to switch contexts. This causes a minor performance hit that you can avoid through a combination of two techniques. First, when creating your textures, try to put all of the images that might be drawn at the same time into the same texture. Second, try to draw objects that use the same image at the same time. For instance, place all tiles for a single level in the same texture file and draw the entire level together before drawing the rest of the scene.

Font Textures

Because OpenGL does not play nicely with the other graphical APIs on the iPhone, we cannot use the same code to draw text in our GLESGameStates as we did in our gsMain and gsTest classes. Instead, we are going to have to draw our text using GLTextures.

There are two ways to accomplish this task. One is to create a texture and draw our letters into it to create the word we want. Although this is great for static words that don't change, our game is likely to have many different words or strings with numbers that change frequently.

Consider the frames-per-second example from earlier; if we were to create a new texture for every frame rate number, we would quickly run out of memory. Instead, we could create a larger texture containing the digits 0 through 9. When we need to draw our frames-per-second number, we choose a subsection of the texture and draw only the portion we need for each digit. This is an application of the optimization we described earlier: combining many images into one texture. This is a much more efficient way to draw text in OpenGL, and the one we will use.

Specifically, we will create a large dictionary texture that contains all of the letters, numbers, and symbols we need, as well as the code to draw the appropriate sections of the texture to the screen when we want to render a string.

We have done this for you in the GLFont class. You do not need to understand what is going on in every line, but we will offer an overview.

Because GLFont will ultimately contain a GL_TEXTURE_2D texture and the code to draw it, we start by inheriting from the GLTexture class. Next, we add a custom initialization function named initWithString.

In the initWithString function, the GLFont class uses the Quartz2D API to create an image buffer in memory and render all of the letters to it. It has parameters that allow you to specify a font name and size, as well as a second function with extended parameters to specify color and stroke.

While we are rendering each letter into the image buffer, we will store the exact size and position of each character for use later when we want to draw strings to the screen. The data associated with each character is called a *glyph*, and we store our glyphs in an array called fontdata.

Once the image buffer is filled in using Quartz2D, we call the GLTexture initialization function to convert it for use with OpenGL, remembering to release the now unnecessary Quartz2D image buffer.

Finally comes the drawString function, which accepts the string to draw and a CGPoint to indicate where to draw to the screen, starting at the bottom left of the string. For each character in the input string, the function looks up the appropriate glyph in the fontdata array and draws a subsection of our GLTexture to the screen, remembering to add an *x* offset after each character is drawn.

It is very easy to use this class:

```
//Initialize the font for use in a constructor
GLFont* tex = [GLFont alloc];
[tex initWithString:@"
abcdefghijklmnopqrstuvwxyzABCDEFGHIJKLMNOPQRSTUVWXYZ1234567890.!?, "
fontName:@"Helvetica" fontSize:15.0f];

//Draw a string to the screen in a Render function
[tex drawString:@"I love monkeys!" atPoint:CGPointMake(20, 300)];
```

Keep in mind that, just like GLTexture, you must use GLFont in conjunction with a valid GLESGameState.

As a convenience function, we have added a defaultFont function to our Resource Manager to create and return a GLFont with default parameters. You can customize the string to contain whatever characters you need in your displays.

Example State

To show off all of the work we have done, let's create an example state that shows the use of the GLESGameState, GLTexture, and GLFont classes:

1. Before we can use any OpenGL ES code, we need to add the *OpenGLES.framework* and *QuartzCore.framework* files to our project. A *.framework* file is similar to a *.lib* file in Windows programs, or an *.so* file in Linux. Right-click the *frameworks* folder in the project browser on the left of your Xcode window, select Add→Existing Framework, and find *OpenGLES.Framework*. If you cannot find it, you are in the wrong folder, so start in */Developer/Platforms/* and search for the latest iPhone SDK folder followed by */System/Library/Frameworks/OpenGLES.framework*.

2. Select Xcode file→New File→Cocoa Touch Classes→NSObject subclass, and name the new class gsTextureTest.

3. Add **#include "GameState.h"** to the top of *gsTextureTest.h*.

4. Modify *gsTextureTest.h* so that the gsTextureTest class inherits from GLESGameState instead of NSObject.

5. The default constructor from GSLESGameState will do all the necessary setup automatically, so all we need is a Render function that will handle the drawing code. Technically, you could put all of this in the Update function, but it's a good practice to keep your rendering code separate from your update logic. To begin, Render will have the basic code needed to clear the background and commit our graphics to the screen:

```
-(void) Render {
    //clear anything left over from the last frame, and set background color.
    glClearColor(0xff/256.0f, 0x66/256.0f, 0x00/256.0f, 1.0f);
    glClear(GL_COLOR_BUFFER_BIT);

    //Render textures here

    //you get a nice boring white screen if you forget to swap buffers.
    [self swapBuffers];
};
```

Notice the glClearColor and glClear function calls. Both of these are OpenGL functions. You can use OpenGL directly in your code; however, you won't need to do this often.

6. Now we are going to add some spice to our Render function. We want to draw some text and images using defaultFont and the *scissors.png* and *drawregion.png* files in *Chapter3Framework.zip*. To make things interesting, we will move the scissors texture left and right, and draw only a portion of the drawregion texture:

```
//some rendering offsets
int yspacing = -24, line = 0, yoff = 360;
int leftcolumn = 10;

//test our GLFont
[[g_ResManager defaultFont] drawString:@"Font ok."
        atPoint:CGPointMake(leftcolumn, yoff+yspacing*line++)];

//draw the scissors image with a label
[[g_ResManager defaultFont] drawString:@"GLTexture test:"
        atPoint:CGPointMake(leftcolumn, yoff+yspacing*line++)];
//make the image waggle back and forth.
float x = (1+sin([[NSDate date] timeIntervalSince1970]))
                * self.frame.size.width / 2;
[[g_ResManager getTexture:@"scissors.png"]
        drawAtPoint:CGPointMake(x, yoff+yspacing*line)];
yoff -= [[g_ResManager getTexture:@"scissors.png"] contentSize].height;

//draw the clipped drawregion image with a label
[[g_ResManager defaultFont] drawString:@"Clipped image test:"
        atPoint:CGPointMake(leftcolumn, yoff+yspacing*line++)];
[[g_ResManager getTexture:@"drawregion.png"]
        drawInRect:CGRectMake(leftcolumn, yoff+yspacing*line, 20, 20)
  withClip:CGRectMake(15, 30, 20, 20) withRotation:0];
```

As you can see, we are using the defaultFont provided by the Resource Manager, and can easily draw "Font ok." text to the screen.

Next, we draw another string to label our second test. Our starting point is the line following the previous string, because we increment our line variable each time we use it to calculate a location. We compute an *x* position offset from the center of the screen as a sine wave of the current time (don't worry too much about the math behind this). We grab our *scissors.png* texture from the Resource Manager and call drawAtPoint using that offset. For convenience, we also modify our yoff variable to move down a number of pixels equal to the height of the image. (If we replaced *scissors.png* with a different image here, this assignment statement would automatically resize the *y* offset of the next drawing test.)

Finally, we draw a third string to label the last test. We grab *drawregion.png* from our Resource Manager and draw it with the drawInRect: withClip function. Notice that we leave the rotation at zero; you could easily modify this to add rotation based on time (as we did with the *x* position of our *scissors.png* image). Everything is working so far, so let's move on to the next feature.

7. Add a touchesEnded function to allow this state to change to a Main menu state we will create later on:

```
-(void)touchesEnded:(NSSet*)touches withEvent:(UIEvent*)event
{
    UITouch* touch = [touches anyObject];
    NSUInteger numTaps = [touch tapCount];
    if( numTaps > 1 ) {
        [m_pManager doStateChange:[gsMainMenu class]];
        //we will create gsMainMenu at the end of this chapter
    }

}
```

The Sound Engine

There are typically two purposes for playing a sound in a game application: background music and sound effects. Both end up at the same place, the speakers (or headphones), but due to their different requirements, they need two different routes to get there.

Sound effect files tend to be very short, most of them between one and 10 seconds long, and they don't take up much memory, partly because their sound quality can be lower than that of music. For our application, we require that they play as soon as we request them to play with little to no latency (so that they are relevant to what is happening on the screen), and we may need to play many of them at once.

However, music files tend to be longer (on the order of one or more minutes) and much larger. So large, in fact, that they need to be compressed to reduce their size, thus the popularity of the *.mp3* file format. Unfortunately, that also means they need to be uncompressed when we want to play the file, which requires additional CPU usage. Since we don't need to play more than one music file at the same time, this is acceptable.

Just as with graphics, the iPhone provides multiple APIs for sound playback. Your decision of which to use will depend on the problem you are trying to solve. For example, OpenAL is good at playing short sound effect files with as little latency as possible, while Audio Queue can be used for playing music from compressed file formats.

A lot of code goes into setting all this up, but Apple has provided some example code in the form of *SoundEngine.h* and *SoundEngine.cpp*, which we have incorporated into our framework. Although the body of work is C++ code, Xcode can compile Objective-C, standard C, and C++ in the same project. Note, however, that the C++ code is entirely contained in the *.cpp* file and that all of the *.h* interfaces are standard C functions so that the C++ code can be easily used within Objective-C code.

As we mentioned earlier, we have written ResourceProvider functions that act as an interface to this code to make it even simpler to use, by handling the loading and unloading of sound resources automatically.

Example State

Just as with the example state for rendering, we want to create an example state to show our new sound functionality. This state will be a little different from the last one: because we do not need to use any OpenGL rendering, we will create a normal GameState and use Interface Builder to add severalUIButtons to it.

Specifically, we will create a button that plays a sound effect file, *tap.caf*; another button that plays a looped music file, *social.mp3*; a button that stops the music file; and a button that switches state to the Main menu state:

1. Add the *OpenAL.framework* and *AudioToolbox.frameworks* files in the same manner as you added the *OpenGLES.framework* file earlier.

2. Select Xcode file→New File→User Interfaces→View XIB and name the file *soundtest.xib*.

3. Select Xcode file→New File→Cocoa Touch Classes→NSObject subclass and name the new class gsSoundTest.

4. Add **#include "GameState.h"** to the top of *gsSoundTest.h*.

5. Modify *gsSoundTest.h* to have the gsSoundTest class inherit from GameState instead of NSObject.

6. Add an IBOutlet to *gsSoundTest.h* to represent the UIView:

   ```
   IBOutlet UIView* subview;
   ```

7. Add four IBActions to *gsSoundTest.h* to represent the actions that will take place when each button is pressed:

   ```
   -(IBAction) playCafSfx;
   -(IBAction) playMp3;
   -(IBAction) stopMusic;
   -(IBAction) back;
   ```

8. Modify the initWithFrame function in *gsSoundTest.m* to load the *soundtest.nib* file:

   ```
   -(SoundTest*) initWithFrame:(CGRect)frame
                  andManager:(GameStateManager*)pManager
   {

       if (self = [super initWithFrame:frame andManager:pManager]) {
           NSLog(@"SoundTest init");
           //load the soundtest.xib file here.
           //this will instantiate the 'subview' uiview.
           [[NSBundle mainBundle] loadNibNamed:@"soundtest"
                               owner:self options:nil];
           //add subview as... a subview.
           //This will let everything from the nib file show up on screen.
           [self addSubview:subview];
       }

       return self;
   }
   ```

9. Implement the `IBAction` functions we defined to play the sound effect file, play the music file, stop the music, and return to the Main menu state:

```
-(IBAction) playCafSfx
{
    [g_ResManager playSound:@"tap.caf"];
}

-(IBAction) playMp3
{
    [g_ResManager playMusic:@"social.mp3"];
}

-(IBAction) stopMusic
{
    [g_ResManager stopMusic];
}

-(IBAction) back {
    [m_pManager doStateChange:[gsMainMenu class]];
}
```

 Have you noticed that the sound interface we created is function-based instead of object-oriented? The Resource Manager will give us a `GLTexture` object or `GLFont` object, but why is there no `SoundObject`?

Although it makes sense to treat textures like objects (to manipulate properties such as height and width, and choose which way to draw them), sound playback is much simpler. Typically, you want a sound to play in a fire-and-forget manner. You don't need to know how long it is or the present position of a sample that is currently playing. All you want it to do is play or stop sounds and let the sound engine do the rest.

The Data Store

The final feature we must add to our framework is the ability to store and load data, such as the player's sound preferences and game progression.

On some platforms, we would be required to create a binary file format to store our data manually using filesystem I/O; however, the iPhone provides the `NSUserDe faults` API, which allows us to store key-value pairs (similar to the Registry in Windows) of the following types: `NSData`, `NSString`, `NSNumber`, `NSArray`, and `NSDictionary`. We have added an interface to perform these tasks easily in `ResourceManager`.

Storing Simple Data

The simplest data we will want to store is a Boolean variable to indicate whether the user wants game sounds to be on or off. We can store it as an `NSNumber` in the following manner:

```
[g_ResManager storeUserData:[NSNumber numberWithBool:TRUE]
            toFile:@"soundPrefs"];
```

This will save the NSNumber value of TRUE with a key name of "soundPrefs". Then we can exit the application knowing that value has been saved to disk. To retrieve it the next time we start up, we'll use the following code:

```
BOOL mySoundPref = [[g_ResManager getUserData:@"soundPrefs"] boolValue];
```

This will load the NSNumber value associated with the key "soundPrefs" and convert it to a BOOL, which will have a value of TRUE because we stored it on our previous application run.

You can use this method for any of the data types, leading to more interesting combinations. For instance, to store a list of high scores, you could create an NSDictionary whose NSString keys represent names and whose NSNumber values represent the scores. You could then store that NSDictionary and retrieve it again later on.

Storing Complex Data

As the player progresses through a game, he may unlock new levels, gain new weapons and equipment, or achieve new high scores. He may even wish to save his exact position and all other game entities in the middle of game play if a phone call interrupts him.

Having to translate all of this data from objects in memory to NSNumber or NSDiction ary types would be inefficient. However, the NSData type allows us to store a buffer with arbitrary memory content using the storeUserData function.

After serializing the data you wish to save into a buffer in memory, use the following code to store dataSize bytes of data into NSUserDefaults:

```
int dataSize;
void* progressionData = myGameSaveFunction(&dataSize);
[g_ResManager storeUserData:
            [NSData dataWithBytes:progressionData length:dataSize]
            toFile:@"gameSave1"];
```

And to retrieve the buffer from memory, issue the following:

```
const void* savedData = [[g_ResManager getUserData:@"gameSave1"] bytes];
```

Example State

Now we will create the third example state. Similar to the sound example, we do not need to use OpenGL to render any elements, so we will inherit from the regular GameState class and use Interface Builder to add UI elements.

Specifically, we want to show that we can store a preference to persistent memory and recall that value the next time our application runs. So, we will add a UISwitch to represent the preference, as well as a UIButton to allow the user to return to the Main menu:

---

1. Select Xcode file→New File→User Interfaces→View XIB and name the file *storagetest.xib*.

2. Select Xcode file→New File→Cocoa Touch Classes→NSObject subclass and name the new class `gsStorageTest`.

3. Modify *gsStorageTest.h* so that the class inherits from `GameState` instead of `NSObject`.

4. Add `#include "GameState.h"` to the top of *gsStorageTest.h*.

5. Add two `IBOutlets` in *gsStorageTest.h*, one for the view you will load from *storagetest.xib* and one for the `UISwitch` inside that view:

```
IBOutlet UIView* subview;
IBOutlet UISwitch* toggle;
```

6. Add two `IBActions` in *gsStorageTest.h* to represent the actions that take place when the `UISwitch` and `UIButton` are pressed, as well as a function to run some additional unit tests:

```
- (void) runTests;
- (IBAction) toggled;
- (IBAction) back;
```

7. Modify the `initWithFrame` function in *gsStorageTest.m* to load the *storagetest.nib* file, initialize the state of your `UISwitch` with `getUserData`, and call the `runTests` function:

```
-(gsStorageTest*) initWithFrame:(CGRect)frame
                andManager:(GameStateManager*)pManager
{

    if (self = [super initWithFrame:frame andManager:pManager]) {
        NSLog(@"storagetest init");
        //load the storagetest.xib file here.
        //this will instantiate the 'subview' uiview.
        [[NSBundle mainBundle] loadNibNamed:@"storagetest"
                            owner:self
                            options:nil];
        //add subview as... a subview.
        //This will let everything from the nib file show up on screen.
        [self addSubview:subview];
    }
    //load the last saved state of the toggle switch.
    toggle.on = [[g_ResManager getUserData:@"toggle.on"] boolValue];
    [self runTests];

    return self;
}
```

8. Implement the `IBAction` functions to switch to the Main menu state, and update the state of the `UISwitch` with `storeUserData`:

```
-(IBAction) back {
    [m_pManager doStateChange:[gsMainMenu class]];
}
```

```
-(IBAction) toggled {
    //we can't directly store a bool, but we can store a nsnumber with a bool.
    [g_ResManager storeUserData:
            [NSNumber numberWithBool:toggle.on]
            toFile:@"toggle.on"];
}
```

9. Implement the runTests function to unit-test more complex aspects of data storage:

```
-(void) log:(NSString*)str {
    //just dump to console.
    NSLog(str);
}

-(NSString*)passfail:(BOOL)pass{
    return pass?@"(pass)":@"(fail)";
}

//unit tests for data storage.
//Anything that comes out as (fail) is problematic.
-(void) runTests {
    {
        NSData* nonexistantfile = [g_ResManager getUserData:@"notfound"];
        [self log:[NSString stringWithFormat:@"%@ load non existant file: %@",
                        [self passfail:nonexistantfile==nil],
                        nonexistantfile]];

        BOOL fileexists = [g_ResManager userDataExists:@"notfound"];
        [self log:[NSString stringWithFormat:@"%@ non existant file test: %d",
                        [self passfail:!fileexists],
                        fileexists]];
    }

    {
        NSString* savedString = @"some saved text.";
        BOOL saveok = [g_ResManager storeUserData:
                [savedString dataUsingEncoding:NSUnicodeStringEncoding]
                                toFile:@"savetest"];
        [self log:[NSString stringWithFormat:@"%@ save result: %d",
                [self passfail:saveok], saveok]];

        BOOL fileexists = [g_ResManager userDataExists:@"savetest"];
        [self log:[NSString stringWithFormat:@"%@ existant file test: %d",
                [self passfail:fileexists], fileexists]];

        NSString* loadedString = [[NSString alloc] initWithData:
                                    [g_ResManager getUserData:@"savetest"]
                                    encoding:NSUnicodeStringEncoding];
        [self log:[NSString stringWithFormat:@"%@ load result: %@",
                [self passfail:
                    [loadedString isEqualToString:savedString]], loadedString]];

        [loadedString release];
    }
```

```
        {
            NSString* savedString = @"another saved text.";
            NSString* loadedString = [g_ResManager getUserData:@"savetest2"];
            if(loadedString == nil){
                [self log:@"Restart app to test loading from persistent storage.
    If you already have, then something might have failed."];
            } else {
                [self log:
                    [NSString stringWithFormat:@"%@ second save test loaded as %@",
                    [self passfail:
                        [loadedString isEqualToString:savedString]], loadedString]];
            }
            [g_ResManager storeUserData:savedString toFile:@"savetest2"];
        }
    }
```

That last step was fairly complicated, so let's walk through it.

The first two functions are simply for utility; log merely sends a string to NSLog() that can be viewed from the debug output window (you can access the debugger console with the hotkey Shift-Apple-Y), and passfail converts a BOOL value into the text "(pass)" if its value is TRUE or "(fail)" if its value is FALSE.

The runTests function consists of three separate code blocks. The first one focuses on testing the existence of a nonexistent userData file named *notfound*. The first time your application runs, there will be no stored user data. It is necessary to check for the existence of the data first so that you can store a default value if your application is being run for the first time.

The second code block stores an NSString to a user data store named *savetest*. After storing the data, the code calls userDataExists to prove that the data now exists inside persistent memory. Finally, the code reloads the string from memory and tests that the loaded string is exactly the same as the original string.

The third code block shows what happens when you try to load a string that does not exist the first time the application is run, but will exist afterward.

The Skeleton Application

By now, we should have a well-rounded framework with all of the basic functionality to begin creating our game. In addition, we have a number of example states showing how to use each feature available. Before we move on to the next chapter, we should create a skeleton application that ties all of the states together to show off our work.

Since we already have the framework and example states, all we need to do is create a Main menu state that will allow us to navigate to each example. The fastest way to do this is with Interface Builder:

1. Select Xcode file→New File→User Interfaces→View XIB and name the file *gsmainmenu.xib*.

2. Select Xcode file→New File→Cocoa Touch Classes→NSObject subclass and name the new class gsMainMenu.

3. Modify *gsMainMenu.h* so that the class inherits from GameState instead of NSObject.

4. Add **#include "GameState.h"** to the top of *gsMainMenu.h*.

5. Add an IBOutlet to *gsMainMenu.h* for the view that you will load from *gsmainmenu.xib*:

   ```
   IBOutlet UIView* subview;
   ```

6. In *gsMainMenu.m*, override initWithFrame: andManager: to manually load *gsmainmenu.xib* and set up the subview:

   ```
   -(gsMainMenu*) initWithFrame:(CGRect)frame
           andManager:(GameStateManager*)pManager
   {
       if (self = [super initWithFrame:frame andManager:pManager]) {
           //load the gsmainmenu.xib file here.  this will
           //instantiate the 'subview' uiview.
           [[NSBundle mainBundle] loadNibNamed:@"gsmainmenu"
                       owner:self options:nil];
           //add subview as... a subview.  This will let everything
           //from the nib file show up on screen.
           [self addSubview:subview];
       }
       return self;
   }
   ```

7. Open *gsmainmenu.xib* in Interface Builder.

8. In the Identity Inspector for File's Owner, set Class to gsMainMenu.

9. Right-clicking on File's Owner should now show subview available as an outlet. Drag a link from subview to the View object.

10. Double-click the View object to begin editing it.

11. Drag and drop three Round Rect Buttons from the Library to the middle of the View.

12. Label them "Graphics", "Sound", and "Data Store" (you do not need an exit button because the iPhone's Home button is assumed to perform that functionality).

13. Add IBActions for each button to *gsMainMenu.h*:

    ```
    - (IBAction) doGraphicsTest;
    - (IBAction) doSoundTest;
    - (IBAction) doStorageTest;
    ```

14. Link each button to its action in Interface Builder.

15. In *gsMainMenu.m*, make each action call doStateChange:

    ```
    - (IBAction) doGraphicsTest {
        [m_pManager doStateChange:[TextureTest class]];
    }
    ```

16. Change the example states to return to `gsMainMenu` when double-tapped.

Now build the skeleton application and marvel at all that you have accomplished. Nothing is holding you back from writing your first game on the iPhone.

Conclusion

We have now completed the foundation for making a great iPhone game. This framework can be used for any kind of game engine, be it 2D or 3D, first-person or top-down, casual or hardcore. Now let's put it to work!

CHAPTER 4

2D Game Engine

Finally, the good stuff! The first three chapters of this book introduced the basics involved in programming for the iPhone and the concepts behind a game engine. We even laid out a nice framework to get us started. All that's left is to make our game... but wait, aren't we forgetting something? What kind of game are we going to make? Before we start coding away, we need to have a plan. We need a game design.

Game Design

The first step in coming up with a good game design is brainstorming. What will the game look like, and how will it feel to play the game? What are the goals, and how will you keep players entertained? Remember that as much fun as it is to make a game, the end result needs to be something that's fun to play.

To begin, we'll need to keep in mind the special considerations of the iPhone:

- Touch-screen input
- Limited resolution and memory
- Play sessions that are short and can be interrupted at any time by a phone call

This means we need to come up with a design that incorporates:

- A simplistic input scheme
- Efficient use of memory for graphics and sound
- Game play that is broken into short segments that can easily be stopped and resumed

To fulfill all of these requirements, we will create a 2D tile-based engine. *Tile-based* means the level background will be composed of a limited number of square tiles that are repeated and put together to form the level (this allows us to create a large level that uses only a small amount of texture memory). Most 2D games are static (the screen does not scroll at all—think puzzle games), side-scrolling (think *Super Mario Bros.*), or top-down (like *Zelda*). A puzzle game is going to be too limiting in terms of AI logic, and most side-scrolling games are too demanding in terms of user input, so top-down best fits our needs. And since this is an O'Reilly book, we'll borrow from the theme of O'Reilly animals.

With these parameters in mind, let's create *O'Reilly's Wildlife Adventure*. As the name suggests, this will be an adventure game involving wild animals. Players will need to help our main character, Tom O'Reilly, as he tends to the animals of a wild animal park. Each "level" will represent a different animal pen, which will nicely segment game play and allow us to challenge players in unique ways with each type of animal they encounter. Tom will handle various special objects as he deals with each animal.

This game design probably won't win any major awards, but it will definitely cover all of the major facets of game development for the iPhone.

Feature List

Now that we have finished brainstorming, it's time to nail down exactly what we need to bring this design into reality.

Graphical layout

To render the game, we will need to draw:

- The level background
- The main character
- Several different types of animals
- Any random objects that may appear in a level

If the levels are larger than the screen, we will need to be able to scroll our view into the world to keep the player centered on the screen.

Input

We will need to interpret user input to:

- Control the main character
- Create an AI engine to control the animal behaviors
- Code up some physics to handle the movement and interaction of those entities with each other and the level

We will also need game logic to determine when goals have been met and store the player's progress.

Display

Apart from drawing the world, we may need to overlay additional information in a heads-up display (HUD) for things such as:

- The player's condition
- Notification of any special items that have been picked up
- Possibly a button to open a pause menu

Furthermore, we will probably need to display some text for dialogs if our main character has anything interesting to say.

Game progress

So far, we've discussed only what goes on during game play. We will also need to add:

- Code to link the levels together and show game progression
- Something like a map that lets players choose what level to play next and unlocks new areas as they complete old ones

Putting it all together, we have the following technical feature list:

- A 2D tile-based render engine with scrolling capability
- Animated sprite entities for the main character, animals, and possibly level entities
- Functions to handle user input to control the main character
- Animal entity logic for several types of animals (such as lions, crocodiles, and emus)
- Physics to allow entities to move where they should, and not where they shouldn't (such as into other entities)
- Level logic to determine when goals have been met and to store the player's progress through the game
- A HUD for important information, including character dialogs
- A menu that allows players to select what level to play and displays their progression through the game

User Input Scheme

As we mentioned earlier, the touch-screen feature of the iPhone means user input has to be a major focus of game design. Specifically, there are three problems that our game design should try to avoid.

The first problem to avoid is requiring accurate touches. When a player touches the screen, she is actually touching many pixels at once; the iPhone will estimate the center pixel among those pixels and events will correspond to just that one pixel. It is important to make touchable interfaces (such as buttons) or in-game objects large enough that an inaccurate touch event will still find its mark if the player touched close enough. Therefore, we should use a rule of thumb (pun intended) that touchable objects should be at least 44 × 44 pixels.

The second problem to avoid is causing the player to cover the screen with her hand while trying to use the screen for input. This is one of the major downsides to a touch-screen interface; because both input and output happen on the same surface, they end up fighting each other for space. One way to solve this is to require as little input from the user as possible. Another is to take user input only in nonessential parts of the screen, or nonessential application states—states where fast response to game actions is not required.

The third problem to avoid is requiring many different types of touches. The iPhone can record not only single and double taps but also finger dragging. With a little work, it is even possible to detect when the player forms symbols (such as a circle or square) with her finger. However, it is important to keep in mind that game play can get frantic, and complex input schemes will frustrate players if they cannot quickly and easily communicate their intended actions to the game.

We chose a top-down design to help reduce the amount of user input activity needed to play the game. Specifically, with a top-down view, we can keep the camera zoomed out far enough that the player can tap an area of the level she wants to move to, and the game will plot out a path and move the character for her. In this way, one simple input (tapping a part of the level) is translated into a series of more complex movements (move forward, turn right, move forward, turn left, move forward), saving the player from a lot of busy work.

However, movement is not the only type of input that will be required during game play. We may also need to handle special actions such as jumping, picking up items, and anything else the game requires. We can handle these in a similar fashion to movement: by translating a simple command into an intelligent behavior. Specifically, we know that if the player touches an area of the level the character is not standing in, we should move the character to that point. However, if she taps the square the character is already standing in, we can treat it as a special command.

But how do we know what that special command is? By determining the context in which the command is used. If the character is standing on the edge of a gap when the player taps, we could consider this as a command to jump across the gap. If instead the character is standing next to a door, we could consider this as a command to open the door. Based on the proximity of the character to a special feature of the level, tapping the character will cause the character to interact with that feature. Such actions are considered *context-sensitive*.

This allows us to have a system that can produce a lot of complex behavior, but the input system remains absolutely simple. In fact, the player needs to know only two motions: tap the area you want the character to move to, or tap the character itself to perform a context-sensitive action.

Learning Curve

By now, we have a basic understanding of the structure of the game world (top-down, tile-based, with entities moving about) and how the user will interact with it (by tapping the level or the character). It is time to come up with some level concepts. However, an important part of level design is to consider the game's learning curve.

When a player first picks up your game, she will not be an expert at it. In fact, learning how to play your game will be part of the fun for her. But if the first levels she encounters are too challenging, she will become frustrated easily and stop playing. On the other hand, if she masters your game in the first five minutes, she will get bored and put it down.

Therefore, it is important to design the levels in such a fashion that the player is neither bored nor overwhelmed. Typically, you should try to introduce one new concept (or a combination of two previously introduced concepts) per level to ensure that players stay awake.

Level 1

Our first level will involve merely walking about, with no context-sensitive actions or fear of death. However, if the player only had to walk from one side of the level to the other without a challenge, she would get bored. So, we will give her something to chase to motivate her to keep playing.

A mother emu's chicks have wandered from the nest and our character will have to chase them in the right direction. This will also give us a chance to work on some flocking AI.

Level 2

Our second level will continue with the movement-only-centered activity, but will increase the intensity of the game.

Specifically, we will ask the player to walk across a habitat filled with sleeping lions to the back of the cave to grab a McGuffin. A *McGuffin* is a nonsense term that means "something that moves the plot."* Basically, we need a reason to send our main character to the back of a lion's cave. It doesn't have to be a good reason, just a reason. That's what the McGuffin is for. If the player avoids the lions, the level will be easy. If she gets too close, the lions will wake up and swipe at her. This will allow us to work on some multistate AI (sleeping and chasing).

Level 3

The third level will dial back the intensity, but it will introduce a new concept. Here, we'll teach the player how to use the context-sensitive actions by providing her with button objects she can interact with to change the level.

We will set up the level as a puzzle: a grid of cells (3 × 3) will contain a cat and a mouse, as well as cheese below a control room that contains three buttons and the main character. Between each cell is a door that can only be opened by pressing the corresponding button from the control room.

---

* Film director Alfred Hitchcock was famous for using the term.

The goal is to open the doors in such a way that the mouse reaches the cheese without meeting the cat. This will show the flexibility of our game engine, being able to create a casual puzzle type of game play experience.

Level 4

The fourth level will focus on using the context-sensitive action method of input in a time-sensitive setting. We will place a McGuffin at the top end of the level past several streams of water that must be crossed.

To do this, we will place logs in the streams that the player can jump on, using the context-sensitive action. The player will have to move quickly, however, as the logs will slowly sink and disappear into the water, requiring a series of decisive jumps.

And if that weren't enough, we will also have crocodiles patrolling the waters, jumping and snapping at the player if she gets too close.

At this point, we are ready to start implementing. Please download the Chapter 4 example code from *https://sourceforge.net/projects/iphonegamebook/files/*.

Tile Engine

The first step in constructing our game will be to focus on the foundation of the game world: the tile engine. The tile engine is responsible for loading the tiles that represent the level and drawing them to the screen. If the level is larger than the viewable area of the screen, we will keep track of a "camera offset" that will be used to draw the portion of the level we are interested in, as well as to draw the rest of the objects on top of the level with the same offset.

Unique Tiles

To begin, we will start with an image that represents our level (see Figure 4-1). This image was constructed out of tiles that are 32 × 32 pixels wide and high. The level is 15 tiles wide by 25 tiles high, or 375 tiles total. However, because it was created from a small set of tiles, we need to load only the unique tiles into memory; we need only 32 tiles (see Figure 4-2).

That's more than 90% less memory! However, we're also going to need to store some data that tells us which unique tile image to use when rendering the level. So, in addition to the unique tile image, we will also need an index array, such as:

```
1,0,0,0,0,0,0,0,0,0,0,0,0,0,0,2
1,0,0,0,0,11,12,13,14,15,0,0,0,0,2
1,0,10,0,0,16,17,18,19,20,0,0,0,0,2
1,0,0,0,0,21,22,23,24,25,0,0,4,0,2
1,0,0,0,0,0,0,0,0,0,0,0,0,0,0,2
1,0,0,0,0,0,0,0,0,0,0,0,0,0,0,2
1,0,0,0,0,0,0,0,0,0,0,0,0,0,0,2
```

```
1,0,0,0,0,10,0,0,0,4,0,0,0,0,2
1,0,4,5,0,0,0,0,0,0,0,0,0,0,2
1,0,0,10,0,0,0,0,0,0,0,0,7,0,2
1,0,0,0,0,0,0,0,0,0,0,0,0,0,2
1,0,0,0,0,0,0,0,0,0,0,0,0,0,2
1,0,0,0,0,0,0,0,0,0,0,0,0,0,2
1,0,0,0,0,5,6,0,0,0,0,0,0,0,2
1,3,4,0,0,10,0,0,0,0,0,0,0,0,2
1,0,0,0,0,0,0,0,0,0,8,9,0,0,2
1,0,0,0,0,0,0,0,0,0,10,0,0,0,2
1,0,0,0,0,0,0,0,0,0,0,0,0,0,2
1,0,0,0,0,0,0,0,0,0,0,0,10,8,2
1,0,0,0,0,0,0,0,0,0,0,0,0,0,2
1,0,0,0,0,0,0,0,4,0,0,0,0,0,2
1,0,0,0,3,4,0,0,0,0,0,9,0,0,2
1,0,0,0,0,0,0,0,0,0,5,6,0,0,2
1,0,0,0,0,0,0,0,0,0,0,0,0,0,2
1,0,0,0,0,0,0,0,0,0,0,0,0,0,2
```

The preceding code describes the tile indexes of a 15 × 25-tile map. The top-left tile uses the second frame (index "1" because indexes start at "0"). The next frame uses frame index "0," and so on.

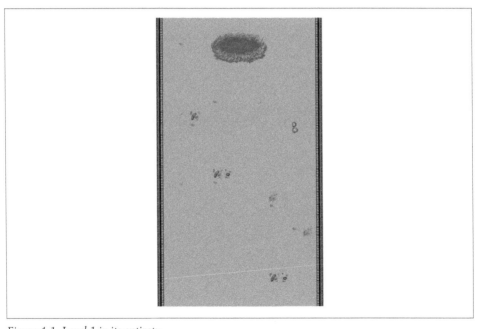

Figure 4-1. Level 1 in its entirety

Figure 4-2. Unique tile strip for Level 1

Drawing Tiles

As we discussed in "Animation" on page 46, sprites are textures that contain multiple images that should be drawn in succession to represent an animation. Each image in the sprite texture is called a *frame*. However, the class we presented in Chapter 3 for rendering textures, GLTexture, is not suitable for drawing frames.

Specifically, we want to consider the unique tile strip (Figure 4-2) to be like a film strip. Each frame is exactly the same width, so finding the location of a single frame in the texture is as easy as x = frame*frameWidth; where frameWidth is the same as the tile size.

The iPhone also limits us to a maximum of 1,024 for both the width and the height of the texture. That means that if our unique tiles are 32 × 32 and we have more than 32 tiles in either direction (because 32 * 32 = 1,024), we have to wrap them to keep our image width or height from exceeding 1,024.

 The OpenGL ES implementation on the iPhone will try to automatically scale down any texture larger than 1,024 in height or width. This could cause unintended side effects for any images that are too large; if you are noticing problems with your textures, make sure they aren't too big.

That means the calculation for the frame offset becomes:

```
int x = (frame * tileSize) % 1024;
int row = (( frame * tileSize ) - x) / 1024;
int y = row * tileSize;
```

Because of the number of mathematical operations involved in calculating this position, it is more efficient to store the results after the first calculation and reuse them, rather than recalculating the frame for each tile in every loop. Therefore, we will create a Tile class that can store the offset into a GLTexture, like so:

```
//Tile.h
typedef enum {
    UNWALKABLE = 1,
    WATER = 2,
    EMUTEARS = 4,
} PhysicsFlags;

@interface Tile : NSObject {
    NSString* textureName;
    CGRect frame;
    PhysicsFlags flags;
}

@property (nonatomic, copy) NSString* textureName;
@property (nonatomic) CGRect frame;

- (void) drawInRect:(CGRect)rect;
- (Tile*) initWithTexture:(NSString*)texture withFrame:(CGRect) _frame;

@end
```

```
//Tile.m
@implementation Tile

@synthesize textureName;
@synthesize frame;

- (Tile*) init {
    [super init];
    flags = 0;
    return self;
}

- (Tile*) initWithTexture:(NSString*)texture withFrame:(CGRect) _frame
{
    [self init];
    self.textureName = texture;
    self.frame = _frame;
    return self;
}

- (void) drawInRect:(CGRect)rect {
    [[g_ResManager getTexture:textureName]
                   drawInRect:rect
                   withClip:frame
                   withRotation:0];
}

- (void) dealloc {
    [super dealloc];
}

@end
```

Notice the PhysicsFlags enumeration. We will use this later for entity-to-world collision detection.

TileWorld Class

With the unique tile index array data, we can now write a class that will render the level to the screen using the Tile class. To do this, we will create a new class named Tile World that a GLESGameState can use. When the GameState is initialized, it will create the TileWorld and load the level data; when the GameState is rendering, it will tell the TileWorld to draw itself before anything else.

This class needs to keep a list of tiles, along with a rectangle that describes what portion of the screen to render those tiles to. In addition, our levels may be larger than the viewable area, so we will need to keep a "camera" offset to pan our rendering to display the portion of the level we want to see:

```
//TileWorld.h
//global tile size.
#define TILE_SIZE 32
```

```
@class Tile;
@class Entity;

@interface TileWorld : NSObject {
    Tile*** tiles;
    CGRect view; //typically will be the same rect as the screen.  in pixels.
considered to be in opengl coordinates (0, 0 in bottom left)
    int world_width, world_height; //in tiles.
    int camera_x, camera_y; //in pixels, relative to world origin (0, 0).
                            // view will be centered on this point.

    NSMutableArray* entities;
}

- (TileWorld*) initWithFrame:(CGRect) frame;
- (void) loadLevel:(NSString*) levelFilename
          withTiles:(NSString*)imageFilename;

- (void) draw;
- (void) setCamera:(CGPoint)position;

//utility function
- (CGPoint) worldPosition:(CGPoint)screenPosition;

- (void) addEntity:(Entity*) entity;
- (Tile*) tileAt:(CGPoint)worldPosition;
- (BOOL) walkable:(CGPoint) point;
```

There are a number of things to note here before we move on to the implementation.
First, what is that TILE_SIZE definition? We stated earlier that we would be using 32 ×
32 pixel tiles. This definition helps us avoid *magic numbers*.

A magic number is a certain numeric value that is used over and over again in code,
and it is bad because you cannot tell when, for example, a value of 32 is used to represent
a tile size or some other concept. It's also bad because if you wanted to change the tile
size to some other value, such as 16, you'd have to do a search and replace, being careful
to replace only the instances of 32 that represent tile size. You should always use a
define for values instead of magic numbers, to make your intended use clear.

The next important piece of code is the Tile*** tiles; line. This represents a dynamically allocated 2D array of Tile pointers. Because the tile engine could be used to
represent a level of any width or height, we must allocate the tiles dynamically.

Finally, you will notice the NSMutableArray* entities; definition. This array will keep
a list of objects we wish to draw in every frame. Because objects in front should be
drawn on top of objects behind them, we need to sort those objects and draw them in
order (from back to front). We also need to offset the rendering position of those objects
by the same camera offset the level tiles are being drawn with.

You can view the implementation of the TileWorld class in the *TileWorld.mm* file.

Loading

Let's hone in on the `loadLevel:` function, which accepts a text file in the following format:

```
[height]x[width]

[comma separated tile texture indexes]

[comma separated tile physics flags]
```

First, it loads the file contents into an `NSString`. Next, it parses out the width and height values from the first line by separating them using the `componentsSeparatedByString:` function of `NSString` to grab the characters to the left and right of the x character. Then it calls the `intValue` function to parse the string into an integer value for each.

Once we have the width and height of the level in tiles, we know how many `Tile` object pointers must be allocated. This is done in the `allocateWidth: height:` function.

Next, we parse through the file and create a new `Tile` object for each tile in the level, initializing it with a `CGRect` representing the frame position of the unique tile index found in the *.txt* file, as we discussed in "Drawing Tiles" on page 104.

Once all of the tiles have been created, we skip past the second blank line and start parsing the physics flags. For each tile, we read in the value and initialize the `flags` property of the corresponding `Tile` object.

Finally, we can release the original file data. Remember, since we have allocated the `Tiles` array and objects, we will need to deallocate them when we unload the level.

Rendering

Now that we have the `Tiles` initialized, we can render the level. Keep in mind that the `TileWorld` instance will be a member of a `GLESGameState` class, which will be calling the `draw:` function:

```
-(void) draw
{
    CGFloat xoff = -camera_x + view.origin.x + view.size.width/2;
    CGFloat yoff = -camera_y + view.origin.y + view.size.height/2;
    CGRect rect = CGRectMake(0, 0, TILE_SIZE, TILE_SIZE);
    for(int x=0;x<world_width;x++){
        rect.origin.x = x*TILE_SIZE + xoff;

        //optimization: don't draw offscreen tiles.
        //  Useful only when world is much larger than screen,
        //  which our emu level happens to be.
        if(rect.origin.x + rect.size.width < view.origin.x ||
          rect.origin.x > view.origin.x + view.size.width) {
            continue;
        }
```

```
        for(int y=0;y<world_height;y++){
            rect.origin.y = y*TILE_SIZE + yoff;
            if(rect.origin.y + rect.size.height < view.origin.y ||
                rect.origin.y > view.origin.y + view.size.height) {
                continue;
            }
            [tiles[x][y] drawInRect:rect];
        }
    }
    if(entities){
        [entities sortUsingSelector:@selector(depthSort:)];
        for(Entity* entity in entities){
            [entity drawAtPoint:CGPointMake(xoff, yoff)];
        }
    }
}
```

First we calculate the offset between the world and the viewable area of the screen. We are basically transforming between world coordinates and screen coordinates.

As an optimization, we also initialize a rectangle the size of a tile for use in the Tile object's drawInRect: function. Rather than creating the rectangle for each tile, we can set it up outside the for loop and have to change only the *x* and *y* positions, saving us some processing power.

You may recall from Chapter 2 that another form of graphics optimization is culling. Inside the for loop, we begin by culling any columns of Tiles that wouldn't show up in the viewable area. Then we start the inner for loop to draw the actual Tiles, first being sure to cull any individual tiles in that row that are outside the viewable area.

Now we get back to the entities array. We will discuss the Entity class in more detail later, but recall that entities need to be sorted and drawn in order from back to front so that they overlap each other correctly. Because the entities variable here is an NSMutableArray we can use the sortUsingSelector method which allows us to apply a comparison function we've written for this purpose.

The comparison function is expected to be called as a message on one object, with a single parameter being an object of the same type that should be compared. The return value must be NSOrderedAscending, NSOrderedSame, or NSOrderedDescending based on the result of the comparison.

A default comparison function is available for use with simple types such as NSString and NSNumber. However, because we are comparing entities, we must write a custom comparison.

Our custom function is named depthSort: and is located in the *Entity.m* file:

```
- (NSComparisonResult) depthSort:(Entity*) other {
    if (self->worldPos.y > other->worldPos.y) return NSOrderedAscending;
    if (self->worldPos.y < other->worldPos.y) return NSOrderedDescending;
    //the logical thing to do at this point is return NSOrderedSame, but that
    //causes flickering when two items are overlapping at the same y. Instead,
```

```
        //one must be drawn over the other deterministically... we use the memory
        //addresses of the entities for a tie-breaker.
        if (self < other) return NSOrderedDescending;
        return NSOrderedAscending;
    }
```

The function compares the y values of the objects, returning NSOrderedAscending if the "other" Entity has a smaller y value. Recall that y = 0 at the top of the screen, so the smaller the y value, the farther "up" on the screen the object will be drawn. We want things closer to the bottom of the screen to be considered "close" and things at the top to be considered "far," so returning the objects in ascending order by y coordinate will make sure that entities that are higher on the screen (farther away) will be drawn first, and entities lower on the screen (closer) will be drawn last (thereby showing on top of the others).

Camera

We mentioned that the tiles are able to be offset so that the viewable area shows the part of the level we are interested in. We call it the camera offset because it's like a camera panning around inside the level area. In particular, we want to be able to set the camera offset to follow our main character as he walks around the level.

By calling setCamera: on our TileWorld with a target position (in world coordinates), we can calculate the offset necessary to draw the tiles so that they will be visible within the screen coordinates. If we offset a point within the tile rectangle by the negated value of that point, it will show up at the top left of the viewable area.

However, we want the main character to show up in the center of the screen, not the top left. Furthermore, if the character walks close to the left side of the world, rather than staying in the middle of the screen (thereby causing the viewable area to extend beyond the level and show empty space), we want to force the camera to stay within the bounds of the level and instead cause the character to leave the center of the screen and get close to the edge. The same condition applies for the top, bottom, and right sides of the screen. Therefore, when the intended camera position is sent to setCamera:, we do a bounds check on each side of the viewable area to make sure the camera stays put, like so:

```
-(void) setCamera:(CGPoint)position {
    camera_x = position.x;
    camera_y = position.y;
    if (camera_x < 0 + view.size.width/2) {
        camera_x = view.size.width/2;
    }
    if (camera_x > TILE_SIZE*world_width - view.size.width/2) {
        camera_x = TILE_SIZE*world_width - view.size.width/2;
    }
    if (camera_y < 0 + view.size.height/2) {
        camera_y = view.size.height/2;
    }
```

```
        if (camera_y > TILE_SIZE*world_height - view.size.height/2) {
            camera_y = TILE_SIZE*world_height - view.size.height/2;
        }
    }
```

Physics

Apart from drawing the tiles and entities at their appropriate offsets, the last feature of the TileEngine is physics. Remember that each Tile in the tiles array has a physics flag that was initialized when we loaded the level file.

During the GameState update function, we will be checking entity-to-world collision by asking the TileWorld for each entity if it is colliding with any tiles that have special physics flags.

To this end, we provide the tileAt: function, which will return the Tile object located at a particular point (in world coordinates). Furthermore, as a convenience, we will also provide the walkable: function to determine whether the Tile has any special physical properties we should worry about.

Animation

Our game will contain a main character and several animated animals. Each of these entities will require one or more animations for each of their behaviors and each of the directions they could be facing during those behaviors. For instance, the main character could have "idle," "walking," and "jumping" animations in the "north," "south," "east," and "west" directions.

Once our artist has rendered each of these, we can assemble them together into a sprite texture similar to the unique tile strip texture we will use for the tile engine map. However, these animations are much more complex than the unique tile strip. See Figure 4-3, for instance, for the images we need to represent a walking emu chick.

Figure 4-3. Emu chick walking animation

As you can see, the emu chick sprite texture has three animations: walking west, walking north, and walking south (we omitted walking east because it can be created by flipping the walking west animation horizontally, which saves precious texture memory).

To make things more complicated, the animations are set up in such a way that some frames should be used multiple times in a single animation sequence. Specifically, the walking west animation should be displayed in the frame sequence 0, 1, 2, 3, 4.

If we had a more complex animation, this format would support something similar to 0, 1, 0, 2, 0, 3..., where the frame indexes are not sequential.

Additionally, we could want some frames to take longer than others, so we should specify how long (in milliseconds) each frame should take: 200, 300, 200, 100, 200, 100, 100, 200. This adds up to an animation sequence that takes 1,400 ms (or 1.4 s) to complete.

To complicate things further, some animations should be looped until we change to a different animation, whereas other animations should play only once and stop. In addition, some animations should specify another animation to switch to as soon as they have completed.

Animation and Sprite Classes

However, our game logic should not have to deal with all of the intricacies of animation programming. We need to encapsulate the animation logic inside an `Animation` class.

To begin, we need a way to specify the animation sequences that an `Animation` object will represent. We could hardcode all of the animation logic, but that would be a lot of work with all of the animals and such, and we would have to throw it away the next time we wrote a game. We could also create a proprietary file format, but then we'd need to write a tool that could take in all of the animation sequences and write them to the file, which is beyond the scope of this book.

Instead, we will use something familiar to Mac developers: the *.plist* file. You already used a *.plist* file to set up certain parameters for your Xcode project. Here we will use a *.plist* file to contain all of our animation sequence data, and we will write an initialization function in our `Animation` class that will read in that data.

Property list

We can use Xcode to create a *.plist* file for animation purposes. We will use the *emuchick.png* file as our texture. Our goal is to describe the "walking left," "walking up," "walking down," and "walking right" animations:

1. From within Xcode, select File→New File to open the New File dialog.
2. From the left column select Other and in the right window select Property List.
3. Type **Animations.plist** for the name and click the Finish button.
4. Select the *Animations.plist* file within Xcode. The .plist editor view will appear.

All items in a property list are added to the root dictionary item, in key-value pairs. You can structure your data by nesting dictionaries or arrays. We are going to structure our animation data by using a dictionary for each sprite texture.

We will begin by adding a dictionary named `emuchick.png`:

1. Right-click the Root row and select Add Row.

2. Replace the "New Item" text with "emuchick.png" in the Key column.

3. Change the Row type to Dictionary by clicking the Type column (it is set to String by default) and selecting Dictionary.

Now we can start adding rows to the emuchick.png dictionary to describe the animations found in this sprite texture:

4. Add a row to the emuchick.png dictionary by right-clicking and selecting Add Row. Make sure you added the row to our dictionary, not the root: the new row should be indented farther to the right than the emuchick.png row is in the Key column.

5. Name the new row "frameCount" and set its type to Number.

6. Set the value for frameCount to 15, since there are 15 frames in the *emuchick.png* texture.

Next, we want to store information about all of the different animations that can be found in this sprite. For each separate animation, we will create a new dictionary below the emuchick.png dictionary:

7. Add another row to the emuchick.png dictionary by right-clicking and selecting Add Row again.

8. Name this one "walkLeft" and set its type to Dictionary. It will represent an animation of the emu chick walking to the left.

Each animation will need to specify a sequence of frames and the animation period for each of those frames. For "walkLeft", we want to use a frame sequence of 0,1,2,3,4 with 100 ms for each frame:

9. Add two rows to the walkLeft dictionary and name them "anim" and "time". Leave their types as String.

10. In "anim", set the value to "0,1,2,3,4", with no spaces.

11. In "time", set the value to "100,100,100,100,100", also with no spaces.

Great; now we have the first sequence done. For the next two, we can actually copy and paste the walkLeft dictionary and rename it to save us some time:

12. Right-click on "walkLeft" and select Copy.

13. Left-click on "emuchick.png", then right-click and select Paste (it is important to have it highlighted by left-clicking before pasting, or your new copy will end up in the wrong place). Double-check that the new copy is a child of emuchick.png; it should be at the same indentation as the original walkLeft dictionary.

14. Rename the first new copy to "walkup" and change the "anim" value to "5,6,7,8,9".

15. Rename the second copy to "walkdown" and change its "anim" value to "10,11,12,13,14".

Now we need a walking right animation. But the sprite has no frames of the emu chick walking to the right. Instead, following our plan when we asked the artist to draw the images, we'll flip the left-facing frames for use in the walking right animation:

16. Copy and paste the `walkLeft` dictionary onto `emuchick.png` once more.

17. This time, add a row to `walkRight`, named "flipHorizontal".

18. Set its type to Boolean and toggle the checkbox that shows up in the Value column. It should be marked with a check, which means the value is set to `true`.

The last piece of data we need to store about the *emuchick.png* animations is an offset value for all of the frames. When we want to draw the emu chick, we don't want to have to figure out how big the frame is and draw from the upper-left corner; instead, we set that value here so that we can automatically offset the graphics. In this case, we want the origin to be at 16,6 within the frame:

19. Add one more row to the `emuchick.png` dictionary.

20. Name this one "anchor" and keep its type as String.

21. Set its value to "16,6".

Now we have a *.plist* file that contains all of the data to represent a series of animations used by an entity. Next, we will create an `Animation` class that will allow us to use this data in our game.

Consider, however, that we do not want to allocate a new `Animation` object for each of our entities. For instance, let's say we have three siren salamanders walking around in our level. Just as they are all using the same `GLTexture` for their image data, they should also use the same `Animation` object for their animation data. You should consider an `Animation` object as a resource such as a texture.

However, certain aspects of the animation should belong to each `Salamander` entity: specifically, the current animation sequence being rendered, and the time since the start of the animation.

To facilitate this, we will also create a `Sprite` class. This class will keep track of the animation data, as well as the exact frame and start time of the animation being rendered.

Animation class

Although the `Animation` class will represent the animation used by an object in our game, it's possible that a single object could have multiple behaviors. In the preceding example, the emu chick had only a walking animation, but it could also have had an idle animation or a sleeping animation.

We call each of these behaviors an animation sequence, and our `Animation` class will keep track of multiple `AnimationSequence` objects.

In the preceding example, the Animation object used by the emu chick would have only one AnimationSequence.

We will start by defining the AnimationSequence class, followed by the Animation class:

```
//Animation.h
@interface AnimationSequence : NSObject
{
    @public
    int frameCount;
    float* timeout;
    CGRect* frames;
    bool flipped;
    NSString* next;
}

- (AnimationSequence*) initWithFrames:(NSDictionary*) animData
                        width:(float) width
                        height:(float) height;

@end

@interface Animation : NSObject {
    NSString* image;
    NSMutableDictionary* sequences;
    CGPoint anchor;
}

- (Animation*) initWithAnim:(NSString*) img;
- (void) drawAtPoint:(CGPoint) point
        withSequence:(NSString*) sequence
        withFrame:(int) frame;

-(int) getFrameCount:(NSString*) sequence;
-(NSString*) firstSequence;

-(AnimationSequence*) get:(NSString*) sequence;

@end
```

The AnimationSequence class keeps track of the number of frames, the time that each frame should be displayed, and (similar to the Tile class) a CGRect to represent the subsection of the GLTexture that represents each frame. It also keeps a Boolean to determine whether the frame should be drawn flipped on the horizontal axis.

The Animation class keeps a string that represents the name of the GLTexture for use with our ResourceManager's getTexture: function, as well as an NSMutableDictionary to keep track of our AnimationSequences. To make things easy, we will use a string as the key value. When we want to access the walking animation sequence, all we have to do is call [sequences valueForKey:"walking"]. Finally, we keep an anchor point that allows us to draw the animation at an offset.

The AnimationSequence class we defined had only one function, an initialization method, which will parse the animation sequence data from a *.plist* file:

```
//Animation.mm
@implementation AnimationSequence

- (AnimationSequence*) initWithFrames:(NSDictionary*) animData
                          width:(float) width
                          height:(float) height
{
    [super init];
    NSArray* framesData = [[animData valueForKey:@"anim"]
                            componentsSeparatedByString:@","];
    NSArray* timeoutData = [[animData valueForKey:@"time"]
                             componentsSeparatedByString:@","];
                             //will be nil if "time" is not present.
    bool flip = [[animData valueForKey:@"flipHorizontal"] boolValue];
    self->next = [[animData valueForKey:@"next"] retain];
    frameCount = [framesData count];
    frames = new CGRect[frameCount];
    flipped = flip;
    for(int i=0;i<frameCount;i++){
        int frame = [[framesData objectAtIndex:i] intValue];
        int x = (frame * (int)width) % 1024;
        int row = (( frame * width ) - x) / 1024;
        int y = row * height;
        frames[i] = CGRectMake(x, y, width, height);
    }
    timeout = NULL;
    if(timeoutData){
        timeout = new float[frameCount];
        for(int i=0;i<frameCount;i++){
            timeout[i] = [[timeoutData objectAtIndex:i] floatValue] / 1000.0f;
            if(i > 0) timeout[i] += timeout[i-1];
        }
    }
    return self;
}

- (void) dealloc {
    delete frames;
    if(timeout) delete timeout;
    [self->next release];
    [super dealloc];
}

@end
```

We begin by grabbing the array of animation frames labeled "anim" from inside the animData dictionary. We do this by passing @"anim" as the key into the valueForKey: function of NSDictionary, which returns a string value. In the same line, we split that string into substrings by separating each section marked by a comma using the componentsSeparatedByString: method of NSString. We do the same thing on the next line, only we grab the "time" entry instead.

We also grab the "flipHorizontal" entry and convert it to a bool value from which we directly initialize our flipped member variable. After that, we get the "next" entry to determine what the next animation sequence should be: if the value is nil, we will simply stop animating; otherwise, we will continue into the next animation sequence automatically.

Next, we want to create a CGRect that represents the section of the GLTexture each frame represents. We know the width and height of the CGRect because they were passed into our function and each frame is the same size. All we need to do is calculate the *x* and *y* offsets based on the frame number of each animation.

We index the framesData array using the objectAtIndex: function and convert each element to an integer to get the frame index. Next, we calculate the *x* and *y* offsets based on the frame height and width. Remember, we need to wrap the frames if the width or height is larger than 1,024.

After we are done creating the frame rectangles, we initialize our timeout array. After indexing the timeoutData array and converting each element into an int (the same as we did earlier), we divide the result by 1,000. We mentioned earlier that the iPhone counts time by seconds, although it allows fractional values. Because the time periods in our *.plist* are in milliseconds, dividing by 1000.0f converts from integer milliseconds to floating-point seconds, which is what we want.

Now we can implement the Animation class. Recall that the Animation class is a resource that multiple Sprite classes will use; it should not store any data used to render a particular instance of an animation, only the list of AnimationSequences. The drawing function should have parameters that specify exactly which frame of which Animation Sequence is currently being requested so that multiple Sprites can render the same animation at different locations of the screen and of the animation.

Let's start by looking at the initialization function:

```
//Animation.mm
- (Animation*) initWithAnim:(NSString*) img {
    NSData* pData;
    pData = [NSData dataWithContentsOfFile:[[NSBundle mainBundle]
                pathForResource:@"Animations" ofType:@"plist"]];
    NSString *error;
    NSDictionary* animData;
    NSPropertyListFormat format;
    animData = [NSPropertyListSerialization propertyListFromData:pData
                mutabilityOption:NSPropertyListImmutable
                format:&format
                errorDescription:&error];

    animData = [animData objectForKey:img];

    GLTexture *tex = [g_ResManager getTexture:img];
    image = img;

    float frameWidth, frameHeight;

    if([animData objectForKey:@"frameCount"]){
        int frameCount = [[animData objectForKey:@"frameCount"] intValue];
```

```
        frameWidth = [tex width] / (float)frameCount;
        frameHeight = [tex height];
    }

    if([animData objectForKey:@"frameSize"]){
        NSArray* wh = [[animData objectForKey:@"frameSize"]
                        componentsSeparatedByString:@"x"];
        frameWidth = [[wh objectAtIndex:0] intValue];
        frameHeight = [[wh objectAtIndex:1] intValue];
    }

    //anchor is the position in the image that is considered the center. In
    //pixels. Relative to the bottom left corner. Will typically be positive.
    //all frames in all sequences share the same anchor.
    NSString* anchorData = [animData valueForKey:@"anchor"];
    if(anchorData){
        NSArray* tmp = [anchorData componentsSeparatedByString:@","];
        anchor.x = [[tmp objectAtIndex:0] floatValue];
        anchor.y = [[tmp objectAtIndex:1] floatValue];
    }

    NSEnumerator *enumerator = [animData keyEnumerator];
    NSString* key;
    sequences = [NSMutableDictionary dictionaryWithCapacity:1];

    while ((key = [enumerator nextObject])) {

        NSDictionary* sequencedata = [animData objectForKey:key];
        if (![sequencedata isKindOfClass:[NSDictionary class]]) continue;

        AnimationSequence* tmp = [[AnimationSequence alloc]
                        initWithFrames:sequencedata
                        width:frameWidth
                        height:frameHeight];

        [sequences setValue:tmp forKey:key];
        [tmp release];
    }

    [sequences retain];

    return self;
}
```

The initWithAnim: function accepts the name of an image as its only parameter. This will be used to grab the associated animation from within the *Animations.plist* file, as well as the GLTexture by the same name.

We start by using an NSData pointer to grab the contents of the *Animations.plist* file. Next, we convert it into an NSDictionary for easy access of the data inside using the propertyListFromData: method of the NSPropertyListSerialization utility class.

However, the NSDictionary we just got contains all of the animations in the *.plist* file, and we want only the animation that corresponds to the image name passed into our initialization function. We grab the subsection with [animData objectForKey:img], re-assigning it to our NSDictionary pointer. We don't need to worry about a memory leak while doing this because the original NSDictionary returned by propertyListFrom Data: is put into an auto-release pool before it's handed to us.

Now that we have only the data that pertains to this animation, we will extract the Animation and AnimationSequence information from it. For the Animation class, we need the data that applies to all of the AnimationSequences, including the frame height and width and the anchor offset.

The rest of the entries into the dictionary comprise AnimationSequence data. However, we don't know what their names are or how many there will be, so we need to use an NSEnumerator to iterate across all of the entries. We do this by calling keyEnumerator: on the animData dictionary.

We also need a place to store the AnimationSequences we create, so we initialize our sequences variable as an empty NSMutableDictionary. Since we are calling alloc on sequences here, we need to remember to release it in the dealloc function, as well as all of the entries inside it.

Next, we start the while loop to iterate through all of the keys in our animData dictionary. The entries are not in a particular order, so we need to be sure to skip any entries that we have already read (and therefore are not AnimationSequence dictionaries). We know that any entry that is an NSDictionary will represent an AnimationSequence, so we check the type of entry using isKindOfClass:. If the entry is not an NSDictionary, we skip it.

Finally, we know we have an AnimationSequence dictionary. We grab it from animData using objectForKey: and then send it into a newly allocated AnimationSequence object. Once the AnimationSequence is initialized, we can store it into our sequences dictionary. Since we called alloc on the AnimationSequence when we were creating it, we need to call release. Rest assured, however, that it was retained by NSDictionary when we inserted it into sequences.

And now the rendering function:

```
//Animation.mm
- (void) drawAtPoint:(CGPoint) point
        withSequence:(NSString*) sequence
        withFrame:(int) frame
{
    AnimationSequence* seq = [sequences valueForKey:sequence];
    CGRect currframe = seq->frames[frame];
    [[g_ResManager getTexture:image]
        drawInRect:CGRectMake(
                point.x+(seq->flipped?currframe.size.width:0)-anchor.x,
                point.y-anchor.y,
                seq->flipped?-currframe.size.width:currframe.size.width,
                currframe.size.height)
            withClip:currframe
            withRotation:0];
}
```

Compared to the initialization function, rendering is fairly simple. We first grab the AnimationSequence as detailed by the sequence parameter. We then extract the CGRect that represents the portion of a GLTexture that contains the frame we want from the AnimationSequence and store it as currFrame.

Next, we grab the GLTexture from the ResourceManager and call drawInRect:, creating the destination rectangle using the utility function CGRectMake and using currFrame as our source rectangle. Creating the destination rectangle is a little tricky because we have to consider whether the animation is flipped and whether there is an anchor offset. Fortunately, the math is simple, as you can see.

Sprite class

Now that we have an Animation, we can create a Sprite class that will allow us to use it. The Sprite class needs to keep track of what animation it is associated with, which AnimationSequence is currently being drawn, when that sequence started, and what the current frame is.

Because the Sprite class will be used directly in our game code, we are going to make an autorelease constructor instead of the typical init function. We will also need a rendering function that accepts a position to draw the sprite, an update function that will calculate when the current frame needs to change based on the timeout values from the current AnimationSequence, and finally, a way to set which sequence we want to display:

```
//Sprite.h
@interface Sprite : NSObject {
    Animation* anim;
    NSString* sequence;
    float sequence_time;
    int currentFrame;
}

@property (nonatomic, retain) Animation* anim;
@property (nonatomic, retain) NSString* sequence;

+ (Sprite*) spriteWithAnimation:(Animation*) anim;
- (void) drawAtPoint:(CGPoint) point;
- (void) update:(float) time;

@end
```

Notice the @property tag we are using for anim and sequence variables. It will cause a special setter function to be called whenever we assign anything to anim or to sequence. Since retain is one of the keywords, it will automatically be retained when we set these.

Although the default setter is acceptable for anim, we want to specify our own setter function for sequence because whenever the sequence changes we need to reset the sequence_time and currentFrame back to zero. We do this by overloading the setter function named setSequence in the following code.

The implementation of Sprite follows:

```
//Sprite.m
+ (Sprite*) spriteWithAnimation:(Animation*) anim {
    Sprite* retval = [[Sprite alloc] init];

    retval.anim = anim;
    retval.sequence = [anim firstSequence];

    [retval autorelease];
    return retval;
}

- (void) drawAtPoint:(CGPoint) point {
    [anim drawAtPoint:point withSequence:sequence withFrame:currentFrame];
}

- (void) update:(float) time{
    AnimationSequence* seq = [anim get:sequence];

    if(seq->timeout == NULL){
        currentFrame++;
        if(currentFrame >= [anim getFrameCount:sequence]) currentFrame = 0;
    } else {
        sequence_time += time;
        if(sequence_time > seq->timeout[seq->frameCount-1]){
            sequence_time -= seq->timeout[seq->frameCount-1];
        }
        for(int i=0;i<seq->frameCount;i++){
            if(sequence_time < seq->timeout[i]) {
                currentFrame = i;
                break;
            }
        }
    }
}

- (void) setSequence:(NSString*) seq {
    [seq retain];
    [self->sequence release];
    self->sequence = seq;
    currentFrame = 0;
    sequence_time = 0;
}
```

The constructor function needs to be statically accessible (you call it before an object exists, not on an object), so we use + instead of - in the definition. It starts by allocating and initializing a Sprite object.

We then set the animation to the anim variable sent in the parameter. Remember that we declared this as a retain parameter, so it will automatically be retained when we set this, meaning we need to release it in our dealloc function.

We start the first `AnimationSequence` by using a utility function to ask the `Animation` which we should use first and then setting it to `sequence`. This is also a property, but it will be calling our custom setter, the `setSequence:` function.

Finally, we add the new `Sprite` to an `autorelease` pool and return it.

The rendering function is very simple: just pass the point to draw at, the current sequence, and the current frame into the `Animation drawAtPoint:` function we discussed earlier.

The update function needs to start by grabbing a pointer to the `AnimationSequence` we are currently running. Next, we need to check that it has a list of frame times; if it does not, we simply increment the frame every update loop. If we reach the end of the `AnimationSequence`, we start over from the first `Animation`.

If there is frame time information, we need to know whether the current frame should be incremented. The `time` parameter of the update function represents the amount of time that has elapsed since the last call to update, so we can simply add this to the `sequence_time` variable and check whether it is larger than the timeout value of the current frame. We calculate the current frame based on the total `sequence_time` elapsed.

The `setSequence:` function is our overloaded setter function, as we already mentioned. A normal setter function has two jobs: retain the new object being assigned to, and release the old one. Our custom setter will also initialize the `currentFrame` and `sequence_time` to zero so that the new sequence starts at the beginning.

Physics

In our game, physics will be a simple matter of entity-to-world and entity-to-entity collision in two dimensions. In Level 4, we have water tiles, but that will be a special case of entity-to-world.

Entities

What are "entities"? As we mentioned in "Physics Engine" on page 51, the game world consists of the "level," the "player," and the "animals." To simplify things, we will say the game world consists of the "level" and "entities." An entity is anything that exists in the game world within a particular level.

The player is an entity because she is in the world but can move around independently. The animals are also entities that can move around on their own. There can also be stationary entities, such as a button. Because a button has an animation and logic behind it (pressed and unpressed), it cannot be fully represented as merely a part of the tile-engine portion of the level; it must be an entity.

All entities need to have a position, a way to render themselves, and an update function that gets called every frame to allow their internal logic to progress.

We will begin by creating a class named `Entity` (which you already saw referenced in `TileWorld`):

```
//Entity.h
@interface Entity : NSObject {
    CGPoint worldPos;
    CGPoint velocity;
    Sprite* sprite;
    TileWorld* world;

}

@property (nonatomic, retain) Sprite* sprite;
@property (nonatomic) CGPoint position;

- (id) initWithPos:(CGPoint) pos sprite:(Sprite*)sprite;
- (void) drawAtPoint:(CGPoint) offset;
- (void) update:(CGFloat) time;
- (void) setWorld:(TileWorld*) newWorld;

@end
```

Notice the pointer to `TileWorld`. This allows the entity to check for entity-to-world collisions on its own.

The implementation of the `Entity` class is very simple, with the exception of the render function, which adds its position to a camera offset before calling `drawAtPoint:` on its `Sprite`:

```
//Entity.m
- (void) drawAtPoint:(CGPoint) offset {
    offset.x += worldPos.x;
    offset.y += worldPos.y;
     [sprite drawAtPoint:offset];
}
```

The rest of the functions are simple or empty because `Entity` is a base class. We will create other classes that inherit from `Entity` and implement more interesting functionality.

Entity-to-World

Entities that can move but are limited by the physical properties of the level must detect entity-to-world collisions. But first we must have a way to know what physical property each level tile has.

We do this in a way similar to the unique tile indexes of the tile graphics. Just as we had a file with texture indexes for each tile, we can have a file with physics flags for each tile. Our game design incorporates the following physics properties for tiles: normal, impassable, and water. Normal is applied to tiles that can be walked upon, impassable is used for walls and tiles that are otherwise inaccessible to entities, and water is for special tiles that represent water.

Giving values (0 = normal, 1 = impassable, 2 = water), we could represent the first level with the following data:

```
1, 0, 0, 0, 0, 0, 0, 0, 0, 0, 0, 0, 0, 0, 0, 1
1, 0, 0, 0, 0, 0, 0, 0, 0, 0, 0, 0, 0, 0, 0, 1
1, 0, 0, 0, 0, 0, 0, 0, 0, 0, 0, 0, 0, 0, 0, 1
1, 0, 0, 0, 0, 0, 0, 0, 0, 0, 0, 0, 0, 0, 0, 1
1, 0, 0, 0, 0, 0, 0, 0, 0, 0, 0, 0, 0, 0, 0, 1
1, 0, 0, 0, 0, 0, 0, 0, 0, 0, 0, 0, 0, 0, 0, 1
1, 0, 0, 0, 0, 0, 0, 0, 0, 0, 0, 0, 0, 0, 0, 1
1, 0, 0, 0, 0, 0, 0, 0, 0, 0, 0, 0, 0, 0, 0, 1
1, 0, 0, 0, 0, 0, 0, 0, 0, 0, 0, 0, 0, 0, 0, 1
1, 0, 0, 0, 0, 0, 0, 0, 0, 0, 0, 0, 0, 0, 0, 1
1, 0, 0, 0, 0, 0, 0, 0, 0, 0, 0, 0, 0, 0, 0, 1
1, 0, 0, 0, 0, 0, 0, 0, 0, 0, 0, 0, 0, 0, 0, 1
1, 0, 0, 0, 0, 0, 0, 0, 0, 0, 0, 0, 0, 0, 0, 1
1, 0, 0, 0, 0, 0, 0, 0, 0, 0, 0, 0, 0, 0, 0, 1
1, 0, 0, 0, 0, 0, 0, 0, 0, 0, 0, 0, 0, 0, 0, 1
1, 0, 0, 0, 0, 0, 0, 0, 0, 0, 0, 0, 0, 0, 0, 1
1, 0, 0, 0, 0, 0, 0, 0, 0, 0, 0, 0, 0, 0, 0, 1
1, 0, 0, 0, 0, 0, 0, 0, 0, 0, 0, 0, 0, 0, 0, 1
1, 0, 0, 0, 0, 0, 0, 0, 0, 0, 0, 0, 0, 0, 0, 1
1, 0, 0, 0, 0, 0, 0, 0, 0, 0, 0, 0, 0, 0, 0, 1
1, 0, 0, 0, 0, 0, 0, 0, 0, 0, 0, 0, 0, 0, 0, 1
1, 0, 0, 0, 0, 0, 0, 0, 0, 0, 0, 0, 0, 0, 0, 1
1, 0, 0, 0, 0, 0, 0, 0, 0, 0, 0, 0, 0, 0, 0, 1
1, 0, 0, 0, 0, 0, 0, 0, 0, 0, 0, 0, 0, 0, 0, 1
1, 0, 0, 0, 0, 0, 0, 0, 0, 0, 0, 0, 0, 0, 0, 1
```

Not very exciting, but you get the point. Entities cannot enter any of the tiles with a "1," but they can walk freely in any tile with a "0."

Now that we know what each tile is supposed to represent physically, we can perform entity-to-world collision detection (remember the separation between collision "detection" and collision "resolution").

The most naive approach is to do a rectangle-to-rectangle collision between the entity and each level tile. However, this quickly becomes inefficient as you have to perform `levelWidth*levelHeight` checks for all entities at every frame. Fortunately, we can make a number of optimizations.

Since this check will be performed every update loop, we can assume that our entity is in a stable state at the start of our check (because any collisions would have been resolved during the last frame). Therefore, if the entity is not moving (its velocity is zero), we can skip the process altogether (for the current loop).

Meanwhile, if the entity is moving, we only need to check for collisions along its intended path. Even better, if we know that our entities aren't moving faster than one tile length per frame, we only need to check the end of the path on each frame (because it will give the same result as the middle of the path if we're not passing through more than one tile).

Vector Math Primer

Vector math is important for games in both 2D and 3D. If you aren't familiar with vectors, you may need to read up on them. There are several important aspects you should be aware of:

- Vector addition and subtraction

  Vectors can be added or subtracted from other vectors. The result represents what happens when the forces represented by both vectors have an impact:

  V1 = 25, 15

  V2 = 5, 15

  V1 + V2 = 25+5, 15+15 = 30, 30

  V2 – V1 = 5-25, 15-15 = –20,0

- Vector to scalar multiplication

  A vector cannot be multiplied by another vector, but it can be multiplied by a single number (also called a scalar). This represents the intensification of a vector (e.g., multiplying by 2 to move twice as fast in the same direction):

  V1 = 20, 10

  V1 * 3.0 = 60, 30

  V1 * 0.5 = 10, 5

- Vector magnitude

  A vector can be thought of as a direction and a magnitude (or length):

  V1 = 30, 20

  V1.magnitude = sqrt($x^2 + y^2$) = sqrt(30*30 + 20*20) = 36.05

- Vector normalization

  Normalization will take any vector and return a new vector that has the same direction, but a length of exactly "1" unit. This is also called a unit vector:

  V1 = 1,1

  V1.magnitude = sqrt(1*1 + 1*1) = 1.414

  V1.normal = 1/V1.magnitude, 1/V1.magnitude = 0.707, 0.707

  V1.normal.magnitude = sqrt(0.707*0.707 + 0.707*0.707) = 1

Unfortunately for us, the iPhone SDK does not come with a helpful 2D vector class. Therefore, we have to provide our own functions for vector math located in *PointMath.h*:

add
   Performs vector addition on two `CGPoint` vectors

sub
   Performs vector subtraction on two `CGPoint` vectors

scale
   Performs scalar multiplication between a `CGPoint` and a scalar float

distsquared
   Returns the squared magnitude of a `CGPoint` vector

unit
   Returns a unit vector based on a `CGPoint` vector

towards
   A utility function that gets the vector between two `CGPoint`s and derives its unit vector

The following is an example of how we will check for collisions in our entity code using our functions for vector math (remember that the `time` parameter of our update function represents time passed since the last update):

```
CGPoint distThisFrame = scale(velocity, time);
CGPoint projection = add( worldPos, distThisFrame );
Tile* newTile = [world tileAt:projection];
if( overtile == nil || (overtile->flags & UNWALKABLE) != 0 ) {
    //tile is out of bounds or impassable
    projection = worldPos; //don't move
}
worldPos = projection;
```

First we calculate the amount of space that will be moved during this frame. Note that we scale our velocity by the time passed during the last frame, instead of merely using the entire velocity. This is because our speed is in units per second, but our update function is not called once per second (hopefully it's being called 33 times per second). If we used the full velocity, the entities would be moving far too quickly, and more importantly, they would speed up or slow down if our game loop was faster or slower.

Next, we use vector math to add the `distThisFrame` to our current `worldPos` to get the projected position at the end of the current loop. Now we need to check to see whether that projected point is going to be in a safe tile or if it is impassable.

We use the `tileAt:` function of `TileWorld` to grab the tile that is underneath that point. If the point is out of the bounds of the level, it will return nil.

We check to see whether the result is nil or whether it has an `UNWALKABLE` physics flag. If either of these cases is true, we should not let the entity walk onto the tile, so we set the projection to our current position.

Finally, we accept the projection vector as our new current position.

Special Tiles

Although impassable tile collisions can simply be resolved as soon as they are detected, other special types of tiles need extra game logic. To handle these situations, we can send the entity a message when it collides with a certain type of tile. This allows us to write code to allow entities to handle special tiles in their own way.

If a hippopotamus is walking on land and collides with a water tile, it can move to a swimming state and keep going. In contrast, a cougar might decide it doesn't want to get wet and the AI can use the message to turn the cougar around and find another path.

Entity-to-Entity

Entity-to-world collision is fairly straightforward. Your only goal is to keep entities from entering impassable tiles, and notifying them when they're on special tiles such as water. Entity-to-entity collision, however, is more complex.

With entity-to-entity collision, there are many results from different types of collisions. If an animal touches another animal, we could simply choose not to let the animals pass through each other, or we could ignore the situation if we want to allow animals to walk over each other. Or if they are two different types of animals, they might attack each other.

When collision resolution takes many different forms due to game design, the line between physics code and game logic code gets blurred. Similar to special tiles, we can handle this through special messages alerting entities of events so that the entities themselves can handle the resolution logic.

However, we might also want to resolve these collisions strictly at the GameState level. A single entity knows only as much about the world as we give it access to. However, the GameState envelops the entire world, including all of the entities, the level, and all of the game logic code.

To clarify, consider the following example. For the first level, we want to determine when one of the emu chicks has walked onto the nest at the top of the level. To represent the nest, we will have a special kind of entity called a *trigger area*. A trigger area has a bounding box for determining physical collisions just like a regular entity, but it doesn't necessarily have a graphical representation. Because the nest is already represented in the tiles of the level background, we don't need to draw anything for this trigger area. Instead, we merely perform entity-to-entity collision between emu chicks and the nest trigger area.

However, when we detect this collision, we want to remove the emu entity from the level. Simply sending a message to the entity won't allow it to remove itself. We need the resolution to happen at the GameState level.

In addition, not all entities require collision detection against each other. Using the previous example, although an emu chick should be tested for collision against the nest trigger area, the main character should not be. Because of the wide variety of expected results from entity-to-entity collision, it should be handled on a case-by-case basis.

In the next section, we will examine the implementation of these cases.

Level 1 Implementation

As we stated before, the goal for Level 1 is for the player to control the main character in a way that will herd a flock of emu chicks into their mother's nest.

This will require the following resources:

- A tile level with a clear depiction of a nest and a wide space for the chicks to run around in
- A main character sprite with idle and walking animations
- An emu chick sprite with idle and running animations
- A mother emu sprite that will pace back and forth on the nest

The game logic will include detecting when an emu chick has walked onto the nest and removing it from the world when it does, a nest trigger area for determining when emu chicks have reached the nest, and a level complete state transition when all emu chicks have reached the goal.

AI logic will consist of:

- A very basic emu mother entity that walks back and forth on the nest
- An emu chick entity that will flock together with other emu chick entities and try to run away from the main character

User input will include detecting a single touch on the screen from the player, translating that into world coordinates to detect the target square, and setting the main character's velocity to move toward that square.

gsEmuLevel

To hold our tile engine, entities, and game logic for the first level, let's create a class named gsEmuLevel that inherits from the GLESGameState class.

gsEmuLevel will need to keep track of the TileWorld, the main character entity, the emu flock entities, and the emu mother entity, as well as the level's complete state:

```
@interface gsEmuLevel : GLESGameState {
    TileWorld* tileWorld;
    Tom* m_tom;
    EmuMother* mama;
    Emu** flock;
    int flock_len;
    BOOL win;
```

```
    }
@end
```

TileWorld

In the constructor, we initialize the `TileWorld` object with the level data:

```
- (id) initWithFrame:(CGRect)frame andManager:(GameStateManager*)pManager;
{
    if (self = [super initWithFrame:frame andManager:pManager]) {
        [self setupWorld];
    }
    return self;
}

- (void) setupWorld {
    tileWorld = [[TileWorld alloc] initWithFrame:self.frame];
    [tileWorld loadLevel:@"lvl1_idx.txt" withTiles:@"lvl1_tiles.png"];

}
```

In the render function of our game state, we tell the `TileWorld` to draw itself:

```
- (void) Render {

    //clear anything left over from the last frame, and set background color.
    glClearColor(0xff/256.0f, 0x66/256.0f, 0x00/256.0f, 1.0f);
    glClear(GL_COLOR_BUFFER_BIT);

    [tileWorld draw];

    [self swapBuffers];
}
```

Now that we have a level to walk around in, we need something to walk around in it.

Main Character

To start, we need the main character sprite. We want the main character to walk around or stand still, so we need walking and idle frames for all facings. Again we will use the draw flipped technique for the right-facing frames so that we need only up, down, and left frames on the texture. Figure 4-4 shows the sprite representing Tom O'Reilly.

Figure 4-4. Tom O'Reilly sprite

Once we have the sprite, we can create an `Entity` class to wrap around it. Then we can put this `Entity` object into `gsEmuLevel` where we will initialize it and hook it into the render and update loops. And since Tom is going to be controlled by the player directly, we can hook it up to the user input code as well.

Entity

The Entity class that represents Tom will be named, well, Tom. It is actually quite a simple class, as most of the rendering code will already have been handled by the Entity class it inherits from, and the entity logic will simply be to move toward a square designated by the player:

```
@interface Tom : Entity {
    CGPoint destPos;
}

- (id) initWithPos:(CGPoint) pos sprite:(Sprite*)spr ;
- (void) moveToPosition:(CGPoint) point;

@end
```

The initWithPos function simply calls the Entity initWithPos function and initializes the destPos to be equal to the current worldPos (otherwise, it would be moving when the game loop starts).

The moveToPosition function will be called by the user input code of gsEmuLevel and will simply set the destination position to the given point in world coordinates.

Tom also overrides the update: function inherited from Entity, like this:

```
//Tom.m
- (void) update:(CGFloat) time {
    float xspeed = 200*time, yspeed=200*time; //pixels per second.
```

What is that 200 value? Uh-oh, that's a magic number! We should replace that with a define such as PLAYER_SPEED. Notice how we multiply it by time (like the distThis Frame example earlier) to get the scaled speed per frame. Next, we save the current worldPos in case our attempt at moving fails (because of a wall or the edge of the level):

```
CGPoint revertPos = worldPos;
```

And now we project the entity toward the destination position, first on the *x*-axis followed by the *y*-axis. If our speed causes us to go past the square (fabs(dx) < xspeed), we snap the distance traveled to end exactly at the destination position. Otherwise, we multiply the speed by positive or negative 1 depending on whether we're moving "right" or "left."

```
            float dx = worldPos.x - destPos.x;
            if(dx != 0){
                if(fabs(dx) < xspeed){
                    worldPos.x = destPos.x;
                } else {
                    worldPos.x += -sign(dx)*xspeed;
                }
            }
```

```
float dy = worldPos.y - destPos.y;
if(dy != 0){
    if(fabs(dy) < yspeed){
        worldPos.y = destPos.y;
    } else {
    worldPos.y += -sign(dy)*yspeed;
    }
}
```

Now we check to see whether we have moved to an acceptable tile. If not, we don't want to simply stand still; it would be better to try to slide along the edge of whatever obstacle we have reached. First, we project ourselves using only the new x value, keeping our old y value as though we had no intention of moving in any direction but horizontal; if that projection works, we accept it and move on. If not, we try to project our position only in the y direction; again, if that works, we accept it and move on. Finally, if neither attempt works, we accept our failure and revert to the old position:

```
if(![world walkable:worldPos]){
    if([world walkable:CGPointMake(worldPos.x, revertPos.y)]){
        worldPos = CGPointMake(worldPos.x, revertPos.y);
    }
    else if([world walkable:CGPointMake(revertPos.x, worldPos.y)]){
        worldPos = CGPointMake(revertPos.x, worldPos.y);
    }
    else {
        worldPos = revertPos;
    }
}
```

Now that we know what the new position will be, we should recalculate the way our sprite is facing and update the animation sequence:

```
//calculate current direction
NSString* facing = nil;
if(dx != 0 || dy != 0){
    if(fabs(dx) > fabs(dy)){
        if(dx < 0) {
            facing = @"walkright";
        } else {
            facing = @"walkleft";
        }
    } else {
        if(dy < 0){
            facing = @"walkup";
        } else {
            facing = @"walkdown";
        }
    }
} else {
    facing = @"idle";
}

//if the direction has changed, we also change our animation
if(![sprite.sequence isEqualToString:facing])
```

```
    {
        sprite.sequence = facing;
    }
```

Finally, we tell our sprite to update:

```
    [sprite update:time];
}
```

gsEmuLevel

Now that we have filled out our entity, we can plug it into our level. We already have the m_tom variable defined in the header; all we need to do is use it.

First, we initialize it inside the setupWorld: function by loading the animation, initializing an instance of Tom, and assigning it to our m_tom variable. Then we add m_tom to tileWorld's list of entities to render and we set the camera to point at m_tom's worldPos:

```
//gsEmuLevel.m
Animation* tomanim = [[Animation alloc] initWithAnim:@"tom_walk.png"];
m_tom = [[Tom alloc] initWithPos:CGPointMake(100, 100)
                      sprite:[Sprite spriteWithAnimation:tomanim]];
[tileWorld addEntity:m_tom];
[tileWorld setCamera:m_tom->worldPos];
```

Next, inside Update:, we call m_tom's update: function.

We don't need to add m_tom to the Render: function because TileWorld will have already taken care of it because we added him to the list of entities to render.

Finally, we need to be sure to call release on m_tom in the destructor.

User input

The user input code is very simple. We will receive a call to touchesEnded: when the player taps the screen.

We can get the position (in screen coordinates) of the tap by calling [self touchPosition:touch]. We then convert that position from screen coordinates to world coordinates using the worldPosition: helper function we wrote in the TileWorld class.

Finally, we set the new destination (in world coordinates):

```
    [m_tom moveToPosition:[tileWorld worldPosition:[self touchPosition:touch]]];
```

Emu Chicks

Now we'll let loose the sprite for emu chicks that we introduced in "Animation." We attach that to a new class called Emu which will also inherit from the base Entity class. This will allow us to write the AI code that controls the emus inside the Emu entity.

We want our emu chicks to flock together. There are many ways to implement a flocking algorithm, but they should all exhibit some common behavior:

- Don't stay too close to neighbors at short range.
- Calculate a velocity based on the average velocity of neighbors.

From here, based on the type of flocking behavior you wish to exhibit, you can add more rules. For example, if you wish to keep a tight cloud-shaped grouping, you may add:

- Try to move toward the center of mass of the flock.

In addition to the flocking behavior, we also want to assert two more rules:

- If the main character is nearby, run away from him.
- If the emu mother is nearby, run toward her.

When we write this code in the Emu entity and create multiple instances, we should see emergent behavior from the entities in the form of a flock of emus that will run away from the main character, and run toward their mother if they are in close proximity.

These rules may seem to be in conflict with each other, and in some cases they are; but resolving that conflict is actually rather easy. Since each rule dictates a velocity, we can consider them to all be impulses being added to the emu entity's current velocity. When we calculate all of them and add them together, we get a single velocity that represents the direction in which the emu entity should move.

Entity

The Emu entity class will need a velocity vector to represent its speed and direction. When we calculate our flocking, however, we want to count only the current velocity before applying any new velocities based on the result of the flocking algorithm; therefore, we need to keep a temporary velocity used for flocking calculation, which we name nextVel.

Finally, we also want to add a velocity to individual emus to keep them away from the other emus. That is what collision_tweak is for:

```
@interface Emu : Entity {
    CGPoint velocity;
    CGPoint nextVel;
    CGPoint collision_tweak;
}

- (id) initWithPos:(CGPoint) pos sprite:(Sprite*)spr;
- (void) flockAgainst:(Emu**) others count:(int)count;
- (void) avoidPlayer:(Entity*) mainChar;
- (void) runToGoal:(Entity*) emuMother;
- (void) update:(CGFloat) time;

@end
```

Notice that we have three separate AI functions here, in addition to the update function. The first one, flockAgainst, definitely needs to be separate from update: because it needs to be called on each entity separately before the individual entity behavior should take place.

The next two, `avoidPlayer:` and `runToGoal:`, could technically be wrapped into `update:` if we needed them to be. However, they can each act individually, and therefore make a cleaner design as separate functions; if we were to simply omit a call to one of them, you would still see all of the other set of behaviors you expected to see.

The implementation of `flockAgainst:` is a bit complicated. To start, we will utilize 95% of our current velocity in our next velocity. This represents the fact that things such as changes in flock movement do not happen immediately, but gradually over time. Otherwise, you might see a flock of birds moving together in the sky immediately freeze, then drop to the ground and land:

```
//Emu.m
- (void) flockAgainst:(Emu**) others count:(int)count {

    nextVel = scale(velocity, 0.95f); //carry inertia

    int neighbor_count=0, vel_count = 0;
    CGPoint avg_pos = CGPointMake(0,0), avg_vel=CGPointMake(0,0);
    collision_tweak = CGPointMake(0,0);
```

Next, we will perform calculation of short-range repulsion of neighbors. Rather than repulsing against all emus, we find the nearest and move away from only that one.

For each emu in the flock (not counting ourselves), we first grab the distance between the current emu and the one being flocked against. We keep track of which emu in the flock is closest to this emu, and we also count the average velocity of all flock members that are within two tiles of the current emu. In addition, we count the average position of all flock members within four tiles of the current emu.

By considering only average velocity and positions of emus within a certain radius, we can separate our emus into smaller groups that still flock independently of each other. If those two subflocks were to get close to each other, they would merge into one giant flock again:

```
float nearest_dist=0.0f;
Emu* nearest_emu;
float velCutoff = 2*TILE_SIZE;
float posCutoff = 4*TILE_SIZE;
for(int i=0;i<count;i++){
    if(self == others[i]) continue;
    float distSQ = distsquared(worldPos, others[i]->worldPos);
    if(distSQ < nearest_distSQ || nearest_dist == 0)
    {
        nearest_distSQ = distSQ;
        nearest_emu = others[i];
    }
    if(distSQ < velCutoff*velCutoff)
    {
        vel_count++;
        avg_vel = add(avg_vel, others[i]->velocity);
```

```
        }
        if(distSQ < posCutoff*posCutoff)
        {
            neighbor_count++;
            avg_pos = add(avg_pos, others[i]->worldPos);
        }
    }
```

The preceding code updates our knowledge of the flock as seen from the point of view of the current entity:

- We know which chick is closest, storing it from the others array into next_emu.

- We know the number of velocities to count from other chicks (storing it in vel_count) and the average velocity of all the nearby chicks (in avg_vel).

- We know the number of chicks in the range we need to consider (storing it in neighbor_count for positions and vel_count for velocities) and the average of all their positions and velocities (in avg_pos and avg_vel).

Next, we calculate a velocity that will push us away from the nearest emu so that we maintain a comfortable distance:

```
float emuradius = TILE_SIZE/2;
if(nearest_dist < emuradius*emuradius) {
    CGPoint away = toward(nearest_emu->worldPos, worldPos);
    float overlap = emuradius - sqrt(nearest_dist);
    collision_tweak = scale(away, overlap*0.25f);
}
```

Then we try to move toward the average flock position. Technically, we were calculating only the total position and velocity earlier. We still need to divide it by the number of neighbors to get the average. Once we know where the average position is, we look at our distance from that point and ignore it if we're too close or too far from the flock center. Otherwise, we add a velocity toward the flock center, but we scale it based on how far away it is so that if the emu is close it only waddles, but if the emu is far away it hurries to catch up:

```
//make the sum into an actual average.
avg_pos = scale(avg_pos, 1.0f/neighbor_count);
CGPoint to = toward(worldPos, avg_pos);
float distToFlock = sqrt(distsquared(worldPos, avg_pos));
if(distToFlock > 34 && distToFlock < 128){
    CGPoint accel = scale(to, sqrt(distToFlock -32));
        //using a sqrt(distance) relationship here...
        // (distance) was a bit too exaggerated.
    nextVel = add(nextVel, accel);
}
```

Finally, we want our velocity to emulate the overall flock velocity. However, we want it to represent only a portion of our calculated velocity, so we apply it as a ratio with one part average velocity and 10 parts currently calculated velocity (the repulsion and attraction values we put into nextVel, respectively):

```
    //attract to neighbors' velocity
    if(vel_count > 0) {
        avg_vel = scale(avg_vel, 1.0f/vel_count); //average velocity.
        //take weighted average between avg_vel and nextVel.
        CGPoint sum = add(scale(avg_vel, 1.0f), scale(nextVel, 10.0f));
        nextVel = scale( sum, 1.0f/11.0f );
    }
}
```

Note that this is all stored in `nextVel`—we don't actually apply it to our real velocity yet because this function is about to be called on the rest of the emus in the level and we want them to perform their calculations based on our current velocity, not the new one we just calculated for ourselves.

Next, we look at the logic used to run away from the main character. After the previous function, this should seem familiar:

```
- (void) avoidPlayer:(Entity*) mainChar {
    CGPoint away = toward(mainChar->worldPos, worldPos);
    float dist = sqrt(distsquared(mainChar->worldPos, worldPos));
    if(dist < 64){ //vision radius?
        CGPoint accel = scale(away, 300.0f/dist);
        nextVel = add(nextVel, accel);
    }
}
```

The function to attract the emu toward the emu mother should also be easy to understand now. There is, however, a slight twist: if we are within 30 units of the goal, we also add a repulsive velocity. This makes the emus stand near the emu mother, but not directly on top of her:

```
- (void) runToGoal:(Entity*) emuMother {
    CGPoint away = toward(emuMother->worldPos, worldPos);
    float dist = sqrt(distsquared(emuMother->worldPos, worldPos));
    if(dist < 30){ //vision radius
        CGPoint accel = scale(away, 300.0f/dist);
        nextVel = add(nextVel, accel);
    }
    if(dist > 34 && dist < 128){
        CGPoint accel = scale(away, -0.5f*(dist-32));
        nextVel = add(nextVel, accel);
    }
}
```

Finally, we get to the `update:` function. This generally looks a lot like Tom's `update:` function, except that when the emu encounters an `UNWALKABLE` tile, it chooses a random direction in which to wander off. We also speed up or slow down the walk animation based on the magnitude of the velocity:

```
- (void) update:(CGFloat) time{
    CGPoint revertPos = worldPos;
    velocity = nextVel;
    worldPos = add(worldPos, scale(velocity, time));
    worldPos = add(worldPos, collision_tweak);
    float dx = -velocity.x, dy = -velocity.y;
```

```
Tile* overtile = [world tileAt:worldPos];
if(overtile == nil || (overtile->flags & UNWALKABLE) != 0){
    //can't move here.
    worldPos = revertPos;
    float dir = (random() % 360) / 180.0f * PI;
    float mag = TILE_SIZE*2;
    velocity = PointFromPolarCoord(PolarCoordMake(dir, mag));
}

if(dx != 0 || dy != 0){
    NSString* facing = nil;
    if(fabs(dx) > fabs(dy)){
        if(dx < 0) {
            facing = @"walkright";
        } else {
            facing = @"walkleft";
        }
    } else {
        if(dy < 0){
            facing = @"walkup";
        } else {
            facing = @"walkdown";
        }
    }
    if(![sprite.sequence isEqualToString:facing])
    {
        //NSLog(@"facing %@", facing);
        sprite.sequence = facing;
    }
}
float pixelsmoved = sqrt(dx*dx+dy*dy);
//using distance-based animation for emus instead of time-based
[sprite update:pixelsmoved/1000.0f];
}
```

gsEmuLevel

We already defined a list of Emu entities named flock. We can now insert the emus into
the level. We begin implementing the flock by initializing this array in setupWorld::

```
//gsEmuLevel.m
flock_len = 10;
Emu** emus;
flock = malloc(flock_len *sizeof(Emu*));
for(int i=0;i< flock_len;i++) {
    emus[i] = [[Emu alloc]
        initWithPos:CGPointMake(200, 15*TILE_SIZE)
        sprite:[Sprite spriteWithAnimation:emuanim]];
    [tileWorld addEntity: emus[i]];
}
```

In the preceding code, we decided to use 10 emus to represent the flock, so we allocate
10 Emu pointers—but notice that we used malloc(). That is a C function, not an
Objective-C function. What gives?

As we mentioned before, you can mix C, C++, and Objective-C if you know what you're doing. In this case, we will need to remember to use `free()` to release this array of pointers when `gsEmuLevel` is deallocated. However, we used `alloc` for the `Emu` objects, so first we will iterate through that list and call `release` on each one.

Next, we iterate through the list and initialize 10 new `Emu` objects, remembering to add them to `TileWorld` to be rendered. In `Update:`, we first call `flockAgainst:` on each flock member. Once we complete that, we can call `avoid:`, `goal:`, and `update:` to finalize their AI calculations and update their position and sprites:

```
for(int i=0;i<flock_len;i++){
    [flock[i] flockAgainst:flock count:flock_len];
}
bool winning = true;
for(int i=0;i<flock_len;i++){
    [flock[i] avoid:m_tom];
    [flock[i] goal:mama];
    [flock[i] update:time];
}
```

Again, we do not need to add anything to `Render:` because `TileWorld` will already render all of the emus for us.

Emu Mother

The goal of the level is to lead the emu chicks to the nest where their mother is waiting for them. We will represent the mother as an entity and limit her movements to the area of the nest; therefore, we will not need an additional entity to represent the nest. Simply colliding with the mother will mean the emu chick is over the nest.

All we need spritewise is for the emu mother to walk to the left and right and occasionally perform an idle animation such as looking about (see Figure 4-5).

Figure 4-5. Emu mother sprite

The entity AI will be just as simple as that:

```
typedef enum EmuMotherState {
    EM_WALKING = 0,
    EM_IDLING,
} EmuMotherState;

//EmuMother is a subclass of Emu, because we want
// to reuse Emu's update method.
@interface EmuMother : Emu{
    EmuMotherState state;
```

```
        float state_timeout;
        CGRect bounds; //where we will wander around.
    }

    @end
```

We define an enumeration to represent the two possible states the emu mother can be in: walking and idling. We also inherit from Emu rather than Entity because we want to reuse the Emu's update function.

We will use the state_timeout variable to determine when to switch between walking and idling.

The bounds CGRect will represent an area the emu mother can walk in (notice that this is being used for AI and not for physics detection).

We initialize the emu mother with a hardcoded bounds area:

```
    - (id) initWithPos:(CGPoint) pos sprite:(Sprite*)spr {
        [super initWithPos:pos sprite:spr];
        bounds = CGRectMake(144,687, 192, 64);
        return self;
    }
```

Next, we need an update: function that can move the emu mother between idle and walking states, and keep her within the bounds rectangle if she is walking.

Because we inherit from Emu we can use all of the same variables for AI, including velocity and nextVel. We begin by setting nextVel to our current velocity and calling the Emu class update: function. This will move our entity forward, stopping if it hits any UNWALKABLE tiles (such as the fences on the left and right sides of the level), and set our walking animation sequence with the appropriate facing. Then we make sure we didn't walk out of bounds, and snap our position back if we did.

Next, we check to see whether time has expired on our current AI state; if so, we toggle to the next one. If we were previously idling, we choose a random direction and start walking. If we were walking, we start idling:

```
    - (void) update:(CGFloat) time {
        nextVel = velocity;
        CGPoint revertPos = worldPos;
        [super update:time];
        state_timeout -= time;
        if(worldPos.x < bounds.origin.x ||
           worldPos.x > bounds.origin.x+bounds.size.width ||
           worldPos.y < bounds.origin.y ||
           worldPos.y > bounds.origin.y + bounds.size.height
        ){
            //wandered too far.
            worldPos = revertPos;
            state_timeout = 0.0f;
        }
        if(state_timeout <= 0.0f){
            switch (state) {
```

```
case EM_IDLING:
{
    //pick a random direction for wandering.
    float dir = (random() % 360) / 180.0f * PI;
    float mag = TILE_SIZE*4;
    velocity = PointFromPolarCoord(PolarCoordMake(dir, mag));
    if(fabs(velocity.x) < fabs(velocity.y)){
        //make primary movement horizontal, because we don't
        //have up/down walk cycles for the emu mother.
        float tmp = velocity.x;
        velocity.x = velocity.y;
        velocity.y = tmp;
    }
    state = EM_WALKING;
    state_timeout = (random() % 1000) / 1000.0f * 1.5f + 0.5f;
}
break;
case EM_WALKING:
    //idle a while.
    velocity = CGPointMake(0,0);
    state = EM_IDLING;
    state_timeout = (random() % 1000) / 1000.0f * 1.5f + 0.5f;
    break;
    }
  }
}
```

This behavior looks pretty convincing when we run it.

Game Logic

Now that we have all of the elements necessary, we can write game logic to figure out when the player reaches the win state. In the case of gsEmuLevel, the win state is achieved when all of the Emu entities are near the EmuMother.

We can implement this check in the Update: function of gsEmuLevel by hijacking the Emu update loop and checking the distance from mama for each emu:

```
bool winning = true;
for(int i=0;i<flock_len;i++){
    [flock[i] update: timeElapsed];
    if( distsquared(mama.position, flock[i].position) >
                EMU_WIN_DISTANCE*EMU_WIN_DISTANCE)
    {
        winning = false;
    }
}
```

We begin by assuming the win state is true and proceed by determining whether any of the 10 Emu entities are *not* close enough to the EmuMother. We do this by checking to see whether the distance between the mama and the current emu is larger than some number EMU_WIN_DISTANCE.

Notice we are doing something strange, though; we're actually checking whether the distance squared is greater than `EMU_WIN_DISTANCE` squared. This is a common speed optimization that becomes apparent when you look at the math involved in calculating distance.

The formula for the distance C between points A and B is:

$$(A.x - B.x)^2 + (A.y - B.y)^2 = C^2$$

Because we are trying to get C, the code would look like this:

```
int resultC = sqrt( (A.x - B.x)* (A.x - B.x) + (A.y - B.y)* (A.y - B.y) );
```

That formula requires four subtractions, two multiplications, one addition, and a call to the `sqrt()` function. Without getting into CPU architecture, addition and subtraction operations are very fast and a multiplication operation takes only slightly longer, but `sqrt()` is very slow in comparison.

Fortunately, with a little math magic, we can get rid of the call to `sqrt()`. The trick is that we don't care about the actual value of the distance; we care only about whether it is greater than some comparison value. If we simply remove the call to `sqrt()`, we get C squared, which is fine for our purposes if the value we compare it to is also squared! Therefore, simply comparing `distSquared(...)` > `EMU_WIN_DISTANCE` * `EMU_WIN_DISTANCE` will provide the same results in half the time.

If any of the `Emu` objects are too far away, our `checkWinState` will get set to `false` and when we get out of the loop, we'll know not to set the `win` condition to `true`:

```
if(winning && ! win) {
    win = true;
    m_tom.celebrating = true;
}
```

If we have found a winning state and we haven't already declared ourselves the winner, we set `win` to `true` and tell Tom to start celebrating.

Sound

The main sound effect we want for this level is to hear the emu chicks peeping as they search for their mother. Unfortunately, we don't have an emu farm nearby, so we're going to have to use a chicken sound instead.

Fortunately, our players aren't likely to be able to tell the difference. We don't need an accurate sound; we just need one that makes the player feel like she is chasing a flock of avian babies.

We have added a sound called *trimsqueak.mp3* to our project and we will play it looped in the background music for this level. In *gsEmuLevel.m*, add the following lines of code to the bottom of `setupWorld`:

```
[g_ResManager stopMusic];
[g_ResManager playMusic:@"trimsqueak.mp3"];
```

The first line will stop whatever music may have been playing before (from the Main menu), and the second plays the sound we want for this level.

Level 2 Implementation

The goal for Level 2 is for the player to navigate to the back of a cave of sleeping lions, pick up the McGuffin, and return alive.

This will require the following resources:

- A tile level showing the inside of a cave.
- The same main character sprite from before, with added death animations.
- A lion sprite, including sleeping, napping, waking, and attacking animations. We will include both lion and lioness for visual variety, but they will behave the same.
- A McGuffin object, such as a coin or a star.

The game logic will include determining when the player has reached the McGuffin ("level complete") or has been eaten by a hungry lion ("level failed").

AI logic will consist of a lion entity. The lions will be strewn across the cave floor while sleeping, forcing the player to weave between them to get to her goal. Occasionally, they may wake up and look around. If they spot the main character, they will swipe at him; and if he gets hit, the player loses.

User input will be the same as Level 1, with no changes.

gsLionLevel

If our levels were basically the same as far as game logic and user input, with only the tile level and entities changing, we would reuse the same GLESGameState class for each level.

But because each of our levels will exhibit strongly different game logic, and in some cases user input, the best way to represent them is by separating each into its own class.

Therefore, we will create a new class named gsLionLevel that inherits from GLESGameState. We can copy and paste the TileWorld and user input code from gsEmuLevel. When initializing the Tom entity, we can use the same code, just modifying the start position to the bottom of our level:

```
@interface LionLevel : GLESGameState {
    TileWorld* tileWorld;
    Tom* m_tom;
    Lion** m_lions;
    int lions_length;
    Entity* m_mcGuffin;
}
```

The Tom class here is exactly the same as the last level. Lion is a new entity class we'll create to represent the lions in the level. And the rest of this code should be easily recognizable by now, so we'll move on.

TileWorld

The level we create for our TileWorld class should represent a cave full of lions with a space in the back for the McGuffin to lie, something similar to Figure 4-6.

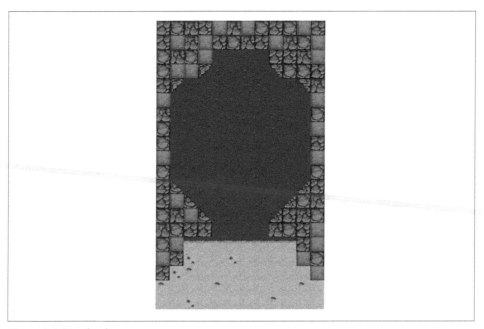

Figure 4-6. Lion level

Again you can see the unique tile strip that will be loaded (see Figure 4-7).

Figure 4-7. Lion level unique tiles

Here are the contents of the *lvl2_idx.txt* file which includes the tile indexes and physics flags:

```
12x20
10,11,9,10,8,9,8,11,10,11,8,10
10,8,9,8,10,11,9,10,8,9,11,8
11,9,11,8,1,1,0,1,10,10,9,8
11,8,8,14,0,0,0,1,15,11,11,10
```

```
10,14,1,1,0,1,0,0,1,1,15,9
8,1,1,0,0,0,1,0,0,1,1,8
9,1,1,2,1,2,2,1,0,1,1,11
11,1,1,2,1,1,2,1,0,1,1,8
11,1,1,1,2,1,1,1,0,1,1,10
8,1,2,1,1,2,1,1,2,1,1,8
11,1,2,1,1,1,2,2,1,1,1,11
10,12,2,2,1,1,1,1,1,1,13,10
10,8,12,2,2,1,1,2,1,13,11,9
11,9,8,12,2,2,2,1,13,10,9,11
9,11,10,10,1,2,2,1,9,11,10,8
11,8,7,6,7,6,7,6,7,6,10,8
8,10,4,3,3,4,3,3,3,3,8,11
10,4,5,3,3,3,3,3,3,3,3,8
5,3,3,3,5,3,3,3,3,3,5,3
3,3,4,3,3,3,3,3,5,3,3,3

1,1,1,1,1,1,1,1,1,1,1,1
1,1,1,1,1,1,1,1,1,1,1,1
1,1,1,1,0,0,0,0,1,1,1,1
1,1,1,1,0,0,0,0,1,1,1,1
1,1,0,0,0,0,0,0,0,0,1,1
1,0,0,0,0,0,0,0,0,0,0,1
1,0,0,0,0,0,0,0,0,0,0,1
1,0,0,0,0,0,0,0,0,0,0,1
1,0,0,0,0,0,0,0,0,0,0,1
1,0,0,0,0,0,0,0,0,0,0,1
1,0,0,0,0,0,0,0,0,0,0,1
1,1,0,0,0,0,0,0,0,0,1,1
1,1,1,0,0,0,0,0,0,1,1,1
1,1,1,1,0,0,0,0,1,1,1,1
1,1,1,1,0,0,0,0,1,1,1,1
1,1,0,0,0,0,0,0,0,0,1,1
1,1,0,0,0,0,0,0,0,0,1,1
1,0,0,0,0,0,0,0,0,0,0,1
0,0,0,0,0,0,0,0,0,0,0,0
0,0,0,0,0,0,0,0,0,0,0,0
```

McGuffin

As we described earlier, the McGuffin is a very simple object. It merely sits in place until the player comes along to pick it up. To that end, we can simply use the Entity class initialized with the McGuffin sprite.

Since there is no AI to deal with, just game logic for detecting player-to-McGuffin collision, we'll move on.

Main Character

Tom will move and act the same as in the first level, but he'll need additional code to handle being attacked by lions. We add the ability to play back a dying animation sequence, and some flags to disable moving around while the character is dead.

The dying flag is simply a Boolean, added to *Tom.h*:

```
bool dying; //flag for when death animations are playing.
            // set in dieWithAnimation, used in update to modify movement
            // and facing code.  Does not reset.
```

We then need a method to start the dying process:

```
//used on player death.
// Caller can pass in special death animations per situation,
// such as drowning or mauling.
- (void) dieWithAnimation:(NSString*) deathanim {
    if(!dying){ //You only die once.
        dying = true;
        sprite.sequence = deathanim;
    }
}
```

Next, we need to modify Tom's update method. We need to make sure the character doesn't move around while dying, and the easiest way to do that is to just reset speed to 0 while in the dying state:

```
- (void) update:(CGFloat) time {
    float xspeed = 200*time, yspeed=200*time; //pixels per second.

    if(dying){
        //you're not a zombie, hold still.
        xspeed = yspeed = 0;
    }
```

We also need to make sure the dying animation isn't clobbered by other character animations. We do this near the end of the update method:

```
    if(dying){
        //let the dying animation proceed as specified in the animation.plist.
    } else {
        if(![sprite.sequence isEqualToString:facing])
        {
            sprite.sequence = facing;
        }
    }

    [sprite update:time];
}
```

Lion Entities

The challenge of sneaking around the sleeping lions is the whole point of this level. To make this fun, we need to ensure that the player will have to go near the lions, while also making sure to give the player plenty of visual feedback about the current state of each lion.

Specifically, we will give the lions the following AI states:

Sleeping

While sleeping, the lions will not be awakened no matter how close the main character gets to them. After a random period of time, the lions will move to the Napping state.

Napping

If the player gets close to a napping lion, the lion will move to the Alert state. If the lion is not alerted after a period of time, it will return to the Sleeping state.

Alert

The lion is still lying down, but it has both eyes open and its head up, looking around for the main character. If he is in the lion's cone of vision, the lion will move to the Attacking state.

Attacking

The lion has spotted the character and is swiping at him. If the lion is near the character, the character will become incapacitated and the player will fail the level.

We will arrange the lions on the level so that there is only a little space between them for the player to creep through. The player will have to wait and watch for the right time to move, being careful not to walk onto any of the lions, or get too close to a napping lion, or be within the field of vision of an alert lion.

The lions do not move, and although they are several tiles wide, they will be facing only left or right (so we do not need "up" and "down" facing frames, and we can mirror the frames, so we really need only one set of "left" facing animations). Notice again that the sprite is wrapped at 1,024 pixels (see Figure 4-8).

Figure 4-8. A ferocious lion

Entity

The `Lion` class will inherit from `Entity`. We will define an enumeration that specifies all of the different AI states the lion can be in. We will also use a `float` to count the amount of time the lion has been in a state (so that we can decide when to switch from sleeping to napping, etc.) and an integer to keep track of how much the player has disturbed the lion's sleep by being too close. Finally, the lions can be facing left or right, which we will keep track of with the `flip` bool (if `flip` is `true`, they are facing to the right):

```
typedef enum LionState {
    ASLEEP = 0,
    WAKING,
    ALERT,
    ATTACKING
} LionState;
```

```
@interface Lion : Entity {
    LionState state;
    float state_time;
    int m_rage;
    bool flip;
}

- (id) initWithPos:(CGPoint) pos sprite:(Sprite*)spr;
- (void) wakeAgainst:(Entity*) other;
- (void) obstruct:(TileWorld*)world;

@end
```

Notice the wakeAgainst: and obstruct functions. In each frame, we will check the distance between the player and the lion to see whether it should wake up, invoking the wakeAgainst: function if it should.

In addition, we want to make sure the player does not walk through the lions. If these were entities that could move about, that would require entity-to-entity collision detection between the player and all of the lions. However, since the lions are stationary, we can cheat: each time a lion is created, it will access the TileWorld to get the two tiles it is on top of, and set their physics flags to UNWALKABLE. That is what the obstruct function will do.

Let's look at the implementation of this class. First, we have a utility function that gives us the AnimationSequence names that should be used for each state the lion can be in. If the lion is flipped we need to call the corresponding -flip sequences:

```
- (NSString*) animForState:(LionState) s {
    NSString* states[] = {
        @"asleep",
        @"waking",
        @"alert",
        @"attacking",
    };
    NSString* states_flip[] = {
        @"asleep-flip",
        @"waking-flip",
        @"alert-flip",
        @"attacking-flip",
    };
    return (flip?states_flip:states)[s];
}
```

Next, we have a useful function for switching states. Because we want to make sure to change not only the state variable but also the sprite animation, and additionally reset the state_time and rage counter whenever we change state, we tuck all of those operations into one tidy function:

```
- (void) setState:(LionState) s {
    state = s;
    sprite.sequence = [self animForState:s];
    state_time = 0;
```

```
    m_rage = 0;
}
```

The initialization function is short and sweet. We accept a new position, sprite, and facing, and set our initial AI state to ASLEEP. Remember that the setState: function sets our sprite sequence, state_time, and rage counters for us so that we don't need to worry about initializing them:

```
- (id) initWithPos:(CGPoint) pos sprite:(Sprite*)spr facingLeft:(bool)faceleft
{
    [super initWithPos:pos sprite:spr];
    flip = !faceleft;
    [self setState:ASLEEP];
    return self;
}
```

The update function is the heart of our lion AI code. It begins by counting up the elapsed state_time. We then branch through a switch statement based on our current state. If we are asleep, we will periodically and randomly check to see whether we should wake up or keep sleeping. If we are waking, we will periodically and randomly decide to switch to the ALERT state, back to the ASLEEP state, or neither. If we are alert but our rage counter is empty, we will fall back to the WAKING state after two seconds have elapsed. And finally, if we are attacking but our rage counter is empty, we will return to the ALERT state after two seconds:

```
- (void) update:(CGFloat) time {
    state_time += time;
    switch (state) {
        case ASLEEP:
            //5 times a second, take a 2% chance to wake up.
            if(state_time > 0.2f){
                if(random() % 1000 < 20){
                    [self setState:WAKING];
                } else {
                    state_time = 0;
                }
            }
            break;
        case WAKING:
            if(state_time > 0.2f){
                if(random() % 1000 < 20){
                    [self setState:ALERT];
                } else if(random() % 1000 < 20){
                    //narcoleptic lions.
                    [self setState:ASLEEP];
                } else {
                    state_time = 0;
                }
            }
            break;
        case ALERT:
            if(state_time > 2.0f && m_rage == 0){
                [self setState:WAKING];
```

```
                }
                break;
            case ATTACKING:
                if(state_time > 2.0f && m_rage == 0){
                    [self setState:ALERT];
                }
                break;
            default:
                break;
        }
        [sprite update:time];
    }
```

But none of this code has anything to do with the player's proximity to the lion yet. To check the proximity between the lion and the player, we need a pointer to the player. Therefore, we have another function that will be called on each loop (in addition to the update function) to perform that duty:

```
- (bool) wakeAgainst:(Entity*) other {
    //each state has a different triggering radius...
    // you can get closer to sleeping lions,
    // and should stay further from alert lions.
    float vision[] = {
        TILE_SIZE, TILE_SIZE*2, TILE_SIZE*3, TILE_SIZE*3,
    };
    float distSQ = distsquared(self.position, other.position);
    if(dist < vision[state]*vision[state]){
        m_rage++;
    } else {
        m_rage--;
        if(m_rage < 0) m_rage = 0;
    }

    //how much rage is needed to advance to the next rage state
    int ragemax[] = {
        1, 20, 20, 20,
    };

    if(m_rage > ragemax[state]){
        if(state == ATTACKING){
            m_rage = ragemax[state];
            //can't rage more.
        } else {
            [self setState:state+1];
        }
    }
    //attack hit detection against the player.
    if(state == ATTACKING){
        CGPoint attackoffset = CGPointMake(-TILE_SIZE, 0);
        if(flip){
            attackoffset.x = - attackoffset.x;
```

```
        }
        attackoffset = add(worldPos, attackoffset);
        float dist = distsquared(attackoffset, other.position);
        if(dist < 64*64){
            //kill player.
            return true;
        }
    }
    return false;
}
```

First, we have an array called `vision` with values that represent the distance at which the lion can sense the character's presence, corresponding to which state the lion is in. When sleeping, he will be disturbed only by the character standing right next to him, but when he is alert, he will see the character from three squares away.

Next, we calculate the distance (squared) from the character and compare it to the appropriate vision level (again squared). If the character is in range, the rage counter increases; otherwise, it decreases. We need to be sure to cap it at 0 on the low end, but we don't have to cap the high end here.

When the rage counter increases past a certain point, we will change states. That point is based on our current state, so just like `vision`, we will use another array of values to represent this. When the lion is `ASLEEP`, the player needs to be within range for only one update loop before the lion switches to `WAKING`. If the lion is `WAKING`, it will wait for the rage counter to reach 20 before switching to `ALERT`, and the same from `ALERT` to `ATTACKING`. If the lion is already `ATTACKING`, it has no greater recourse, so we will cap the rage counter.

If the lion is attacking, we need to check whether the player is within attack range. We check the player's position against the front of the lion. We have to take the `flip` variable into account here, and modify the check position if the lion is flipped. When the player is within attack range, we simply return `true` from `wakeAgainst`; it will be up to the caller to actually kill the player.

The values in `vision` and `ragemax` directly affect game play. If we were to increase the vision range of the lion or decrease the rage limits between states, we would make the game much harder for the player. Conversely, changing these values in the opposite direction would make it easier. These are the kinds of values game designers want to be able to play with to "tweak the game"; tuning them to get the feel just right.

In fact, if we wanted to add a "difficulty level" feature to allow the player to choose between playing the game in "easy mode" or "hard mode," we could tweak these values one way or the other based on the difficulty the player selected.

And lastly, the `obstruct:` function simply grabs the two tiles the lion is hovering over and sets their flags to `UNWALKABLE`, like so:

```
- (void) obstruct:(TileWorld*) world {
    Tile* t = [world tileAt:worldPos]; //right square
    t->flags |= UNWALKABLE;
    //left square, so offset x by -TILE_SIZE
    t = [world tileAt:CGPointMake(worldPos.x-TILE_SIZE, worldPos.y)];
    t->flags |= UNWALKABLE;
}
```

gsLionLevel

Integrating the `Lion` class into our `gsLionLevel` requires that we modify the `setupWorld:` and `update:` functions.

In `setupWorld:`, we begin by hardcoding the position and direction of our lions. If we were reusing this state for multiple levels, it would be worth it to load these values from a resource file instead of hardcoding them. But we're not, so we don't.

Next, we allocate the `Animation` and an array of lion pointers. We then iterate that array and create and initialize each `Lion` entity similar to the way we did the `Emu` entities from the previous level, but with a twist. We are using the hardcoded positions and facings and are randomly selecting between the male and female lion textures when we initialize our `Sprite` for each lion.

Wrapping up, we add each `Lion` entity to the `TileWorld` for rendering purposes and then call the `obstruct:` function from before to make sure the player can't walk over them:

```
int lion_positions[] = {
    2,11,
    4,13,
    4,14,
    5,11,
    5,9,
    6,12,
    8,14,
    8,8,
    9,13,
    9,9,
    10,12,
};
bool lion_faceleft[] = {
    false,
    true,
    true,
    false,
    true,
    false,
    true,
    true,
    false,
```

```
        true,
        true,
};
int lioncount = 11;

Animation* lionanim = [[Animation alloc] initWithAnim:@"lion.png"];
Lion** lions;
lions = malloc(lioncount*sizeof(Lion*));
for(int i=0;i<lioncount;i++) {
    Lion* otherlion = [[Lion alloc]
      initWithPos:
            CGPointMake((left+lion_positions[i*2+0])*TILE_SIZE,
                        (bottom+lion_positions[i*2+1])*TILE_SIZE)
        sprite:[Sprite spriteWithAnimation:random()%100<25?lionanim:lioness]
        facingLeft:lion_faceleft[i]];

    [tileWorld addEntity:otherlion];
    [otherlion obstruct:tileWorld];
    lions[i] = otherlion;
}
[lionanim autorelease];
m_lions = lions;
lions_length = lioncount;
```

The change to the update function is very simple; just call the wakeAgainst: and update: functions and we're finished plugging in the lions:

```
for(int i=0;i<lions_length;i++){
    if([m_lions[i] wakeAgainst:m_tom]){
        [self onFail];
        [m_tom dieWithAnimation:@"dying"];
    }
    [m_lions[i] update:time];
}
```

Game Logic

Unlike the previous level, we have two end states in Level 2. If a lion swipes the main character, we will go to the level failed state. However, if the main character reaches the McGuffin and returns to the bottom of the level, we will advance to the level completed state.

First, we must determine when the player touches the McGuffin and remove it from the TileWorld render list to represent that the player has "picked it up." Next, we determine when the player is back at the cave mouth and start celebrating.

You can find this code in the Update: function of the gsLionLevel class:

```
if(m_goal && distsquared(m_tom.position, m_goal.position) < 32*32){
    //grab the macguffin and rush for the door.
    [tileWorld removeEntity:m_goal];
    [m_goal release];
    m_goal = nil;
}
```

```
    if(m_goal == nil && m_tom.position.y < 8*TILE_SIZE){
        //clear to the door, so win.
        m_tom.celebrating = true;

    }
```

Sound

When the lion takes a swipe at the player, we want to play a sound effect. We will inject this code directly into the setState: function of the Lion class:

```
- (void) setState:(LionState) s {
    state = s;
    sprite.sequence = [self animForState:s];
    state_time = 0;
    m_rage = 0;
    if(state == ATTACKING){
        [g_ResManager playSound:@"tap.caf"];
    }
}
```

Level 3 Implementation

The third level is a puzzle. The main character is located in a room at the top of the level that contains three buttons. He will accomplish his goal or fail while staying in that room. The rest of the level consists of nine cells connected with gates that are controlled by the buttons in the upper room. Inside the cells are a mouse, a cat, and cheese. The cat is located in the upper-left cell, the mouse in the upper right, and the cheese in the bottom left.

The player must move the main character to press the buttons in a way that will open gates for the mouse, allowing it to reach the cheese while avoiding the cat. Each time the player opens a gate next to the cell occupied by the mouse, the mouse will move into the open cell. Afterward, the cat will move into a random cell as well. If the cat and mouse end up in the same cell, the cat will eat the mouse and the player will lose. If the mouse ends up in the cell with the cheese, the player will win.

This will require the following resources:

- A tile level showing the upper room and the nine cells, divided by walls. The walls between each cell should include an open space because the gates will be entities that are drawn on top of the walls, not a part of the tile level.
- The Tom sprite we used before.
- The button entities, with unpressed and pressed frames. There will be three buttons, each a different color.
- The gates (one vertically and one horizontally aligned), open and closed, with colored lights to indicate which buttons they will work with.

- The mouse sprite.
- The cat sprite.
- The cheese sprite.

Since this level is a puzzle, the game logic here will be more complex than previous levels. There is still only one way to enter the win state (when the mouse reaches the cheese) and only one way to enter the lose state (when the cat captures the mouse), but we must also control the buttons and gates from the GameState level.

The AI logic will consist of the cat and the mouse. The mouse is simple: when a door opens, the mouse will move to the next cell. The cat will decide a random cell to move to and will open its own gate.

User input will be similar to Level 2, but now we will add a context-sensitive action. When the user touches the screen above the player's avatar, we will check to see whether the touch is near a button; that context determines whether we react. Specifically, if the avatar is near a button, the resulting game change will be activated.

gsMazeLevel

Again, we will create a new GLESGameState class to represent our level:

```
#define buttons_length 3

@interface MazeLevel : GLESGameState {
    TileWorld* tileWorld;
    Tom* m_tom;
    Tom *cat, *mouse;
    Entity* cheese;
    MazeDoor* door[2][2][3];
    MazeButton* buttons[buttons_length];
    MazeState state;

    //todo; mcGuffin* cheese;
}

@end
```

As you can see, there are many types of entities in this level. As usual, we have Tom acting as the player's avatar. We also have our trusty TileWorld behind the scene and the McGuffin entity (in this case, named cheese). Our new actors will be the CAT and MOUSE along with the MazeDoor and MazeButton.

There will be one CAT and one MOUSE. They will each start in different corners of the "maze" portion of the level, and they will be controlled directly by the game logic.

There will be three MazeButtons, all accessible to the player at the top of the level in the "control room" area. When the player performs a context-sensitive action, it will trigger game logic that sets off one of the buttons and the corresponding MazeDoor.

There are nine cells, and there is a MazeDoor between each cell.

TileWorld

Figure 4-9 shows the TileWorld for Level 3.

Figure 4-9. Level 3 mockup

The level map doesn't have any simple duplicated tiles, so it gets sliced up into the tile strip in Figure 4-10.

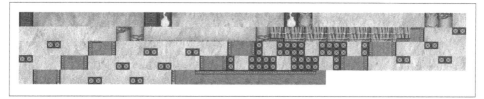

Figure 4-10. Level 3 tiles

Here is the *lvl3_idx.txt* tile index and physics information ("1" represents impassable and "0" represents normal tiles):

```
10x15

0,1,2,3,4,5,6,7,8,9
10,11,12,13,14,15,16,17,18,19
20,21,22,23,24,25,26,27,28,29
30,31,32,33,34,35,36,37,38,39
```

```
40,41,42,43,44,45,46,47,48,49
50,51,52,53,54,55,56,57,58,59
60,61,62,63,64,65,66,67,68,69
70,71,72,73,74,75,76,77,78,79
80,81,82,83,84,85,86,87,88,89
90,91,92,93,94,95,96,97,98,99
100,101,102,103,104,105,106,107,108,109
110,111,112,113,114,115,116,117,118,119
120,121,122,123,124,125,126,127,128,129
130,131,132,133,134,135,136,137,138,139
140,141,142,143,144,145,146,147,148,149

1,0,0,0,0,0,0,0,0,1
1,0,0,0,0,0,0,0,0,1
1,0,0,0,0,0,0,0,0,1
1,0,0,0,0,0,0,0,0,1
1,0,0,0,0,0,0,0,0,1
1,1,1,1,1,1,1,1,1,1
0,0,0,0,0,0,0,0,0,0
0,0,0,0,0,0,0,0,0,0
0,0,0,0,0,0,0,0,0,0
0,0,0,0,0,0,0,0,0,0
0,0,0,0,0,0,0,0,0,0
0,0,0,0,0,0,0,0,0,0
0,0,0,0,0,0,0,0,0,0
0,0,0,0,0,0,0,0,0,0
0,0,0,0,0,0,0,0,0,0
```

Notice that the physics flags define only the control room area the player will be bounded by. There is nothing to represent the cell walls that the cat and mouse must stay in. This is because their positions will be entirely defined by game logic; we will not need entity-to-world collision detection for them.

Buttons

The MazeButton entity itself is very simple. It merely shows an on or off state. It will render the states using the appropriate color for each button, which are all placed in one sprite for the usual efficiency in image loading. Because the buttons will be the target of a context-sensitive action, we will also need a way to determine whether each button is eligible for an action based on its proximity to the player's avatar:

```
//MazeButton.h
@interface MazeButton : Entity {
    int color;
}

- (id) initWithPos:(CGPoint) pos sprite:(Sprite*)spr color:(int)col;
//used to trigger the pressed animation.
- (void) press;
//used to determine if this button is under the specified entity
- (bool) under:(Entity*)other;

@end
```

The integer will store which color the button represents; this will be useful both for displaying the appropriate sprite and for letting the game logic know which button was pressed during a context-sensitive action:

```
MazeButton.m
@implementation MazeButton

- (id) initWithPos:(CGPoint) pos sprite:(Sprite*)spr color:(int)col {
    [super initWithPos:pos sprite:spr];
    color = col;
    [self press]; //probably should start with up image.  using down for now...
    return self;
}

static const NSString* down[] = {
        @"down",
        @"down-green",
        @"down-red",
    };


- (void) press {

    sprite.sequence = down[color];
}

- (bool) under:(Entity*)other {
    return distsquared(worldPos, other.position) < TILE_SIZE*TILE_SIZE;
}

@end
```

Initialization consists of storing the color and calling the press function.

The press function sets the sprite to render the appropriate color animation. Based on the sprite data in the .plist for buttons.png, the "down" animation will automatically reset to the "up" animation once it is complete.

Finally, the under: function will return true if the player is within one tile of the button when the function is called.

Doors

Similar to the MazeButton class, MazeDoors will also be very simple:

```
@interface MazeDoor : Entity {
}

- (id) initWithPos:(CGPoint) pos sprite:(Sprite*)spr ;

@end
```

This entity holds the sprite that represents the door at various states of being opened, closed, opening, closing, and closed with a colored light. However, since the door entity itself does not control these states (rather, the game logic will), we do not need special code in this class beyond initialization:

```
- (id) initWithPos:(CGPoint) pos sprite:(Sprite*)spr
{
    [super initWithPos:pos sprite:spr];
    sprite.sequence = @"closed";
    return self;
}
```

The initialization function simply sets the first animation of the door as closed and leaves the rest to our game logic.

Cat and Mouse

The cat and mouse entities reuse the Tom class because the animation sequences are the same. Meanwhile, they have no direct AI. The AI is located in the game logic and merely commands the entities in the same way as user input commands Tom.

We could have named the Tom class the "externally controlled avatar" to make it more general. But that just sounds silly.

User Input

This level's context-sensitive action will take place inside the touchesEnded: function. This time, instead of immediately calling moveToPosition on Tom when we receive a single tap, we will check the distance between the tap and each button. If it is within a certain distance, we will interpret the input as a command to activate the action associated with the button. Therefore, we search on the three buttons and perform the appropriate game logic if we find one near enough to the touch:

```
- (void) touchesEnded:(NSSet*)touches withEvent:(UIEvent*)event
{
    UITouch* touch = [touches anyObject];
    CGPoint touchpos = [tileWorld worldPosition:[self touchPosition:touch]];
    float dist = distsquared(touchpos, m_tom.position);
    if(dist < 30*30){
        if(state != WAITING_FOR_PLAYER) return;
        //figure out if the player has stomped a button.
        int buttonpressed = -1;
        for(int i=0;i<buttons_length;i++){
            if([buttons[i] under:m_tom]){
                [buttons[i] press];
                buttonpressed = i;
                break;
            }
        }
        if(buttonpressed == -1) return;

/// code snipped - performing game logic

    }
```

```
        } else {
            [m_tom moveToPosition:touchpos];
        }
    }
```

Game Logic

Most of the code in this level is going to be about game logic. In fact, apart from the random relocation of the cat entity, there is no AI. The game proceeds purely on user input and the rules of the maze game.

To begin, we'll explicitly list all of the states the maze game can be in:

```
typedef enum MazeState {
    MOVING_MOUSE=0,
    MOVING_CAT,
    WAITING_FOR_PLAYER,
    GOT_CHEESE, //winning state
    MOUSE_KILLED, //losing state
} MazeState;
```

We start in the WAITING_FOR_PLAYER state as we are waiting for the player to walk over to a button and activate it. Once the player has made her selection, we will enter the MOVING_MOUSE state as we open the corresponding door and move the mouse into the next cell.

When that is complete, we must determine whether the mouse has reached the cheese, in which case, we can move to the GOT_CHEESE state.

Otherwise, the game will automatically advance to the MOVING_CAT state, where we will randomly open a door and move the cat into a new cell.

Lastly, we determine whether the cat has entered the same cell as the mouse, and if so, we enter the MOUSE_KILLED state; otherwise, we return to the WAITING_FOR_PLAYER state and the cycle begins anew.

Initialization

Armed with this simple state machine, we can initialize our game. As usual, we place our initialization code into the setupWorld: function.

We begin by allocating the TileWorld. Because this level was designed to fit the screen exactly, without the need to scroll, we can set the camera to (0, 0) and not have to update it again.

Next, we allocate the main character as usual, placing him in the top control room area:

```
- (void) setupWorld {
    tileWorld = [[TileWorld alloc] initWithFrame:self.frame];
    [tileWorld loadLevel:@"lvl3_idx.txt" withTiles:@"lvl3_tiles.png"];
    [tileWorld setCamera:CGPointMake(0, 0)];
```

```
Animation* tomanim = [[Animation alloc] initWithAnim:@"tom_walk.png"];
m_tom = [[Tom alloc] initWithPos:CGPointMake(5.0f*TILE_SIZE, 12*TILE_SIZE)
                      sprite:[Sprite spriteWithAnimation:tomanim]];
[tileWorld addEntity:m_tom];
[tomanim autorelease];
```

The main character is followed by the cat, mouse, and McGuffin entities:

```
Animation* catanim = [[Animation alloc] initWithAnim:@"cat.png"];
cat = [[Tom alloc] initWithPos:CGPointMake(2*TILE_SIZE, 8*TILE_SIZE)
                  sprite:[Sprite spriteWithAnimation:catanim]];
[tileWorld addEntity:cat];
[catanim release];

Animation* mouseanim = [[Animation alloc] initWithAnim:@"mouse.png"];
mouse = [[Tom alloc] initWithPos:CGPointMake(8*TILE_SIZE, 8*TILE_SIZE)
                    sprite:[Sprite spriteWithAnimation:mouseanim]];
[tileWorld addEntity:mouse];
[mouseanim autorelease];


Animation* goalanim = [[Animation alloc] initWithAnim:@"mcguffin.png"];
cheese = [[Entity alloc]
          initWithPos:CGPointMake(2*TILE_SIZE, 2*TILE_SIZE+0.1f)
          sprite:[Sprite spriteWithAnimation:goalanim]];
[tileWorld addEntity:cheese];
[goalanim autorelease];
```

Now we begin adding the cell doors. As you may notice from the level mockup, the
cells are all drawn without doors. This lets us overlay the door sprites onto the scene,
allowing them to show the unobstructed passages underneath when they are opened.

There are nine cells, with a door between every two adjacent cells. That means two
rows of three vertically aligned doors, and two columns of three horizontally aligned
doors.

The central square has one door that doesn't open. We've made this compromise in
the design so that we need only three buttons; it's not worth adding a fourth button
just so that one cell can have a fourth door:

```
Animation* vertdoor = [[Animation alloc] initWithAnim:@"mazedoor.png"];
for(int x=0;x<2;x++){
    for(int y=0;y<3;y++) {
        door[0][x][y] =
            [[MazeDoor alloc] initWithPos:
                CGPointMake((3*x+3.5f)*TILE_SIZE, (3*y+1.0f)*TILE_SIZE)
                             sprite:[Sprite spriteWithAnimation:vertdoor]];
        [tileWorld addEntity:door[0][x][y]];
    }
}
[vertdoor autorelease];

Animation* horizdoor = [[Animation alloc] initWithAnim:
                                    @"mazedoor-horizontal.png"];
```

```
for(int x=0;x<3;x++){
    for(int y=0;y<2;y++) {
        door[1][y][x] =
            [[MazeDoor alloc] initWithPos:
                CGPointMake((3*x+2.0f)*TILE_SIZE, (3*y+3.5f)*TILE_SIZE)
                        sprite:[Sprite spriteWithAnimation:horizdoor]];
        [tileWorld addEntity:door[1][y][x]];
    }
}
[horizdoor autorelease];
```

Three buttons are located within the control room area. They need to be spaced out enough so that only one button is ever eligible for a context-sensitive action at any given time:

```
Animation* buttonanim = [[Animation alloc] initWithAnim:@"buttons.png"];
for(int i=0;i<buttons_length;i++){
    buttons[i] =
        [[MazeButton alloc] initWithPos:
            CGPointMake((2.5f+2.5f*i)*TILE_SIZE,12*TILE_SIZE)
                    sprite:[Sprite spriteWithAnimation:buttonanim] color:i];
    [tileWorld addEntity:buttons[i]];
}
[buttonanim release];
```

Finally, because we are starting in the WAITING_FOR_PLAYER state, we need to show colored lights above the doors leading out of the mouse's current cell. We are going to have to perform this action a lot, so let's create a function named decorateDoors to handle this feature:

```
    state = WAITING_FOR_PLAYER;
    [self decorateDoors];
}
```

Context action

We already showed the code in touchesEnded that detects when players have performed a context-sensitive action; now we will examine the game logic that gets triggered when they do:

```
if(state != WAITING_FOR_PLAYER) return;
//figure out if the player has stomped a button.
int buttonpressed = -1;
for(int i=0;i<buttons_length;i++){
    if([buttons[i] under:m_tom]){
        [buttons[i] press];
        buttonpressed = i;
        break;
    }
}
if(buttonpressed == -1) return;

//perform action.
NSArray* moves;
int angle;
```

```
    moves = [self possibleMoves:mouse];
    if(buttonpressed < [moves count]){
        angle = [[moves objectAtIndex:buttonpressed] intValue];
        //open the chosen door
        [self doorFrom:mouse.position inDirection:angle].sprite.sequence = @"opening";

        //un-decorate the other possible doors.
        for(NSNumber* n in moves){
            int i = [n intValue];
            if (i==angle) continue;
            [self doorFrom:mouse.position inDirection:i].sprite.sequence = @"closed";
        }

        //move the char through the open door.
        CGPoint mousepos = mouse.position;
        //int angle = random() % 4;
        mousepos.y += TILE_SIZE*3*cheapsin[angle];
        mousepos.x += TILE_SIZE*3*cheapcos[angle];
        [mouse moveToPosition:mousepos];
        //wait for the mouse to stop moving.
        state = MOVING_MOUSE;
    }
```

After determining which button the player pressed, we call the **press** function on that button to show graphically that the button has been pressed.

Remember, each cell has either two or three doors. (One wall in the central cell has a door that doesn't open, as we explained earlier.) That means corner cells, which have only two adjacent cells, will have only two possible moves, whereas the side and center cells will have three.

After retrieving the list of possible moves the player could have made, we check to see whether the button that was pressed corresponds to one of those moves. If the mouse is in a corner cell and the third button is pressed, it would fail this test and we would not open any doors. If you look ahead, you will see that the state is set to MOVING_MOUSE only if this test passed. That means the player can press the wrong button and see it depressed, but no door will open and she will still be able to choose a different button.

Next, we retrieve the direction of the door from the **moves** array and use it to open the corresponding door. Retrieving the right door is slightly complicated, so we place it inside a subfunction that can return a door based on a cell and a direction from that cell:

```
- (MazeDoor*) doorFrom:(CGPoint) pos inDirection:(int) angle {
    int x = gamepos(pos.x);
    int y = gamepos(pos.y);
    if(angle == 1 || angle == 3){
        //moving left/right will find horizontal column doors only
        if(angle == 1) x--;
        return door[0][x][y]; //3 columns of 2 rows
    } else {
        //moving up/down will find verticle row doors only
```

```
        if(angle == 2) y--;
        return door[1][y][x];
        //x and y are reversed for horizontal doors,
        //so that we can squeeze 2x3 of them in.
    }
}
```

Once we have a door opening, we should remove the colored lights from the other possible doors by setting their animations to "closed".

Finally, we determine the new mouse position and send it to the mouse actor, similar to the way we send the main character to a position when the player taps the screen.

Update

In the `Update:` function, we use a `switch` statement based on our current `MazeState` to perform the appropriate logic:

```
//clockwise from straight up, in opengl coords.
int cheapsin[] = { 1, 0, -1, 0 };
int cheapcos[] = { 0, -1, 0, 1 };

- (void) Update {
    float time = 0.033f;

    //move mouse, wait to stop.
    //move cat, wait to stop.
    //decorate doors, wait for button push.
    switch (state) {
        case MOVING_MOUSE:
```

In the `MOVING_MOUSE` state, we will be waiting for the mouse to finish moving (it was already told to begin moving at the start of the state when the player pressed one of the buttons). Once the mouse has reached its destination cell, we will check to see whether it found the cheese and move to the `GOT_CHEESE` state if it has.

Otherwise, we need to start moving the cat. We list the possible directions in which the cat can move and randomly select one. We then open the corresponding door and walk through it, just like we told the mouse to do in the `touchesEnded:` function:

```
            if([mouse doneMoving]){
                if (distsquared(mouse.position, cheese.position) < 16) {
                    //todo: win.
                    state = GOT_CHEESE;
                    NSLog(@"win condition triggered.");
                } else {
                    //time to move the cat.
                    NSArray* moves = [self possibleMoves:cat];
                    int angle = [[[moves
                            objectAtIndex:random()%[moves count]] intValue];

                    MazeDoor* door_tmp = [self doorFrom:cat.position
                                    inDirection:angle];
```

```
                door_tmp.sprite.sequence = @"opening";

                //move the char through the open door.
                CGPoint catpos = cat.position;
                //int angle = random() % 4;
                catpos.y += TILE_SIZE*3*cheapsin[angle];
                catpos.x += TILE_SIZE*3*cheapcos[angle];
                [cat moveToPosition:catpos];
                state = MOVING_CAT;
            }
        }
        break;
    case MOVING_CAT:
```

In the `MOVING_CAT` state, we are waiting for the cat to finish walking to its new cell. Once it has, we should determine whether the cat caught the mouse, in which case, we move to the `MOUSE_KILLED` state; otherwise, we return to `WAITING_FOR_PLAYER`:

```
        if([cat doneMoving]){
            if(distsquared(mouse.position, cat.position) < 16){
                //todo: lose.
                state = MOUSE_KILLED;
                NSLog(@"lose condition triggered.");
            } else {
                [self decorateDoors];
                state = WAITING_FOR_PLAYER;
            }
        }
        break;
    default:
```

The rest of the states do not require special processing in the update function. `WAITING_FOR_PLAYER` is just waiting for the player to activate a button, and the `GOT_CHEESE` and `MOUSE_KILLED` states are our win and lose states:

```
        //nothing interesting here...
        break;
    }

    [m_tom update:time];
    [cat update:time];
    [mouse update:time];
    for(int i=0;i<2;i++){
        for(int x=0;x<2;x++){
            for(int y=0;y<3;y++){
                [door[i][x][y] update:time];
            }
        }
    }
    for(int i=0;i<buttons_length;i++){
        [buttons[i] update:time];
    }
    //[tileWorld setCamera:[m_tom position]]; //unnecessary for this level
}
```

Finally, we make sure to update all of our entities so that they can animate their sprites.

Sounds

When the player presses a button, we want to play a click sound effect. We will add the code into the `press:` function of the `MazeButton` class:

```
static const NSString* down[] = {
        @"down",
        @"down-green",
        @"down-red",
    };


- (void) press {

    sprite.sequence = down[color];
    [g_ResManager playSound:@"tap.caf"];
}
```

Level 4 Implementation

Level 4 features the timing of jumps across log platforms while avoiding crocodile enemies. Like before, we will be focusing on context-sensitive actions (the jump action will require the same user input as pressing buttons did in the previous level), but this time we use it to cross special water tiles.

This level will require the following sprites:

- A tile level consisting of a series of solid ground patches separated by water tiles
- The same Tom sprite as before, adding the "jump" animation
- A log sprite with "floating" and "sinking" animations
- A crocodile sprite with "swimming" and "attacking" animations
- A plant sprite to make the level look like an overgrown swamp

The game logic will include detecting loss and win states. The two ways to lose in this level are to fall into water or to get eaten by a crocodile. The way to win is to reach the end of the level and grab the McGuffin.

The AI will consist of logs that sink when the character lands on them and crocodiles that jump out of the water and snap at the character if the character jumps over them.

We will need to update the Tom class to support the new jump behavior. He is allowed to jump upward (in the positive direction on the y-axis) as long as either solid ground or a log is within three tiles in that direction.

User input will be the same as in the preceding level, except that instead of searching for buttons, we will search for the edge of a platform or a log to jump to.

gsRiverLevel

As in the previous levels, we will create a new class that inherits from GLESGameState:

```
@interface RiverLevel : GLESGameState {
    TileWorld* tileWorld;
    Tom* m_tom;
    Rideable* log[log_length];
    Croc *croc[croc_length];
    Entity* m_goal;
    int state;
}
```

This level reuses the TileWorld, Tom, and Entity classes from earlier. We also introduce the Rideable class for floating log platforms and Croc to represent the crocodiles.

TileWorld

The tile world should look like Figure 4-11.

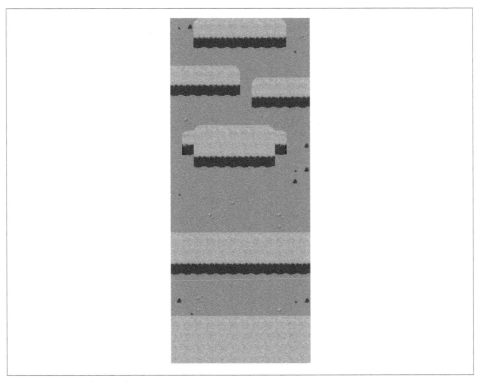

Figure 4-11. Level 4 mockup

Figure 4-12 shows the unique tiles.

Figure 4-12. Level 4 tiles

And here is the *lvl4_idx.txt* file:

```
12x30
11,11,11,11,11,11,11,11,11,11,11,11
16,17,5,6,6,6,6,6,6,7,11,11
11,11,3,3,3,3,3,3,3,3,11,12
11,11,9,9,9,9,9,9,9,9,16,11
11,11,11,11,11,11,11,11,11,11,11,11
6,6,6,6,6,7,11,11,11,11,11,11
3,3,3,3,3,3,11,5,6,6,6,6
9,9,9,9,9,9,11,3,3,3,3,3
11,11,11,11,11,11,11,9,9,9,9,9
11,12,11,11,11,11,11,11,11,11,11,11
11,13,5,6,6,6,6,6,7,15,11,11
11,2,1,1,1,1,1,1,1,4,11,17
11,8,3,3,3,3,3,3,3,10,11,11
11,11,9,9,9,9,9,9,9,11,16,17
11,11,11,11,11,11,11,11,11,11,17,11
16,11,11,11,11,11,11,11,11,11,11,11
11,11,11,11,11,12,11,11,11,11,11,11
11,11,11,12,11,11,11,11,11,12,11,11
11,11,11,11,11,11,11,11,11,12,11,11
6,6,6,6,6,6,6,6,6,6,6,6
1,1,1,1,1,1,1,1,1,1,1,1
3,3,3,3,3,3,3,3,3,3,3,3
9,9,9,9,9,9,9,9,9,9,9,9
11,11,11,11,11,11,11,11,11,11,11,11
17,11,12,11,11,11,11,11,11,11,16,17
11,16,12,11,11,11,11,11,11,12,11,11
6,6,6,6,6,6,6,6,6,6,6,6
1,1,1,1,1,1,1,1,1,1,1,1
1,1,1,1,1,1,1,1,1,1,1,1
1,1,1,1,1,1,1,1,1,1,1,1

3,3,3,3,3,3,3,3,3,3,3,3
3,3,0,0,0,0,0,0,0,0,3,3
3,3,0,0,0,0,0,0,0,0,3,3
3,3,3,3,3,3,3,3,3,3,3,3
3,3,3,3,3,3,3,3,3,3,3,3
0,0,0,0,0,0,3,3,3,3,3,3
3,3,3,3,3,3,3,0,0,0,0,0
3,3,3,3,3,3,3,3,3,3,3,3
3,3,3,3,3,3,3,3,3,3,3,3
3,3,3,3,3,3,3,3,3,3,3,3
3,3,0,0,0,0,0,0,0,3,3,3
3,0,0,0,0,0,0,0,0,0,3,3
3,3,0,0,0,0,0,0,0,3,3,3
```

```
3,3,3,3,3,3,3,3,3,3,3,3,3
3,3,3,3,3,3,3,3,3,3,3,3,3
3,3,3,3,3,3,3,3,3,3,3,3,3
3,3,3,3,3,3,3,3,3,3,3,3,3
3,3,3,3,3,3,3,3,3,3,3,3,3
3,3,3,3,3,3,3,3,3,3,3,3,3
0,0,0,0,0,0,0,0,0,0,0,0,0
0,0,0,0,0,0,0,0,0,0,0,0,0
0,0,0,0,0,0,0,0,0,0,0,0,0
3,3,3,3,3,3,3,3,3,3,3,3,3
3,3,3,3,3,3,3,3,3,3,3,3,3
3,3,3,3,3,3,3,3,3,3,3,3,3
3,3,3,3,3,3,3,3,3,3,3,3,3
0,0,0,0,0,0,0,0,0,0,0,0,0
0,0,0,0,0,0,0,0,0,0,0,0,0
0,0,0,0,0,0,0,0,0,0,0,0,0
0,0,0,0,0,0,0,0,0,0,0,0,0
```

In this level, we use the physics flag **3** to represent water tiles.

Crocodiles

The crocodile includes three frames of swimming, three frames of beginning the attack, and six frames of jumping out of the water to snap at the player's character. This is unrealistic behavior for a crocodile, but at the risk of misrepresenting nature, it gives the player an exciting explanation for why she just lost.

The definition of the Croc class includes an integer that tracks the direction of the crocodile (it flips between 1 and −1 as the crocodile turns around at the edge of the level) and a CGRect representing the bounds of the croc that the player must avoid:

```
@interface Croc : Entity {
    int direction; //-1 or 1, for pacing back and forth across the level.
    CGRect bounds; //used for hit detection on jumping player.
}

- (bool) under:(CGPoint)point;
- (void) attack:(Entity*) other;

@end
```

The interesting functions in the Croc class include under:, attack:, and update:. The under: function will return true if the given point collides with the crocodile's bounds (offset by its current position):

```
- (bool) under:(CGPoint)point {
    if(
        point.x > self.position.x + bounds.origin.x &&
        point.x < self.position.x + bounds.origin.x + bounds.size.width &&
        point.y > self.position.y + bounds.origin.y &&
        point.y < self.position.y + bounds.origin.y + bounds.size.height
        ) return true;
    return false;
}
```

The `attack:` function is used when the crocodile is found underneath the player's character. We are using the current sprite to represent the AI state of the `Croc`. Only if it is in the "idle" or "idle-flip" animation is the crocodile ready to attack. If it is, we snap its position to be directly underneath the player's character and then start the attacking animation:

```
- (void) attack:(Entity*) other {
    if([sprite.sequence isEqualToString:@"idle"] ||
       [sprite.sequence isEqualToString:@"idle-flip"])
    {
        worldPos.x = other.position.x;
        sprite.sequence = direction==1?@"attack-flip":@"attack";
    }
}
```

The `update:` function simply moves the crocodile to the left or right, depending on its direction, being sure to flip around if it reaches either side of the world:

```
- (void) update:(CGFloat) time {
    [super update:time];
    if([sprite.sequence isEqualToString:@"idle"] ||
       [sprite.sequence isEqualToString:@"idle-flip"])
    {
        //pace back and forth.
        float speed = time*200; //in pixels per second.
        float nextx = speed*direction + worldPos.x;
        if(nextx < 0 || nextx > world.world_width*TILE_SIZE){
            direction = -direction;
            //-1 is @"idle", 1 is @"idle-flip"
            sprite.sequence = direction==1?@"idle-flip":@"idle";
        } else {
            worldPos.x = nextx;
        }
    }
}
```

Logs

The `Rideable` class is like the `Croc` class, but it is even simpler as it doesn't move about:

```
@interface Rideable : Entity {
    CGRect bounds;
}

- (bool) under:(CGPoint) point;
- (void) markRidden:(Entity*) rider;

@end
```

Just like the `Croc` class, the `Rideable` class keeps track of a physics boundary. The `under:` function here is the same as `Croc`'s.

The `markRidden:` function will cause the log to start sinking if a pointer to an entity is passed or to begin rising if the entity is null:

```
- (void) markRidden:(Entity*) rider {
    if(rider){
        sprite.sequence = @"sinking";
    } else {
        sprite.sequence = @"rising";
    }
}
```

Tom

For this level, we will add new functionality to the Tom class—two new member variables and two functions to the header file:

```
//Tom.h
@interface Tom : Entity {
    CGPoint destPos; //tom-specific
    bool dying;

    bool inJump;
    Rideable* riding;
}

//... code snipped

- (void) jump;
@property (nonatomic, readonly) bool inJump;
```

The inJump bool will be true when we are currently jumping, false otherwise. The game logic can use this during the physics simulation to know whether we should check for collision with water.

The new Rideable pointer will be empty most of the time, but when the player is on a log, it will point to that entity. This will allow us to walk to the left or right while on a Rideable platform.

First, we modify the walkable: function to consider whether we are jumping, walking, or riding:

```
- (bool) walkable:(CGPoint) point {
    if(inJump) return true;
    if(riding == nil) return [world walkable:point];
    else return [riding under:point];
}
```

We also modify the moveToPosition: function to prevent new destinations from being input while in the middle of a jump action:

```
- (void) moveToPosition:(CGPoint) point {
    if(inJump) return; //freeze input while already jumping.
    destPos = point;
}
```

Next, we add a check in our update: function just above NSString* facing = nil; to handle the transition from jumping to landing on a platform:

```
        if(inJump){
            if([self doneMoving]){
                [riding markRidden:self];
                inJump = false;
            }
        }
    }
```

And finally, we implement the jump function itself:

```
- (void) jump {
    if(inJump) return; //freeze input while already jumping.
    if(![world walkable:worldPos]){
        //search for a walkable tile in the +y direction to jump to.
        //   take the first within 2 tiles.
        for(int i=1;i<=2;i++){
            if([world walkable:CGPointMake(worldPos.x, worldPos.y+i*TILE_SIZE)])
            {
                inJump = true;
                destPos = CGPointMake(worldPos.x, worldPos.y+i*TILE_SIZE);
                if(riding){
                    [riding markRidden:nil];
                    riding = nil;
                }
                return;
            }
        }
    }

    NSArray* nearby = [world entitiesNear:worldPos withRadius:4*TILE_SIZE];
    for(Rideable* e in nearby){
        if(e == riding) continue; //ignore the log we are already on.
        //ignore things we can't ride on.
        if(![e isKindOfClass:[Rideable class]]) continue;
        CGPoint pos = CGPointMake(worldPos.x, e.position.y-1);
        if(![e under:pos]) {
            //NSLog(@"not lined up to make jump.");
            continue;
        }
        float dy = e.position.y - worldPos.y;
        if(
            dy > TILE_SIZE*3 //too far to jump
            ||
            dy < 0 //ignore logs behind us, only jump forward.
        ){
            //NSLog(@"too far to jump");
            continue;
        }
        inJump = true;
        if(riding){
            [riding markRidden:nil];
            riding = nil;
        }
        riding = e;

        destPos = pos;
        return;
```

```
        }
        NSLog(@"jump failed to initiate");
    }
```

First, we make sure the jump function reacts only if we are not already jumping. Next, we search for a jump position. The current implementation of jump allows movement only in the up direction, so we only need to search upward (otherwise, we would search based on the direction we are currently facing).

First, we search upward for a passable tile to land on. If we find one, we set it as our destination position, turn on our inJump flag, and if we are currently attached to a Rideable platform, we detach it and return from our function.

If we didn't find solid ground to land on, we begin searching for Rideable entities. From within the jump function, we don't have access to RiverLevel's Log array, but we do have a pointer to the TileWorld with which we can call entitiesNear: to retrieve a list of entities within a given radius of the player.

To weed out the entities that are not eligible platforms, we use the isKindOfClass function on each entity to determine whether they are instances of Rideable.

If they are Rideable, we project a vertical line to determine whether jumping straight up would land on the log. If not, we continue our search. Otherwise, we tune our search further and determine whether the object is within jumping distance (three tiles).

If the object is too far, we continue our search. If it's within range, we mark our avatar as jumping, set our new destination, detach from the previous platform (if any), and attach to the new platform.

User Input

For this level, we want the context-sensitive action to call the new jump function on Tom:

```
-(void)touchesEnded:(NSSet*)touches withEvent:(UIEvent*)event
{
    UITouch* touch = [touches anyObject];
    CGPoint touchpos = [tileWorld worldPosition:[self touchPosition:touch]];
    float dist = distsquared(touchpos, m_tom.position);
    if(dist < 30*30){
        [m_tom jump];
    }
    if(![m_tom inJump])
    {
        [m_tom moveToPosition:[tileWorld worldPosition:
                                    [self touchPosition:touch]]];
    }
}
```

Notice that rather than simply using an if-else pair here, we check to see whether Tom is inJump after telling him to jump. This is because calling jump does not always result in a jump. If Tom is not in a place where he can jump, he won't. In those cases, we still want to allow the player to move even small amounts (otherwise, we could wind up in a situation where Tom is two pixels away from a place he can jump from, but the player can't get him to move there because the code is trying to interpret the move request as a jump action).

Game Logic

This level's game logic will be heavily focused on physics. If Tom finds himself standing on a water tile, he will fall and drown; the player loses the level. This can occur only when standing on a log for too long because our jump function doesn't allow the player to jump into the water. Tom faces another hazard while jumping across water, however: if he jumps over a croc, he will get chomped and lose the level.

Furthermore, while the character is jumping, we should avoid collision tests against the level for the water flag. Also, if the character has landed, we still need to check collisions for Rideable platforms before we decide he has collided with water.

Initialization

Our initialization continues as usual with the setup of TileWorld and our various entities (with hardcoded positions) inside the setupWorld function:

```
- (void) setupWorld {
    tileWorld = [[TileWorld alloc] initWithFrame:self.frame];
    [tileWorld loadLevel:@"lvl4_idx.txt" withTiles:@"lvl4_tiles.png"];

    Animation* tomanim = [[Animation alloc] initWithAnim:@"tom_walk.png"];
    m_tom = [[Tom alloc] initWithPos:CGPointMake(100, 100)
                        sprite:[Sprite spriteWithAnimation:tomanim]];
    [tileWorld addEntity:m_tom];
    [tomanim autorelease];

    int log_position[log_length*2] = {
        4,5,
        3,7,
        5,13,
        2,15,
        8,15,
        7,16,
        4,21,
        9,22,
        2,23,
        7,26,
    };

    Animation* loganim = [[Animation alloc] initWithAnim:@"log.png"];
    for(int i=0;i<log_length;i++){
        log[i] = [[Rideable alloc] initWithPos:
                        CGPointMake(
                            log_position[i*2+0]*TILE_SIZE,
                            log_position[i*2+1]*TILE_SIZE )
                        sprite:[Sprite spriteWithAnimation:loganim]];
```

```
        [tileWorld addEntity:log[i]];
        log[i].sprite.sequence = @"idle";
    }
    [loganim autorelease];


    int croc_position[croc_length*2] = {
        8,5,
        5,13,
        9,16,
        4,21,
        10,26,
    };

    Animation* crocanim = [[Animation alloc] initWithAnim:@"croc.png"];
    for(int i=0;i<croc_length;i++){
        croc[i] = [[Croc alloc] initWithPos:
                        CGPointMake(
                            croc_position[i*2+0]*TILE_SIZE,
                            croc_position[i*2+1]*TILE_SIZE+11)
                        sprite:[Sprite spriteWithAnimation:crocanim]];
        [tileWorld addEntity:croc[i]];
    }
    [crocanim autorelease];

    int bush_position[] = {
        16,16,
        16,112,
        16,272,
        16,304,
        16,336,
        16,784,
        48,592,
        304,592,
        304,912,
        320,752,
        368,48,
        368,272,
        368,304,
        368,336,
    };
    int bush_count=14;

    Animation* bushanim = [[Animation alloc] initWithAnim:@"plant.png"];
    for(int i=0;i<bush_count;i++){
        Entity* bush = [[Entity alloc] initWithPos:
                            CGPointMake(
                                bush_position[i*2+0],
                                bush_position[i*2+1])
                            sprite:[Sprite spriteWithAnimation:bushanim]];
        [tileWorld addEntity:[bush autorelease]];
    }
    [bushanim release];

    Animation* goalanim = [[Animation alloc] initWithAnim:@"mcguffin.png"];
```

```
    m_goal = [[Entity alloc] initWithPos:CGPointMake(192,896)
                          sprite:[Sprite spriteWithAnimation:goalanim]];
    [tileWorld addEntity:m_goal];
    [goalanim autorelease];

    [tileWorld setCamera:m_tom.position];

}
```

If you've studied the previous three levels, this code should be familiar.

Update

Now we need to update the player and the logs to determine whether the player's character has fallen in the water. We also need to check the crocodiles to determine whether the character has been attacked and the McGuffin to determine whether the player has completed the level successfully:

```
- (void) Update {
    float time = 0.033f;
    if(endgame_state != LOSING)
        [m_tom update:time];
    for(int i=0;i<log_length;i++){
        [log[i] update:time];
    }

    for(int i=0;i<croc_length;i++){
        [croc[i] update:time];
        if(m_tom.inJump && [croc[i] under:m_tom.position]){
            [croc[i] attack:m_tom];
            //NSLog(@"lose, crikey!");
            [m_tom dieWithAnimation:@"dying"];
            [super onFail];
        }
    }

    if(m_tom.riding && [m_tom.riding.sprite.sequence isEqualToString:@"sunk"])
    {
        [m_tom dieWithAnimation:@"dying"];
        [super onFail];
        //NSLog(@"lose");
    }

    if(m_goal && distsquared(m_tom.position, m_goal.position) < 32*32){
        [super onWin];
        //NSLog(@"win");
    }

    [m_goal update:time];

    [tileWorld setCamera:[m_tom position]];
}
```

This code ends by updating the camera.

Sounds

When the player jumps, we want to play a "boing" sound effect. We add the code into the jump function of the Tom class:

```
- (void) jump {
    if(inJump) return; //freeze input while already jumping.
    if(![world walkable:worldPos]){
        for(int i=1;i<=2;i++){
            if([world walkable:CGPointMake(worldPos.x, worldPos.y+i*TILE_SIZE)])
            {
                inJump = true;
                [g_ResManager playSound:@"tap.caf"];
                destPos = CGPointMake(worldPos.x, worldPos.y+i*TILE_SIZE);
                //worldPos = desPos;
                if(riding){
                    [riding markRidden:nil];
                    riding = nil;
                }
                return;
            }
        }
    }

    //... code snipped
}
```

Game State Serialization

Now that we have implemented our levels, we need a way to show the progression between them and a way to jump between levels and the menu. This presents us with three tasks:

- We need to store an integer value that represents how many levels have been unlocked.
- When the player completes a level *for the first time*, we need to increment that value.
- From our Main menu, we list all of the playable levels; we want to gray out the links to levels that are currently locked.

Initialize Storage

We begin by adding the integer to our persistent storage in the Game2DAppDelegate class. Therefore, we will add the following to our applicationDidFinishLaunching: function:

```
//Game2DAppDelegate.m
//setup default save data.
if([g_ResManager getUserData:ProgressionSavefile] == nil){
    //progression will store the unlocked level count, from 0..3.
    [g_ResManager storeUserData:[NSNumber numberWithInt:0]
                toFile:ProgressionSaveFile];
}
```

where ProgressionSaveFile is defined as:

```
#define ProgressionSaveFile @"progression"
```

End Game

Within our GLESGameStates, we have already written code to determine win and loss states. Now we will write some functions that all of our levels can use to handle user input and rendering for the end states (win or lose) and increment the progression integer.

We modify the GLESGameState class:

```
@interface GLESGameState : GameState {
    int endgame_state;
@private
    float endgame_complete_time;
}

//... code snipped

#define ENDGAME_GAME_IN_PROGRESS 0
#define ENDGAME_WINNING 1
#define ENDGAME_LOSING 2
#define ENDGAME_HOLD_TIME 2.0f

- (void) onWin:(int)level;
- (void) onFail;
- (void) renderEndgame;
- (void) updateEndgame:(float)time;
- (void) touchEndgame;

@end
```

We want to keep track of whether the GameState is still in progress, or has completed with a win or loss condition. We will also keep a time counter so that we can automatically return to the Main menu after displaying the win or loss result for a number of seconds as defined by ENDGAME_HOLD_TIME.

First, we must initialize our new variables:

```
-(id) initWithFrame:(CGRect)frame andManager:(GameStateManager*)pManager;
{
    if (self = [super initWithFrame:frame andManager:pManager]) {
        // Initialization code
        [self bindLayer];
        endgame_state = ENDGAME_GAME_IN_PROGRESS;
        endgame_complete_time = 0;
    }
    return self;
}
```

Next, we implement the onWin function, where we actually try to increment the progression variable (making sure to do so only if the level has not yet been completed):

```
- (void) onWin:(int)level{
    if(endgame_state == ENDGAME_GAME_IN_PROGRESS){
        int unlocked = [[g_ResManager
                            getUserData:ProgressionSavefile] intValue];
        if(level >= unlocked){
            //when we beat a level, unlock the next level.
            unlocked = level+1;
            //note: we could do something special on unlocked==4
            [g_ResManager storeUserData:[NSNumber numberWithInt:unlocked]
                            toFile:ProgressionSavefile];
        }
        endgame_state = ENDGAME_WINNING;
        [g_ResManager stopMusic];
        [g_ResManager playMusic:@"march.mp3"];
    }
}
```

We grab the value from our `ResourceManager` with `getUserData:` and convert it to an integer. Then we determine whether the current level has not yet been passed; if so, we increment the value and save it back into persistent storage. Regardless, we set our `endgame_state` to `ENDGAME_WINNING` and play a triumphant winning march.

If the level completes with a fail, we simply set the `endgame_state` to `ENDGAME_LOSING`:

```
- (void) onFail{
    if(endgame_state == ENDGAME_GAME_IN_PROGRESS){
        endgame_state = ENDGAME_LOSING;
    }
}
```

In our `render` function, we perform a spiffy zoom and rotation effect on either the "level complete" or "level failed" image. Once a time period has passed, we also display a "tap to continue" message to cue the player that tapping the screen will now return her to the Main menu. We expect the various `GameState`s to call this function on their own, at the end of their own render functions, for this to be overlaid in front of their contents:

```
- (void) renderEndgame{
    if(endgame_state == WINNING) {
        [[g_ResManager getTexture:@"levelcomplete.png"]
        drawAtPoint:
            CGPointMake(self.frame.size.width/2, self.frame.size.height/2 - 64)
        withRotation:min(endgame_complete_time, 0.25f)*4*2*180
        withScale:min(endgame_complete_time, 0.25f)*4];
    } else if (endgame_state == LOSING) {
        [[g_ResManager getTexture:@"levelfailed.png"]
        drawAtPoint:
            CGPointMake(self.frame.size.width/2, self.frame.size.height/2 - 64)
        withRotation:min(endgame_complete_time, 0.25f)*4*2*180
        withScale:min(endgame_complete_time, 0.25f)*4];
    }
    if(endgame_complete_time > 2.0f){
        [[g_ResManager getTexture:@"taptocontinue.png"]
        drawAtPoint:
            CGPointMake(self.frame.size.width/2, self.frame.size.height/2 - 128)
        ];
```

```
        }
    }
```

The update and touch functions will count the amount of time that has passed since
we entered an end condition and allow the player to change state only if that time has
passed:

```
- (void) updateEndgame:(float) time{
    if(endgame_state != ENDGAME_GAME_IN_PROGRESS){
        endgame_complete_time += time;
    }
}

- (void) touchEndgame{
    if(endgame_complete_time > ENDGAME_HOLD_TIME){
        [m_pManager doStateChange:[gsMainMenu class]];
    }
}
```

This assumes that all GameState levels want to return to gsMainMenu when they are done.

Now we modify our levels to use these new functions. It will be the same process for
each level, so we will review only one level.

In *LionLevel.m*, we change the Update: function to call onFail if we lost or onWin: if we
have won the level:

```
- (void) Update {

//... code snipped

    for(int i=0;i<lions_length;i++){
        if([m_lions[i] wakeAgainst:m_tom]){
            [self onFail]; //NEW PROGRESSION CODE
        }
        [m_lions[i] update:time];
    }

//... code snipped

    if(m_goal == nil && m_tom.position.y < 8*TILE_SIZE){
        //clear to the door, so win.
        [self onWin:1]; //NEW PROGRESSION CODE
    }

//... code snipped

    [super updateEndgame:time]; //NEW PROGRESSION CODE
}
```

In the Render function, we simply add a call to renderEndgame just above swapBuffers:

```
- (void) Render {
    //clear anything left over from the last frame, and set background color.
    glClearColor(0xff/256.0f, 0x66/256.0f, 0x00/256.0f, 1.0f);
    glClear(GL_COLOR_BUFFER_BIT);
```

```
    [tileWorld draw];

    [super renderEndgame]; //NEW PROGRESSION CODE

    //you get a nice boring white screen if you forget to swap buffers.
    self swapBuffers];
}
```

And finally, in touchesEnded:, we call touchEndgame at the bottom of the function:

```
-(void)touchesEnded:(NSSet*)touches withEvent:(UIEvent*)event
{
    UITouch* touch = [touches anyObject];
    [m_tom moveToPosition:
            [tileWorld worldPosition:[self touchPosition:touch]]];
    [super touchEndgame];
}
```

Modify UI

Now that we have a variable to represent progression, we need to enforce it. We already have an Interface Builder-based GameState with buttons that link to each level. All we need to do is check which ones should be locked and disable them in the initialization of that state.

Inside gsMainMenu.m initWithFrame:, we add the following:

```
-(gsMainMenu*) initWithFrame:(CGRect)frame
            andManager:(GameStateManager*)pManager
{
    if (self = [super initWithFrame:frame andManager:pManager]) {
        [[NSBundle mainBundle] loadNibNamed:@"MainMenu"
                                owner:self
                                options:nil];
        [self addSubview:subview];
    }

    //NEW PROGRESSION CODE
    UIButton* lvls[] = {
        lvl1, lvl2, lvl3, lvl4
    };

    int unlocked = [[g_ResManager getUserData:ProgressionSavefile] intValue];
    for(int i=0;i<4;i++){
        lvls[i].enabled = i <= unlocked;
    }

    return self;
}
```

It's as simple as that!

Conclusion

Congratulations, you have created your first iPhone game! You could make many improvements to this game, including adding new levels and modifying the game play of the current levels. But don't get too distracted because next up is a 3D game!

CHAPTER 5

3D Games

The topic of 3D game programming, including graphics, animation, and physics, is worth years of college courses. A single chapter cannot hope to span the breadth of it. What we can achieve, however, is a simple game that covers the basics of dealing with 3D on the iPhone, and we'll build the steppingstones of more complex work.

We won't offer advice on general 3D programming that you'll probably use in your game, specifically, lighting, triangle-mesh collision detection, skeletal animation, and shaders. Instead, we will focus on topics with special significance for game developers:

- Loading multiple 3D meshes for rendering
- Creating a particle system for special effects
- Using basic 3D math for physics detection
- Using the iPhone's accelerometer as input
- Keeping track of player times

Again, we have provided example source code for the chapter that you should download at *https://sourceforge.net/projects/iphonegamebook/files/*.

Naturally, in this chapter, we will be writing a lot of 3D code. Unfortunately, a primer on 3D graphics is beyond the scope of this book. If you are familiar with OpenGL or Direct3D, you will already have a handle on much of it; if you are not, you may want to look up a primer or continue to read here while paying attention to the more general game-specific issues—particularly, how to use the code we have provided.

To get the most from this chapter, you should have an understanding of the following:

The difference between the Projection matrix and the Model View matrix
   The Projection matrix is used to specify how the 3D scene is rendered to the screen, and the Model View matrix is used to position objects within the scene.

Switching the Projection matrix between orthogonal and perspective projection
   We used orthogonal projection for our 2D game because it renders everything in parallel to the camera; but we will be using perspective projection for our 3D scene

because it will give us a sense of depth by rendering close objects larger than objects that are farther away.

Using `glPushMatrix`, `glPopMatrix`, `glTranslate`, `glRotate`, `glScale`, *and* `glMultMatrix` *to manipulate the Model View matrix*

> `glPushMatrix` and `glPopMatrix` allow us to "save" and later "restore" the state of the Model View matrix. This lets us use `glTranslate`, `glRotate`, and `glScale` and set up the Model View matrix to render a specific object the way we want it, then return to the previous matrix to process other objects. This procedure is conceptually like moving into the local coordinates of the object we want to render, and then returning to world coordinates. And we'll use `glMultMatrix` to perform the same task as `glTranslate`, `glRotate`, and `glScale`, all in one operation.

Basic 3D vector math, such as vector addition, multiplication, dot product, and cross product

> This is just like 2D vectors, but with the extra z dimension thrown in. Now circles are spheres, squares are boxes, and lines are planes, but don't let that intimidate you; we're still taking things one challenge at a time.

The use of quaternions for rotation

> Quaternions represent rotations and can be transformed into a rotation matrix or angle-axis rotation pair. You don't need to know how quaternions work; you just need to know how to use them.

If you understand these concepts, you will be able to figure out the rest as we go.

GLESGameState3D Class

In the preceding chapter, we used OpenGL ES to draw a 2D game. Specifically, we set up the Projection matrix in orthogonal projection mode. However, we need to use perspective projection to draw a realistic 3D environment. There are some other settings we want to change as well; so, rather than reuse the `GLESGameState` class, we will create a new `GLESGameState3D` class to handle our 3D game states:

```
//GLESGameState3D.h
@interface GLESGameState3D : GameState {
    int endgame_state;
    float endgame_complete_time;
}

- (void) startDraw;
- (void) swapBuffers;
- (BOOL) bindLayer;
+ (void) setup;

-(id) initWithFrame:(CGRect)frame andManager:(GameStateManager*)pManager;

- (CGPoint) touchPosition:(UITouch*)touch;

@end
```

If you compare this class to GLESGameState, you'll find them almost identical. That's because they provide the same services—what's changed is how the class provides them.

Specifically, we will need to modify the setup: function to configure the Projection matrix to use a perspective projection instead of an orthogonal one. Instead of calling glOrthof() to set up orthogonal projection, we will call glFrustrumf() to set up perspective projection:

```
//Set the OpenGL projection matrix
glMatrixMode(GL_PROJECTION);
const GLfloat    zNear = 0.1;
const GLfloat    zFar = 3000.0;
const GLfloat    fieldOfView = 60.0;
GLfloat size = zNear * tanf(DEGREES_TO_RADIANS(fieldOfView) / 2.0);
CGRect rect = CGRectMake(0, 0, 320, 480);
glFrustumf(-size, size, -size / (rect.size.width / rect.size.height),
           size / (rect.size.width / rect.size.height),
           zNear, zFar);
glViewport(0, 0, rect.size.width, rect.size.height);
```

Next, we will modify the bindLayer: function to add a depth buffer. A *depth buffer* is used to keep track of which triangles being rendered are in front of or behind others. We didn't need a depth buffer for our last game because we were rendering everything flat to the screen and we assumed whatever was rendered last would be drawn on top of the other images. But unless you want to sort all of the triangles in all of the models that are being drawn to the screen yourself (which would be unnecessary and slow!), you need a depth buffer for your 3D scene.

We start by adding a global GLuint to hold the depth buffer ID next to the global GLuints we are using for the frame and render buffers at the top of the file *GLESGameState3D.m*, like so:

```
//primary context for all opengl calls.
EAGLContext* gles_context;

GLuint                  gles_framebuffer;
GLuint                  gles_renderbuffer;
GLuint                  gles_depthRenderbuffer; //new in Chapter 5
```

Now we can generate a depth buffer in our bindLayer: function, just after we create our render buffer:

```
// first, figure out the height and width of the render buffer
GLint backingWidth, backingHeight;
glGetRenderbufferParameterivOES(GL_RENDERBUFFER_OES,
                       GL_RENDERBUFFER_WIDTH_OES, &backingWidth);
glGetRenderbufferParameterivOES(GL_RENDERBUFFER_OES,
                       GL_RENDERBUFFER_HEIGHT_OES, &backingHeight);
// now generate a depth buffer
glGenRenderbuffersOES(1, &gles_depthRenderbuffer);
glBindRenderbufferOES(GL_RENDERBUFFER_OES, gles_depthRenderbuffer);
// and set up some configuration using the width and height values
```

```
glRenderbufferStorageOES(GL_RENDERBUFFER_OES, GL_DEPTH_COMPONENT16_OES,
                    backingWidth, backingHeight);
glFramebufferRenderbufferOES(GL_FRAMEBUFFER_OES, GL_DEPTH_ATTACHMENT_OES,
                    GL_RENDERBUFFER_OES, gles_depthRenderbuffer);

if(glCheckFramebufferStatusOES(GL_FRAMEBUFFER_OES) !=
                        GL_FRAMEBUFFER_COMPLETE_OES)
{
    DebugLog(@"failed to make complete framebuffer object %x",
                    glCheckFramebufferStatusOES(GL_FRAMEBUFFER_OES));
    return NO;
}
```

You don't have to understand all of the OpenGL functions being used here; it's enough that you know we are adding a depth buffer. If you were to try to render a 3D scene in a GLESGameState instead of a GLESGameState3D, it would probably look pretty weird (assuming it didn't crash)!

POWERVR

As you know, we are using OpenGL ES as our 3D graphics library. On the iPhone, the specific hardware solution that OpenGL ES runs on top of is called POWERVR. The company that makes this chip (Imagination Technologies, or ImgTec for short) has released a supplemental API that you can use to get the most out of its hardware. This API is free to use and available for download from *http://www.imgtec.com/powervr/insider/powervr-sdk.asp*. You can find additional utilities for handling POWERVR at *http://www.imgtec.com/powervr/insider/powervr-utilities.asp*.

For ease of use, we have included the PVRT SDK with our *Chapter5Example.zip* file. We will use PVRT to represent our 3D vectors and matrixes, to load and draw our 3D models, and to perform quaternion rotations (more on quaternions later).

Vectors and matrixes

Conceptually, there is no real difference between using the PVRTVec3 and PVRTMat4 structures versus the simple float[3] and float[16] arrays OpenGL uses. In fact, wherever a float[3] is expected, we can use a PVRTVec3, and wherever a float[16] is expected, a PVRTMat4.

However, the PVRT structs also have overloaded operators, so we can do something such as this:

```
PVRTVec3 vecB = vecA * matrixA; //vector-matrix multiplication
//or this
PVRTVec3 vecC = vecA.cross(vecB); //cross-product
```

We will use the PVRT structs for convenience.

Model format

To take advantage of the POWERVR hardware, ImgTec has created the POD model format. It is a lightweight format that simply aligns the vertex, index, and texture data in the configuration expected by the iPhone's OpenGL ES API.

Source code to use the format is available as part of the PVRT SDK. The class is named `CPVRTModelPOD` and it supports skeletal animation. To make using the class easier, we have created a `Model` class to wrap the `PowerVR` class. You can view the code in *Model.h* and *Model.mm* from the *Chapter5Example.zip* download.

You may notice that we use *.mm* files whenever we create classes that use the PVRT code. The *.mm* format tells Xcode to compile code with support for C++ syntax, which is required for PVRT.

3ds Max plug-in

To make the POD format easy to use, ImgTec has provided plug-ins for Maya and 3ds Max (two of the major modeling programs). Simply load a model in one of the editors and use the PVRGeoPOD plug-in to export the file as a *.pod* file.

If the original model was associated with a texture file, the *.pod* file will retain the same association.

Texture format

In addition to the POD model format, ImgTec has also created the PVR texture format. You can use the PVRTexTool utility to save textures as any format the POWERVR hardware supports.

The POWERVR hardware extends OpenGL to support decompression of the PVR format on the GPU hardware, making it a very efficient texture solution. For our game, we are using PVRTC4bb (PVRT compressed 4 bits per pixel).

Of course, if you are saving a model texture as a *.pvr* file, you will have to modify the *.pod* file to point to the new texture. You can use the PVRShaman utility for that.

Sprite3D

In the 2D game, our `GLTexture` is a resource, and we use a `Sprite` class to represent a unique instance of that texture on the screen.

In our 3D game, we have a similar analogy. The `Model` class is our resource. Therefore, we will create a `Sprite3D` class to represent unique instances of the model on the screen.

For example, consider a simple 3D game where the player flies through a series of hoops. In this case, we have one hoop model that we want to display multiple times. Rather than loading it into memory multiple times (one instance of `Model` for each hoop in the level), we will load it only once and have multiple instances of Sprite3D that all share a pointer to that mesh.

The Sprite3D class will contain a Model pointer, as well as scale, position, and orientation data in the form of a float, a PVRTVec3, and a PVRTQUATERNION, respectively.

As with the Model class, you can view the Sprite3D code in the *Sprite3D.h* and *Sprite3D.mm* files from the *Chapter5Example.zip* download.

Accelerometer

The iPhone provides us with an accelerometer to sense when the player is tilting the phone. To gain access to the output of the accelerometer, we need to conform to the UIAccelerometerDelegate protocol like so:

```
@interface TestState : GLESGameState3D <UIAccelerometerDelegate> {
}
@end
```

Declaring that the TestState class conforms to the UIAccelerometerDelegate protocol means it is expected to handle the - (void)accelerometer:(UIAccelerometer *)accelerometer didAccelerate:(UIAcceleration *)acceleration function.

However, just because we say our class can receive these messages does not mean the messages will automatically be directed to it. We must also set the class as the destination for accelerometer input when we create an instance of it.

We do this by grabbing the global pointer to the UIAccelerometer object and calling the setDelegate: function on it:

```
-(id) initWithFrame:(CGRect)frame andManager:(GameStateManager*)pManager;
{
    [super initWithFrame:frame andManager:pManager];
    [[UIAccelerometer sharedAccelerometer] setUpdateInterval:(1.0 / 100.0)];
    [[UIAccelerometer sharedAccelerometer] setDelegate:self];
    return self;
}
```

While setting a class as the target delegate for accelerometer events, we also set the frequency at which we wish to receive those events using the setUpdateInterval: function.

When we do receive a message in our accelerometer:didAccelerate: function, we will have access to it in the form of a UIAcceleration pointer, which has x, y, and z parameters representing acceleration in each axis direction.

However, we don't want to use this data immediately. The values we get from the accelerometer can be a bit noisy; we need a way to ignore unwanted values.

We will use something called a *low-pass filter*, the idea being that we allow the normal "low-frequency" values to pass through the filter, while getting rid of the random "high-frequency" values. Note that *frequency* here refers to wave frequency and doesn't really mean how often they show up.

It sounds complicated, but in practice it's very simple. Instead of accepting the new acceleration "signal" entirely every frame, we combine a portion of the new signal with a corresponding portion of the old signal. This means that over time any large spikes will get weighted out and the signal will remain steady.

To implement the filter, we choose a value k between 0.0 and 1.0 to represent how much of the new signal we want to keep. We then multiply the new signal by k and add it to $1 - k$ times the old value. If we store the x, y, and z accelerometer values in an array of floats named accel, the code looks like this:

```
#define kFilteringFactor          0.1
- (void)accelerometer:(UIAccelerometer*)accelerometer
        didAccelerate:(UIAcceleration*)acceleration
{
    // accel represents the 'old' signal
    // and acceleration is the 'new' signal
    accel[0] = acceleration.x * kFilteringFactor
                + accel[0] * (1.0 - kFilteringFactor);
    accel[1] = acceleration.y * kFilteringFactor
                + accel[1] * (1.0 - kFilteringFactor);
    accel[2] = acceleration.z * kFilteringFactor
                + accel[2] * (1.0 - kFilteringFactor);
}
```

Now we can use the accel array in our game logic and we won't have to worry about strange spikes in our input values.

3D Game Design

As we did in the preceding chapter, we will want to specify a game design before we implement our game.

Let's create a flight simulation game where the goal is for the player to race through a course of hoops as fast as he can. We will use the iPhone's accelerometer (or "tilt sensor" if you prefer) to control the flight since that will translate well to the feeling of flying. We will also provide a slider bar on the touch screen to provide control over the ship's thrust velocity. Figure 5-1 shows the game concept.

Graphics

We need a 3D model for our ship, and the rings we'll fly through. We will need a skybox to represent the environment we are flying in. And just to enhance visual realism, we will develop a particle system to show the vapor trail as our ship is flying about.

Figure 5-1. Game concept

In addition to the 3D scene, we will also want some 2D elements to represent our heads-up display (HUD). We want to display a clock showing how much time the player is taking, and we will need to show the thruster control in 2D as well.

Ship

We need a 3D model for our ship. Fortunately, plenty of places on the Web provide free models for things such as this. We found a model at *http://www.3Dxtras.com*.

It's not the right format, but we can use the PVRT plug-in for 3ds Max to export the model as a *.pod* file. In addition to saving the shape of the model, the *.pod* file will also store the texture data.

When drawing the ship, we'll position the camera a short distance behind and above it.

Hoops

Similarly, we will need a model for the 3D hoops, but all we need is a simple torus (doughnut) shape. We can easily create the shape and store it to *POD* format using 3ds Max.

To distinguish which hoops have already been passed through, we will shrink hoops as the ship collides with their center.

Skybox

To give a sense of motion, we must create the game so that the player notices a difference in position between two frames of movement. When the ship is facing the rings, their changes in size and shape will show the player's movement through the level, but if the ship turns away from the rings, the player will be without a point of reference.

Therefore, we need a background with a distinguishable pattern so that even when there are no other objects to use as a point of reference, the player can detect the ship's motion as the background shifts around the camera.

A typical solution is to use a *skybox*. To understand the concept of a skybox, imagine you are inside a large cube. Now imagine the interior walls of the cube are painted with scenery. Looking up you see sky, looking down you see ground, and looking around you see the horizon.

The skybox is a good solution for most situations where a 3D scene represents "outdoors" and the sky should be seen.

Particle system

Even with hoops and a skybox, the game world we are creating is still sparse. To add some more visual stimulation, we will show a trail of engine vapors coming from the ship, as well as a kind of explosion when the ship passes through a hoop.

A particle system is something that keeps track of a large number of simple objects. When moving together, these simple objects (or "particles") can represent complex systems, such as fire or smoke. Particle systems are easy to make and look really cool.

For instance, when we use such a system to project a series of particles from the engine of the ship, the player will see them as a stream of exhaust from the ship's engines. By increasing the number of particles generated in relation to the thrust, we can show the engines working harder to give a realistic feel to the game. Like real smoke, our particles will have a beginning and an end; each particle will last a fixed amount of time.

2D elements

Apart from the 3D elements of the game world, we also want to render some 2D HUD elements on top of the screen: one to display the time taken in the current race and another to display a sliding bar that represents the ship's thruster controls.

Input

The controls for our ship are fairly simple. We need to be able to pitch (tilt up and down) and yaw (turn left and right).

Along these lines, another method of controlling a ship is to roll it (spin it about its forward axis), but that won't be necessary for this game.

We will also provide a sliding bar to control the amount of forward velocity.

Accelerometer

The iPhone accelerometer gives us feedback when the phone is tilted or shifted in any direction. When the player tilts the phone to the left or right, the ship will yaw. When the player tilts the phone forward or back, the ship will pitch.

Another motion that elicits accelerometer action is to jerk the iPhone straight up or down. We could have mapped that to the ship's thrust control (speed); however, there are a couple of problems with this.

First, jerking the phone makes it hard to read the screen and is hard to control delicately. Second, unlike tilting, jerking the phone around doesn't give a point of reference to the current state of the control. So instead, we'll provide a separate control.

Thruster

The player can control the ship's speed through a slider bar that we'll draw to the screen. Whenever the player touches the bar, we will adjust the control to that position and adjust the ship's velocity as well.

The thruster will be placed to the side so that it can be controlled by the player's thumb.

Camera

To give the player the best view of the game world, we will render the scene in landscape orientation. As we described earlier, we will put the camera in third-person position, slightly behind and above the ship, to give a clear view of it as it navigates through the level.

By increasing or decreasing the distance of the camera from the ship in relation to the change in the thrust control, we can give another feeling of acceleration in the ship.

Coupled with the particle system and the feel of titling and rotating the phone, these subtle designs add up to a convincing game play feel.

Logic

For this game, we need to keep track of the time the course started as well as the list of rings and how many of them have been passed through.

We can also save the player's time to a list of high scores that can be accessed from the Main menu, increasing the replay value of the game by giving the user a goal to achieve the best score possible.

Implementation

We'll begin by creating a class named RingsState that inherits from GLESGameState3D. Since we plan to receive accelerometer input, we will also conform to the

`UIAccelerometerDelegate` protocol and add an array to store the input. We can start rendering by using a `Sprite3D` to represent our space ship:

```
//RingsState.h
@interface RingsState : GLESGameState3D <UIAccelerometerDelegate> {
    UIAccelerationValue     accel[3];
    Sprite3D *ship;
}
```

Remember that we'll be using PVRT code, which requires C++ compatibility, so our implementation file will have to be in *.mm* format.

First, we need to hook into the `UIAccelerometer` in our `initWithFrame:` function:

```
//RingsState.mm
-(id) initWithFrame:(CGRect)frame andManager:(GameStateManager*)pManager;
{
    [super initWithFrame:frame andManager:pManager];
    [self setupWorld];
    [[UIAccelerometer sharedAccelerometer] setUpdateInterval:(1.0 / 100.0)];
    [[UIAccelerometer sharedAccelerometer] setDelegate:self];
    return self;
}
```

Next, we initialize the ship in the `setupWorld:` function. If you are using the example code, the *ship.pod* and *littlespaceship02DiffuseMap.pvr* files should already have been added to the project in the same manner we added textures in the preceding chapter:

```
- (void) setupWorld {
    ship = [[Sprite3D spriteWithModel:
                    [Model modelFromFile:@"ship.pod"]] retain];
    [ship setScale:4.0f];
}
```

Because we called **retain** on the ship, we will need to let go of it in our **dealloc** function:

```
-(void) dealloc {
    [ship release];
    [super dealloc];
}
```

Now we can modify our render function to draw the ship:

```
- (void) Render {
    //clear anything left over from the last frame, and set background color.
    glClearColor(0xff/256.0f, 0xcc/256.0f, 0x99/256.0f, 1.0f);
    //important to clear the depth buffer as well as color buffer.
    glClear(GL_COLOR_BUFFER_BIT | GL_DEPTH_BUFFER_BIT);

    glLoadIdentity();

    [ship draw];

    //you get a nice boring white screen if you forget to swap buffers.
    [self swapBuffers];
}
```

So far so good, except...if we ran this code now, we might not see the ship at all. That's because we haven't set up the camera yet. By default, the camera is sitting at the origin (0,0,0) and so is the ship, so technically the ship is inside the camera. And because back-face culling is on by default, it won't render the inside of the ship.

We need to set up a camera!

Camera

Because we want to have a third-person camera, we will create a class specifically for keeping track of where the camera should be in relation to the player's ship.

Like the Sprite3D class we already have, the Camera class will need to keep track of position and rotation. Rather than duplicating that code, we will make Camera inherit from Sprite3D and simply leave it invisible instead of attaching a Model to it.

The Camera class will keep track of its offset away from its target (the ship) and provide functionality to apply the camera to the scene:

```
//Camera.h
@interface Camera : Sprite3D {
    PVRTVec3 boom;
    //the follow distance from our view target. used for
    //  rotating about the target while keeping it in view

}

//function to create a camera and set it to autorelease
+ (Camera*) camera;

//applies the camera's position and rotation to the modelview matrix
- (void) apply;

//set the boom vector
- (void) offsetLook:(float)look up:(float)up right:(float)right;

@end
```

The implementation of the class is simple, but it is best understood when seen in practice:

```
//Camera.mm
@implementation Camera

-(void) dealloc {
    [super dealloc];
}

+ (Camera*) camera {
    Camera* retval = [[Camera alloc] init];
    retval->rotate.w = 1;
    return [retval autorelease];
}
```

```
- (void) apply {

    PVRTMat4 view;
    PVRTMatrixRotationQuaternion(view, rotate);
    PVRTMatrixInverse(view, view);

    glTranslatef(-boom.x, -boom.y, -boom.z);
    glMultMatrixf((float*)&view);
    glTranslatef(-translate.x, -translate.y, -translate.z);
}

- (void) offsetLook:(float)look up:(float)up right:(float)right {
    boom.z = look;
    boom.y = up;
    boom.x = right;
}

@end
```

We can now add a Camera pointer to our RingsState class:

```
//RingsState.h
@interface RingsState : GLESGameState3D <UIAccelerometerDelegate> {
    UIAccelerationValue        accel[3];
    Sprite3D *ship;
    Camera *camera;
}
```

which we will initialize in the setupWorld: function after our ship initialization:

```
//RingsState.mm
- (void) setupWorld {
    ship = [[Sprite3D spriteWithModel:
                        [Model modelFromFile:@"ship.pod"]] retain];
    [ship setScale:4.0f];

    camera = [[Camera camera] retain];
    camera.position = ship.position;
    camera.rotation = ship.rotation;
    [camera offsetLook:100.0f up:30.0f right:0.0f];
}
```

And don't forget to deallocate it!

```
-(void) dealloc {
    [ship release];
    [camera release];
    [super dealloc];
}
```

Notice that we set the camera position and rotation to the same as that of the ship. Won't this end up drawing exactly the same as before? Don't worry, the apply function will apply the boom vector to the position of the camera when we are setting up the world rotation and translation, which we will do at the beginning of the Render function:

```
- (void) Render {
    //clear anything left over from the last frame, and set background color.
```

```
glClearColor(0xff/256.0f, 0xcc/256.0f, 0x99/256.0f, 1.0f);
//important to clear the depth buffer as well as color buffer.
glClear(GL_COLOR_BUFFER_BIT | GL_DEPTH_BUFFER_BIT);

glLoadIdentity();

[camera apply];

[ship draw];

//you get a nice boring white screen if you forget to swap buffers.
[self swapBuffers];
}
```

Now we can actually see the ship, as shown in Figure 5-2!

Figure 5-2. Ship model

Note what happens if you change the parameters of the offsetLook: function in setupWorld.

Skybox

Next, we might want to implement the accelerometer input code, but then we wouldn't be able to tell whether it was working because there is nothing else in the scene to compare movement to; so, we will implement the skybox first.

The skybox itself is simply a textured cube model exported to POD format, which we will load with Sprite3D. However, because it is intended to be viewed from the inside, we need to turn off face culling or we won't be able to see the skybox (the same way we couldn't see the ship when the camera was inside it).

Also, unlike other models, we want the skybox to always be behind everything in the scene. So, when we render it, we will need to turn off depth testing as well. This means we will have to draw the skybox before anything else in the scene, even before applying the camera.

With these warnings in mind, we start by adding a `Sprite3D` to the `RingsState` class that will represent our skybox:

```
//RingsState.h
@interface RingsState : GLESGameState3D <UIAccelerometerDelegate> {
    UIAccelerationValue      accel[3];
    Sprite3D *ship;
    Camera *camera;
    Sprite3D *skybox;
}
```

Next, we initialize it in the `setupWorld:` function:

```
//RingsState.mm
- (void) setupWorld {
    ship = [[Sprite3D spriteWithModel:
                       [Model modelFromFile:@"ship.pod"]] retain];
    [ship setScale:4.0f];

    camera = [[Camera camera] retain];
    camera.position = ship.position;
    camera.rotation = ship.rotation;
    [camera offsetLook:100.0f up:30.0f right:0.0f];

    skybox = [[Sprite3D spriteWithModel:
                        [Model modelFromFile:@"skybox.pod"]] retain];
}
```

For use with the example code, the files *skybox.pod* and *skybox_texture.pvr* have already been added to the project.

Let's remember to deallocate the skybox:

```
-(void) dealloc {
    [ship release];
    [camera release];
    [skybox release];
    [super dealloc];
}
```

Finally, we apply the skybox to the world in the Render function immediately after we reset the Model View matrix:

```
- (void) Render {
    //clear anything left over from the last frame, and set background color.
    glClearColor(0xff/256.0f, 0xcc/256.0f, 0x99/256.0f, 1.0f);
    //important to clear the depth buffer as well as color buffer.
    glClear(GL_COLOR_BUFFER_BIT | GL_DEPTH_BUFFER_BIT);

    glLoadIdentity();
```

```
//grab the camera's matrix for orienting the skybox
PVRTMat4 view;
PVRTMatrixRotationQuaternion(view, camera.rotation);
PVRTMatrixInverse(view, view);
glPushMatrix();
glMultMatrixf((float*)&view);
glDisable(GL_CULL_FACE);
glDepthMask(GL_FALSE);
[skybox draw];
glDepthMask(GL_TRUE);
glEnable(GL_CULL_FACE);
glPopMatrix();

[camera apply];

[ship draw];

//you get a nice boring white screen if you forget to swap buffers.
[self swapBuffers];
}
```

So, what exactly is going on with this new code? As we mentioned before, we are turning off culling and depth testing to draw the skybox. Since we are doing this before we apply the camera to the world, we will need to manually apply the camera rotation to the skybox or it will seem like the world never rotates (or that it is always the same rotation as our camera, depending on your perspective).

First, we extract a rotation matrix from the quaternion that represents the camera's rotation and invert it. Next, we save the state of the Model View matrix before applying the rotation matrix to it and disabling culling and depth writing.

Now the scene is ready for our skybox, so we render it and then immediately reenable depth writing and culling and restore the Model View matrix to its original state.

We should now have a working skybox (see Figure 5-3). Enjoy the view!

Input

Now we may begin using our accelerometer data. This whole time it has been quietly waiting for us in the accel[3] array we set up inside our RingsState class. To use it, we will modify our Update function to apply rotation to our ship based on the accel values:

```
//RingsState.mm
- (void) Update {

    PVRTVec3 accel_vec(accel[0], accel[1], accel[2]);

    //yaw
    float yaw = accel_vec.x;

    //pitch
    float pitch = accel_vec.y;
```

Figure 5-3. Ship with skybox

First, we wrap the accelerometer data inside a 3D vector to conceptualize the values more easily. As we discussed earlier, when the player tilts the iPhone to the left or right, it will excite the *x*-axis of the accelerometer, which we will use to yaw the ship. Similarly, when the player tilts the iPhone forward or backward, it will excite the *y*-axis of the accelerometer, which we will use to pitch the ship.

Next, we will filter the yaw and pitch values and apply them to the ship. It's the filtering of these values—just how sensitive the ship is and how tightly it turns—that gives us the game play feel we're after.

Also note that when we apply the pitch and yaw values to our ship, we aren't simply rotating the ship around the world's *x*- and *y*-axes, rather we are rotating it around its own local *x*- and *y*-axes:

```
if(fabs(yaw) > 0.15f) //ignore small values
{
    //filter the yaw value and apply it
    yaw = (yaw-sign(yaw)*0.15f)*0.25f
    [ship applyYaw:yaw];
}

if(fabs(pitch) > 0.15f) //ignore small values
{
    //filter the pitch value and apply it
    pitch = (pitch-sign(pitch)*0.15f)*0.25f
    [ship applyPitch:];
}
```

Now that we have rotated the ship appropriately, we are going to set up some code for the next part of our input: the thruster control. When implemented, it will give us a speed value that we can apply to the forward direction of our ship. For now, we will just assume our speed is zero and leave a TODO comment:

```
//get the forward direction of the ship
PVRTVec3 movement_axis(0, 0, -1);
movement_axis = [ship getAxis:movement_axis];

//apply speed and direction to get velocity
float speed = 0.0f; //TODO: get speed from thruster input
PVRTVec3 velocity = speed*movement_axis;

//apply velocity to ship
PVRTVec3 shipPos = ship.position;
ship.position = shipPos + velocity;
```

Finally, we update the camera to follow our ship's position and rotation:

```
//update the camera position and rotation
camera.position = ship.position;
camera.rotation = ship.rotation;

    }
```

As an exercise for the reader, we leave the question: what happens when you don't update the camera's position and/or rotation here?

Building now should show the ship rotating (pitching and yawing) as the player tilts the phone.

Calibration

Notice that you may need to keep the phone flat (parallel to the ground) to keep from rotating; this is because we are fighting with gravity. Holding the phone still but at a tilt will give us constant accelerometer input as gravity pulls on the lower side of the phone differently than the upper side.

But holding the phone flat isn't a comfortable way to play the game. If only we knew at what angle the player wanted to hold the phone, we could figure out the offset and subtract it from the accelerometer input.

Fortunately, we can. We will add an Options screen to the Main menu where the player can calibrate the game. This screen will show a Calibrate button. When the player is holding the phone at a comfortable position and presses the button, we will call storeUserData on our ResourceManager to save the state of the accelerometer input to the device.

We will also add two toggle buttons to allow the user to invert the x- and y-axes; some people might feel that tilting the phone up should point the ship's nose upward, while others may feel that it should rotate the world upward (thereby rotating the ship down). We will give them the ability to play the game either way.

When we initialize our game state, we will load the calibration data and use it in our Update function to normalize the accelerometer input.

You can see the Options screen (see Figure 5-4) in the *Options.xib*, *Options.h*, and *Options.m* files in the *Chapter5Examples.zip*. For now, we will focus on how to use the data in our game.

Figure 5-4. Options screen

First, we will add two PVRTVec3s to our RingsState class to represent the calibrated axis: one for the "up" vector and one for the "right" vector. You may ask why we need to worry about the "right" vector since gravity should apply only to the "up" vector of the phone. This is true, but by also calibrating the "right" vector we allow the player to prefer to hold the phone at a tilted horizontal angle (e.g., if the player wanted to play the game while lying down on his side or to avoid the sun's glare).

We also add two bools to represent the *x*- and *y*-axes' invert preferences:

```
//RingsState.h
@interface RingsState : GLESGameState3D <UIAccelerometerDelegate> {
    UIAccelerationValue      accel[3];
    Sprite3D *ship;
    Camera *camera;

    bool invertX, invertY;
    PVRTVec3 calibrate_axis_right; //right
    PVRTVec3 calibrate_axis_up;
}
```

Next, we have to load the calibration data in the setupWorld: function of the RingsState class:

```
//RingsState.mm
-(void) setupWorld {

//code snipped

    invertY = [[g_ResManager getUserData:@"invertY.on"] boolValue];
    invertX = [[g_ResManager getUserData:@"invertX.on"] boolValue];
```

Then, we extract the inverted axis preferences:

```
    //load accelerometer calibration.
    NSString *calibratedata = [g_ResManager getUserData:@"calibrate"];
    NSArray *tmp = [calibratedata componentsSeparatedByString:@","];
    //considered straight forward
    PVRTVec3 calibrate_axis([[tmp objectAtIndex:0] floatValue],
                            [[tmp objectAtIndex:1] floatValue],
                            [[tmp objectAtIndex:2] floatValue]);
    calibrate_axis.normalize();
```

The axis data is stored in comma-separated format, so after retrieving it using getUser
Data: from our ResourceProvider, we separate the values with the componentsSepara
tedByString: function of NSString. Next, we put the separate components back together inside a PVRTVec3 that represents the "forward" vector of the phone. From this,
we want to extract the "up" and "right" vectors.

Given two vectors, we can use the cross product to find a third vector perpendicular to
the first two. That means we could determine the "right" vector if we had the "forward"
and "up" vectors, or determine the "up" vector if we had the "forward" and "right"
vectors. But we have only the "forward" vector right now, so we need to get creative.

By assuming the "right" vector is parallel to the ground $(0,1,0)$, we can use it to calculate
the "up" vector. And once we have the "forward" and "up" vectors, we can go back
and calculate the correct "right" vector:

```
    calibrate_axis_right = PVRTVec3(0, 1, 0); //right
    calibrate_axis_up = calibrate_axis_right.cross(calibrate_axis);
    calibrate_axis_right = calibrate_axis.cross(calibrate_axis_up);

}
```

Finally, we have what we want, and we can use the calibration axes in the Update:
function:

```
- (void) Update {

    PVRTVec3 accel_vec(accel[0], accel[1], accel[2]);

    //yaw
    float yaw = accel_vec.dot(calibrate_axis_right);
    if(invertX) yaw = -yaw;

    //pitch
    float pitch = accel_vec.dot(calibrate_axis_up);
    if(invertY) pitch = -pitch;
```

```
//code snipped

}
```

By applying the dot product of the calibration axes against the accelerometer vector, we reduce the velocity applied by gravity to zero when holding the phone at the calibrated angle.

Thrusters

Right now our ship can rotate, but it won't move anywhere because the speed is stuck at zero. We need to add a graphical slider bar interface that accepts touch input to adjust the ship's speed from 0% to 100%.

First, we will add a float that represents the current value of the slider bar in *RingsState.h*:

```
//RingsState.h
@interface RingsState : GLESGameState3D <UIAccelerometerDelegate> {
    UIAccelerationValue      accel[3];
    Sprite3D *ship;
    Camera *camera;

    float speed_knob;

// code snipped

@end
```

Next, we initialize the value to zero in the setupWorld function:

```
//RingsState.mm
- (void) setupWorld {

    speed_knob = 0.0f;

// code snipped

}
```

Now we want to draw the slider bar interface. Because this is a 2D interface, we will need to change our Projection matrix to orthogonal projection mode and turn off depth testing.

Since we want the slider drawn on top, we should do it after we draw our 3D scene elements (at the bottom of the Render function). This would also be a good place to draw any other 2D HUD graphics, so we will come back to this code later when we want to render the timer:

```
- (void) Render {

// code snipped

    //Set up OpenGL projection matrix for 2d hud rendering.
```

```
//switch to the projection matrix so we can set up Orthogonal mode
glMatrixMode(GL_PROJECTION);
glPushMatrix(); //save the state of the normal projection matrix
glLoadIdentity(); //clear out the current projection matrix
//set projection mode to Orthogonal
glOrthof(0, self.frame.size.width, 0, self.frame.size.height, -1, 1);

//now switch back to the modelview matrix
glMatrixMode(GL_MODELVIEW);
glLoadIdentity(); //clear the current modelview matrix
glEnableClientState(GL_TEXTURE_COORD_ARRAY); //set up for 2D textures
glEnable(GL_BLEND); //enable transparent blending
glBlendFunc(GL_ONE, GL_ONE_MINUS_SRC_ALPHA);
//disable the depth test so last drawn shows on top
glDisable(GL_DEPTH_TEST);

glcolorf(1.0f,1.0f,1.0f,1.0f); //set default color to opaque white
```

Now that we have configured OpenGL to draw 2D graphics, we can begin displaying our slider. Keep in mind that the player will be holding the phone sideways to view the game in landscape mode, which means our 2D coordinate origin is at the bottom left instead of the top left of the screen. The x-axis is now "up" and the y-axis is now "right."

We need to draw the slider background first so that the slider knob will be displayed on top. Next, we draw the knob, remembering to set the x position based on the value of the speed_knob variable we defined previously:

```
//define some hardcoded values for slider bar position
int ycenter = 40;
int xcenter = self.frame.size.width/2;
int slide_groove = 246; //size of the area the slider knob can appear in.
int xmin = xcenter - slide_groove/2;

//draw the slider background image
[[g_ResManager getTexture:@"slider.png"]
    drawAtPoint:CGPointMake(xcenter, ycenter) withRotation:-90 withScale:1];

//draw the slider knob at the proper position
[[g_ResManager getTexture:@"knob.png"]
    drawAtPoint:CGPointMake(xmin+speed_knob*slide_groove, ycenter)
    withRotation:90 withScale:1];
```

When we are finished rendering our 2D graphics, we must reconfigure OpenGL for 3D so that the next frame will render properly:

```
//end drawing 2d stuff
glEnable(GL_DEPTH_TEST);
glDisable(GL_BLEND);

//switch to the projection matrix and
// restore the Perspective projection mode
glMatrixMode(GL_PROJECTION);
glPopMatrix();
//and switch back to the modelview matrix
```

```
glMatrixMode(GL_MODELVIEW);

//you get a nice boring white screen if you forget to swap buffers.
[self swapBuffers];
}
```

Remember, we always want to be left in Model View matrix mode whenever we are rendering.

Figure 5-5 shows the result; the thruster bar is drawn on top of the scene in 2D.

Figure 5-5. Thruster bar

Finally, we need to handle touch input by responding to touchesBegan:, touches Moved:, and touchesEnded:. We really care only about the position of the touch event on the screen, so we will write one function to handle all three events.

Remember the coordinate origin is in the bottom-left corner with the *x*-axis:

```
- (void) touchSpeedKnob:(UITouch*) touch {
    CGPoint pos = [self touchPosition:touch];
    int xcenter = self.frame.size.width/2;
    int slide_groove = 246; //size of the area the slider knob can appear in.
    int xmax = xcenter + slide_groove/2;
    int xmin = xcenter - slide_groove/2;
    if(pos.x > xmax) pos.x = xmax;
    if(pos.x < xmin) pos.x = xmin;
    speed_knob = (pos.x - xmin) / slide_groove;

}
```

```
-(void)touchesEnded:(NSSet*)touches withEvent:(UIEvent*)event
{
    [self touchSpeedKnob:[touches anyObject]];
}

-(void)touchesBegan:(NSSet*)touches withEvent:(UIEvent*)event
{
    [self touchSpeedKnob:[touches anyObject]];
    [self touchEndgame];
}

-(void)touchesMoved:(NSSet*)touches withEvent:(UIEvent*)event
{
    [self touchSpeedKnob:[touches anyObject]];
}
```

Now the player can slide the knob by touching the screen and the ship reacts by increasing and decreasing velocity.

It bears consideration that some people are left-handed and would benefit from having the slider bar on the left side of the screen. It shouldn't be hard to add another toggle to the Options screen and rearrange the position of the slider bar if you are so inclined.

Rings

By now, we have a 3D scene containing a skybox and a ship. The ship can yaw and pitch and move about the scene. All we need now are the rings that the player will fly through to complete the course.

Each ring will be represented by a Sprite3D. However, in addition to the basic position and orientation of the ring, we also want to add functionality for detecting when the ship has passed through a ring and keep track of the state of the ring as the ship passes through it, making it inactive. Therefore, we create a new Ring class that inherits from Sprite3D:

```
//Ring.h
@interface Ring : Sprite3D {
    int lastDistance;
    PVRTVec3 normal;
    bool active;
}

+ (id) ringWithModel:(Model*)model;
- (bool) update:(float)time collideWith:(Sprite3D*) ship;

@property (nonatomic, readonly) PVRTVec3 normal;
@property (nonatomic, readonly) bool active;

@end
```

The `lastDistance` and `normal` variables are used for collision detection, and `active` is true when the player still needs to pass through the ring. We will call the `update:` function on all the active rings each frame to see whether the ship has passed through them:

```
//Ring.mm
@implementation Ring

@synthesize normal, active;

- (void) forwardX:(float)x Y:(float)y Z:(float)z {
    PVRTVec3 forward(x, y, z);
    forward.normalize();
    normal = forward;
    [super forwardX:x Y:y Z:z];
}
```

First, we override the `forwardX:Y:Z:` function of `Sprite3D` because we want to store the normal. Since the ring model we are using was created in 3ds Max in an orientation such that its radius is on the x-y plane, its normal will be on the local z-axis or "forward" vector.

However, we still want to allow the original functionality for this method, so once we have the normal, we pass a call down to `Sprite3D`:

```
+ (id) ringWithModel:(Model*)model {
    Ring *retval = [[Ring alloc] init];
    retval.model = model;
    return [retval autorelease];
}

- (id) init {
    [super init];
    active = true;
    lastDistance = 1;
    return self;
}
```

The `update:` function will try to detect collision with the `Sprite3D` we pass into the function. Consider that a "ring" is a 2D concept created by mapping a sphere to a 2D plane. Therefore, we will test collision by first checking whether the ship has recently crossed the plane the ring inhabits, followed by detecting whether the ship is currently in the sphere with a radius equal to the ring's and centered at the ring's position.

The detection takes place in two phases: point-plane detection, followed by point-sphere. *Point-plane detection* is performed by applying the dot product of the normal against the distance vector between the plane and the ship. If the result is positive, we consider the point to be "in front of" the plane, whereas if the distance is negative, the point is "behind" the plane. The result is checked against a stored result from the previous frame: if the value suddenly changes from negative to positive or positive to negative, we know it has passed from one side of the plane to the other.

This is similar to back-face culling: for each triangle, the GPU can test whether the camera is in front of or behind the triangle by taking the dot product of the camera position against the triangle's normal vector. If the camera is behind the triangle, it is discarded from the render pipeline.

Point-sphere detection is merely the 3D version of point-circle detection: get the distance of the point from the center of the circle and test that against the circle's radius. The only difference is that the distance formula in 3D adds the z-axis: $d^2 = x^2 + y^2 + z^2$. Again, we make sure to avoid using the slow `sqrt()` function by testing the distance squared against the radius squared.

We could have tested either method first, as both require approximately the same amount of calculation to complete: the dot product used in point-plane is three multiplications and two additions and so is the distance formula in point-sphere. However, since we need to keep track of which side of the ring's plane the player is on, we check the point/plane collision first:

```
- (bool) update:(float)time collideWith:(Sprite3D*) ship {
    bool retval = false;
    float dist = (translate-ship.position).dot(normal);
    int newdist = dist > 0.0f? 1 : -1;
    if(newdist != lastDistance){
        //ship crossed our plane; see if it was within the ring when it did so.
        lastDistance = newdist;
        PVRTVec3 toward = translate-ship.position;
        float distsquared = toward.x*toward.x
                            +toward.y*toward.y
                            +toward.z*toward.z;
        //the torus major radius is 60, minor radius is 10.
        if(distsquared < 50*50)
        {
            //detected a proper fly-through.
            active = false;
            retval = true;
            NSLog(@"detected fly through.");
        }
    }
}
```

Once we know the ship has collided with the ring, we set the ring's `active` flag to `false`. To distinguish between active and inactive rings, we want the inactive ones to shrink. The *ring.pod* file we will be using is actually an animated model that starts with a large torus and ends with a smaller one, so when the ring becomes inactive, we begin the animation by incrementing the frame until it reaches the maximum number of frames we define for rings. The default `Sprite3D` render function will take care to apply the frame to the model when drawing, properly animating the ring:

```
if(!active){
    if(frame < model.numFrames-1)
        frame += 30*time;
```

```
            if(frame > model.numFrames-1)
                frame = model.numFrames-1;
        }

        return retval;
    }

    @end
```

Finally, we return true or false depending on whether a collision took place; this lets the game logic take further action when a ring is passed through.

Layout

Exactly how the rings are placed and oriented will define the course: if they are very close together with tight turns, it will be a very difficult course. If they are spread out and arranged in almost a straight line, the course will be very easy.

We have defined a set of positions and orientations by drawing out the course on a whiteboard, as shown in Figure 5-6 (notice the top and side views are necessary to show all three dimensions).

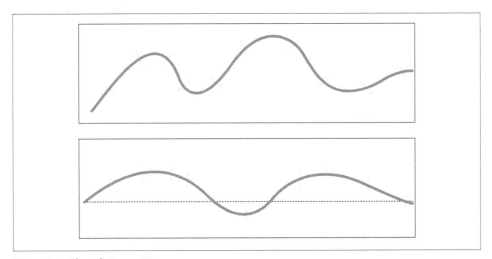

Figure 5-6. Plotted ring positions

We then plotted out and hardcoded these values in the setupWorld: function. If we planned to support multiple levels, we would place the information in a file and load that file in setupWorld: instead.

Implementation

First, we add an array to the RingsState class to hold our rings. Since we know exactly how many rings we will be creating, we can use an array of that size, but if we were loading the data from a file, we would have to allocate a dynamically sized array:

```
//RingsState.h
#define RING_COUNT 11

@interface RingsState : GLESGameState3D <UIAccelerometerDelegate> {
    UIAccelerationValue         accel[3];
    Sprite3D *ship;
    Ring *rings[RING_COUNT];
    Camera *camera;

// code snipped

}
```

Next, we initialize the rings in setupWorld: using the hardcoded data we talked about:

```
RingsState.mm
- (void) setupWorld {

    //these are the hardcoded positions of the rings in the level.
    int positions[] = { //x,y,z
    0, 0, 0,
    154, 100, 132,
    366, 174, 340,
    370, 166, 552,
    152, 114, 674,
    196, -46, 922,
    430, -120, 1116,
    466, 96, 1490,
    200, 168, 1702,
    152, 90, 2008,
    270, -24, 2292,
    };
```

Notice that the increasing z values mean the course moves forward linearly across the z-axis. Since the camera is actually facing the negative z-axis to begin with, we invert the z values when assigning them:

```
    //these are the orientations of the rings in the level.
    int normals[] = { //x,y,z
    64, 51, 64,
    64, 38, 64,
    44, 0, 64,
    -64, -25, 46,
    -60, -35, 64,
    64, -37, 52,
    44, 0, 64,
    -64, 34, 55,
    -49, -19, 64,
    31, -27, 64,
    22, -26, 64,
    };

    Model *ringmodel = [Model modelFromFile:@"ring.pod"];
```

If you are using the example code, the *ring.pod* and *ring.pvr* files have already been added to the project:

```
for(int i=0;i<RING_COUNT;i++){
    rings[i] = [[Ring ringWithModel:ringmodel] retain];
    //flipping z here, because our camera currently faces toward -z.
    [rings[i] setTranslateX:positions[i*3+0]
                            Y:positions[i*3+1]
                            Z:-positions[i*3+2]];
    //apply ring orientations, also with flipped z
    [rings[i] forwardX:normals[i*3+0]
                     Y:normals[i*3+1]
                     Z:-normals[i*3+2]];
}
```

Once we have created and initialized all of the rings, we want to position the ship in front of the first one:

```
ship = [[Sprite3D spriteWithModel:
                [Model modelFromFile:@"ship.pod"]] retain];
[ship setScale:4.0f];

PVRTVec3 tmppos = rings[0].position;
tmppos += -100*rings[0].normal;
ship.position = tmppos;

// code snipped

}
```

We do not need to retain the model explicitly here because the rings will hold on to it themselves. However, we will have to release the rings (see Figure 5-7):

```
-(void) dealloc {
    [ship release];
    [camera release];
    for(int i=0;i<RING_COUNT;i++)
        [rings[i] release];
    [skybox release];
    [super dealloc];
}
```

Particle System

The last graphical element to put in place is the particle system. At its heart, the particle system is just a group of Sprite3Ds flying about in the world. However, for each particle, we need to keep track of not only the model, position, and orientation (all provided by Sprite3D), but also the velocity, life span, and animation speed. Therefore, we will create a new Particle class that inherits from Sprite3D:

```
//Particle.h
@interface Particle : Sprite3D{
    PVRTVec3 _vel;
    float _life; //time, in seconds, that this particle will be around for.
    float _framespeed;
}
```

```
+ (id) particleWithModel:(Model*)model;

- (void) resetLife:(float)life
          velocitiy:(PVRTVec3)vel
          framespeed:(float)framespeed;
- (void) update:(float)time;
- (bool) alive;

@end
```

Figure 5-7. Rings, of course

When a particle is made active, we set its _life variable to a positive number of seconds. As we call **update** on the particle, the life gets ticked away until it reaches zero, at which time, it is considered inactive. The **update:** function also adds the velocity to the position to move the particle along its path:

```
//Particle.mm
@implementation Particle

+ (id) particleWithModel:(Model*)model {
    Particle *retval = [[Particle alloc] init];
    retval.model = model;
    return [retval autorelease];
}

- (id) init {
    [super init];
    [self resetLife:0.0f velocitiy:PVRTVec3(0, 0, 0) framespeed:0];
    self.scale = 0.025f;
    return self;
}
```

```
- (void) resetLife:(float)life
         velocitiy:(PVRTVec3)vel
        framespeed:(float)framespeed
{
    frame = 0;
    _life = life;
    _vel = vel;
    _framespeed = framespeed;
}

- (void) update:(float)time {
    if(!_life) return;
    _life -= time;
    if(_life <= 0.0f){
        _life = 0.0f;
        return;
    }

    frame += _framespeed*time;
    if(frame > model.numFrames){
        frame -= model.numFrames;
    }

    translate += _vel * time;
}

- (bool) alive {
    return _life != 0.0f;
}

- (void) draw {
    if ([self alive])
        [super draw];
}

@end
```

Only active particles will be rendered and updated.

Now we need to keep track of the particles in the RingsState class. We could keep a dynamically sized list of particles, adding and removing them as they are needed. In practice, however, many particles come into use very rapidly and just as quickly go away; it would be inefficient to allocate and deallocate each particle over and over.

Fortunately, the concept of a memory pool is well suited to situations such as this. By preallocating a sufficient number of particles and reusing inactive ones, we can make it so that particles can go in and out of use without thrashing our heap memory. The downside to this is that we will have a maximum number of particles that can be used at any one time.

But because the particle system is used merely for graphical effect, our game will not be adversely affected if we fail to add a particle to the screen. Meanwhile, all we have to do is to wait and one of the previous particles will finish its life span, making room for a new particle in the memory pool.

We implement the memory pool by adding an array of particles to the RingsState class. We will also need to keep track of the models used by our particles; we want one model for the engine exhaust particles and one for the ring explosion particles:

```
//RingsState.h
#define RING_COUNT 11
#define MAX_PARTICLES 100

@interface RingsState : GLESGameState3D <UIAccelerometerDelegate> {
    UIAccelerationValue         accel[3];
    Sprite3D *ship;
    Ring *rings[RING_COUNT];
    Particle *particle[MAX_PARTICLES];
    Model *engine_particle, *ring_particle;
    Camera *camera;
    Sprite3D *skybox;

// code snipped

}
```

We want to preallocate all of the particles in the setupWorld: function. If you are using the example code, *star.pod* and *flare.pod* have already been added to the project. These models don't have any textures on them and will be rendered as semitransparent and double-sided:

```
//RingsState.mm
- (void) setupWorld {

//code snipped

    ring_particle = [[Model modelFromFile:@"star.pod"] retain];
    engine_particle = [[Model modelFromFile:@"flare.pod"] retain];
    for(int i=0;i<MAX_PARTICLES;i++){
        particle[i] = [[Particle particleWithModel:ring_particle] retain];
        [particle[i] resetLife:0 velocitiy:PVRTVec3(0, 0, 0) framespeed:0];
    }
}
```

Don't forget to release the particles and models:

```
-(void) dealloc {
    [ship release];
    [camera release];
    for(int i=0;i<RING_COUNT;i++)
        [rings[i] release];
    for(int i=0;i<MAX_PARTICLES;i++)
        [particle[i] release];
    [engine_particle release];
    [ring_particle release];
    [skybox release];
```

```
    [super dealloc];
}
```

In the Update: function, we will add code to iterate the memory pool and update active particles:

```
- (void) Update {
    float time = 0.033f;
    for(int i=0;i<MAX_PARTICLES;i++){
        [particle[i] update:time];
    }

// code snipped

}
```

Note that we are assuming a frame rate of 30 fps (or 0.033 seconds per frame).

We will also need to render the particles:

```
- (void) Render {
// code snipped
    [ship draw];

    //draw our particles as semitransparent orange.
    glColor4f(1.0f, 0.6f, 0.0f, 0.5f);
    //the particles have simple geometry, and are made
    //to see both sides of polygons, so disable culling
    glDisable(GL_CULL_FACE);
    glBlendFunc(GL_SRC_ALPHA, GL_ONE); //shiny blend
    glEnable(GL_BLEND);
    for(int i=0;i<MAX_PARTICLES;i++){
        [particle[i] draw];
    }
    glDisable(GL_BLEND);
    glEnable(GL_CULL_FACE);
    //reset global color
    glColor4f(1.0f, 1.0f, 1.0f, 1.0f);

// code snipped
```

Before rendering, the first thing we need to do is set the color to a semitransparent orange, since the particles do not have any texture applied to them. Next, we disable face culling so that we can see both sides of the particles. We also set up the blending mode to enable transparency, and we choose a blend function that will give the particle a saturated look. After rendering the particles, we reset the blending, culling, and color to their previous values.

Now we can start adding engine exhaust particles. We want the particles to be created randomly behind each engine and move directly away from the path of the ship at the time they are created. To help us calculate this, we will create a function that generates engine particles:

```
- (void) engineParticleAt:(PVRTVec3) position
            inDirection:(PVRTVec3) axis
            withSpeed:(float) speed
{
    for(int i=0;i<MAX_PARTICLES;i++){ //search the memory pool
        if(![particle[i] alive]){    //find an inactive particle to reuse

            float life = 0.25f;
            [particle[i] resetLife:life
                          velocitiy:axis*(-speed)
                          framespeed:100.0f/life];
```

The first thing our function does is search the memory pool for an inactive particle. If all of the particles in the memory pool are active, we simply fail to create a particle and move on as though nothing happened.

Assuming an inactive particle was found, we reinitialize the particle, giving it life once more. We calculate the velocity to be the forward axis of the engine multiplied by the inverse speed (because we want the particle to go in the opposite direction of the engine). Note that for this to work properly the axis vector needs to be normalized before it gets sent into this function. Otherwise, the particle's speed may be greater than or less than the speed parameter here:

```
            particle[i].position = position+axis*5;
            [particle[i] forwardX:axis.x Y:axis.y Z:axis.z];
            particle[i].model = engine_particle;
            particle[i].scale = 1.0f;
            break;

        }
    }
}
```

We also initialize the position to the location of the engine plus five units in the ship's direction. This is so that the particle "comes into existence" inside the ship and can be seen emerging from the engine. If we simply used the position given to us, the particles would be created outside the ship and the player would notice them "popping" into the world.

Next, we set the orientation of the particle; technically, this does not need to be done for particles that are symmetric. Since we are sharing a memory pool of particles for both engine exhaust and ring explosion particles, we must be sure to reinitialize the model and scale of the particle.

Now, all we need to do is call this method from the Update: function:

```
- (void) Update {
    float time = 0.033f;
    for(int i=0;i<MAX_PARTICLES;i++){
        [particle[i] update:time];
    }

// code snipped
```

```
//generate engine particles
if(speed > 0.0f ) {

    PVRTVec3 engine;

    if((random() % 100) / 100.0f < speed_knob){
        //figure out where the right engine is.
        engine = [ship getAxis:PVRTVec3(5.0f, 0.2f, 3.0f)];
        engine = engine*ship.scale;
        [self engineParticleAt:engine+ship.position
                inDirection:-movement_axis
                withSpeed:speed];
    }

    if((random() % 100) / 100.0f < speed_knob){
        //figure out where the left engine is.
        engine = [ship getAxis:PVRTVec3(-5.0f, 0.2f, 3.0f)];
        engine = engine*ship.scale;
        [self engineParticleAt:engine+ship.position
                inDirection:-movement_axis
                withSpeed:speed];
    }
}

// code snipped

}
```

We want the particles generated to be slightly randomized, and we want more particles to be generated when the thrust is set higher. Therefore, we generate a random percent value and create a new particle only if that value is greater than the current thrust value. If the engine thrust is set to full, the engine has a 100% chance of creating a particle.

Next, we figure out where the ship's engine is located in world coordinates by taking the local offset of the engine from the ship's origin, multiplying it by the ship's current orientation, and adding the ship's position. We also multiply this by the ship's scale (if we scale the ship up or down, we want to be sure the particles will still be drawn at the appropriate location on a bigger or smaller ship).

Finally, we call the engineParticleAt: function to generate the particles. We perform these steps for both engines and voilà—engine exhaust à la mode (see Figure 5-8).

The other use for our particle system is to generate explosion particles when the ship passes through a ring. As with the engine particles, we will create a function specifically for generating ring explosion particles:

```
- (void) ringParticleAt:(PVRTVec3) position inDirection:(PVRTVec3)axis {
    for(int i=0;i<MAX_PARTICLES;i++){
        if(![particle[i] alive]){
            [particle[i] resetLife:1+(random() % 100)/100.0f
                    velocitiy:axis*(200+(random() % 100)-50)
                    framespeed:100+(random()%60)-30];
            particle[i].position = position;
```

```
            particle[i].model = ring_particle;
            [particle[i] setScale:(random() % 100) / 100.0f * 0.25f];
            break;
        }
    }
}
```

Figure 5-8. Engine particles

As we did with the `engineParticleAt:` function, we start by searching the memory pool for an inactive particle to reuse. Unlike the engine particles, we want ring explosion particles to have random life, velocity, animation, and scale values.

We will call this function when the ship passes through a ring; to detect this, we need to call the `update:` function we created before in our `Ring` class. This is done in `RingsState`'s `Update:` function:

```
- (void) Update {

// code snipped

    for(int i=0;i<RING_COUNT;i++){
        if ( rings[i].active && [rings[i] update:time collideWith:ship]){
            //player passed through an active ring
            // so generate explosion particles
            for(int j=0;j<20;j++){
                PVRTVec3 randvec((random()%100)/99.0f-0.5f,
                        (random()%100)/99.0f-0.5f,
                        (random()%100)/99.0f-0.5f);
```

```
            //beware of divide by zero
            if(randVec.x == randVec.y == randVec.z == 0.0f )
                randVec.x = 1.0f;

            randVec.normalize();

            randVec = randVec.cross(rings[i].normal);

            [self ringParticleAt:rings[i].position
                inDirection: randVec + movement_axis];
        }

        //TODO: if this was the last ring, perform game logic

    }
  }
}
```

Each game loop, we will check all of the active rings for collision with the ship. If a collision is detected, we'll generate 20 explosion particles.

For each particle, we generate a random direction vector; we want to normalize the vector, but it is possible that a vector of zero length was created, which could cause a divide by zero (a crash!) if we tried to normalize() it. Therefore, we'll check for the special case and handle it by setting an arbitrary axis (in this case, x) to a nonzero value.

Next, we take the cross product of the random vector and the ring normal; as you know, the cross product generates a vector that is perpendicular to the two input vectors. Since one of the vectors is the ring's normal vector, we know the result will be perpendicular to the ring's normal: it will be somewhere on the ring's local x-y plane at a distance of one unit from the center.

Finally, we initialize the particle at the ring's center position, with a direction pointing away from the center of the ring. Because the ship is passing through the ring and the camera is attached to the ship, the particles generated will quickly fall behind the camera and we won't see most of the debris. Therefore, we also add the forward movement vector of the ship to the particles' direction to keep them in the visible camera area for a little while longer.

Figure 5-9 shows the particles exploding from a ring that was just passed. The ring is not visible (because it is behind the camera) but the particles are.

Logic

By now, we have a fairly intricate game world. The player can fly around and through the course of rings we have set up. All that's left is to keep track of the time it takes to pierce all of the hoops, and switch to an end game state when the player has done so.

We will also record a list of best times. If the player's new time is faster than one of the best times, we insert it into the list, which will be available from the Main menu.

First, we will add floats to keep track of the start and total course times and an integer to indicate how highly ranked the new best time is to the RingsState class:

```
//RingsState.h
@interface RingsState : GLESGameState3D <UIAccelerometerDelegate> {

// code snipped

    double startTime, courseTime;
    int newbest;
}
```

Figure 5-9. Ring particles

As usual, the next step is always to initialize the variables in the setupWorld: function:

```
//RingsState.mm
- (void) setupWorld {

// code snipped

    startTime = [[NSDate date] timeIntervalSince1970];
    courseTime = 0.0f;
    newbest = -1;
}
```

As you can see, we have already started the timer. Now we must be vigilant and wait for the player to complete the course. We left a TODO comment in the Update: function when we implemented the ring explosion particles—we will fill this in now:

```
- (void) Update {

// code snipped
```

```
                 for(int i=0;i<RING_COUNT;i++){
                     if ( rings[i].active && [rings[i] update:time collideWith:ship]){
                         //player passed through an active ring
                         // so generate explosion particles
                         for(int j=0;j<20;j++){

// code snipped

                         }
                         //if this was the last ring, perform game logic
                         bool finished = true;
                         for(int k=0;k<RING_COUNT;k++){
                             if(rings[k].active){
                                 finished = false;
                                 break;
                             }
                         }
                         if(finished){
                             [self onWin];
                         }

                     }
                 }
             }
```

We check all of the rings to see whether any of them are active; if there is even one active ring, we are not yet finished. If the test was passed, we call onWin to handle calculating the course time and to check it against the best times list.

Note that onWin is just like the function we set up in the preceding chapter. We will be implementing the accompanying renderEndGame:, updateEndGame:, and touchEndgame functions as well. But first, the onWin function:

```
- (void) onWin{
    if(endgame_state == 0){
        courseTime = [[NSDate date] timeIntervalSince1970]-startTime;
        newbest = [RingsState insertBestTime:endTime];
        endgame_state = WINNING;
    }
}
```

The course time is calculated by subtracting the current time from the start. We then attempt to determine whether this is a new record with insertBestTime: (which we have not yet implemented); regardless of whether the time is a new best, we enter the WINNING end game state because the level was completed.

Best Times

Our best times will be stored using the ResourceManager storeData: function, just like the accelerometer calibration data. We want to be able to read the list of times in the HighScores state; we also need to be able to compare new values against the list, and possibly insert them, in `RingsState`. Finally, we also want to be able to reset the list to default values to provide a reset option in the `HighScores` (technically we should have named this `BestTimes`) state.

To provide functionality to both classes, we will write these as publicly accessible class methods in the `RingsState` class:

```
//RingsState.h
// code snipped

//maximum number of time entries we want to save
#define MAX_TIMES 10

// code snipped

@interface RingsState : GLESGameState3D <UIAccelerometerDelegate> {

// code snipped

}

+ (NSArray*) bestTimes;
+ (int) insertBestTime:(double) time;
+ (void) defaultBestTimes;

@end
```

First, some default best times, for the player to try to beat:

```
//RingsState.mm
//setup some default best times.
+ (void) defaultBestTimes {
    NSArray *times = [NSArray arrayWithObjects:
        [NSNumber numberWithDouble:40.0],
        [NSNumber numberWithDouble:50.0],
        [NSNumber numberWithDouble:60.0],
        [NSNumber numberWithDouble:70.0],
        nil];
    [g_ResManager storeUserData:times toFile:@"bestTimes"];
}
```

The `defaultBestTimes` method demonstrates how our saved data will be formatted: we are saving a sorted array of `NSNumber`s, each with a double value, to the file *bestTimes*. The best times will be at the front of the array.

The times were chosen from trial and error by playing the game itself: 70 seconds should be rather easy to beat, possibly the first time someone picks up the game. The 40-second time should be achievable after the player gets more comfortable with the controls and layout of the level.

Next, we need to load the best times:

```
//grab the stored best times, and initialize to defaults if needed
//returns an NSArray of NSNumber doubles with sorted best times.
+ (NSArray*) bestTimes {
```

```
        id retval = [g_ResManager getUserData:@"bestTimes"];
        if(retval == nil){
            //no data stored, so setup defaults and try again.
            [RingsState defaultBestTimes];
            return [RingsState bestTimes];
        }
        return retval;
    }
```

Loading is pretty straightforward: we simply grab the stored array. If the load fails, such as when the game is first started and no best times exist, we simply call `defaultBest Times` to set up the data and try loading again.

Now, we can update the best times when the player finishes the level:

```
//returns the slot where time has been inserted into the best times list,
//or -1 if the time didn't make it onto the list.
+ (int) insertBestTime:(double) time {
    NSMutableArray* times = [NSMutableArray
                arrayWithArray: [RingsState bestTimes]];
    NSNumber* timeNumber = [NSNumber numberWithDouble:time];
    //drop the time into the list, and then sort it
    [times addObject:timeNumber];
    [times sortUsingSelector: @selector(compare:)];

    //if we now have too many items in the list, we need to bump off the
    //times from the bottom
    if([times count] > MAX_TIMES){
        NSRange range = NSMakeRange(MAX_TIMES, [times count] - MAX_TIMES);
        [times removeObjectsInRange: range];
    }

    //find out where we inserted the number.
    NSUInteger index = [times indexOfObject: timeNumber];

    //if the number isn't in there, it must not have been good
    //enough, so return -1
    int retval = (NSNotFound == index) ? -1 : index;

    //dump the table back to persistent storage
    [g_ResManager storeUserData:times toFile:@"bestTimes"];
    return retval;
}
```

The first thing we do here is make a mutable copy of the best times array so that we can add or remove times from it. We then add the new time to the end of the list, and re-sort it. After adding the time, we need to make sure we're not trying to save too many best times, so we trim the end of the list to get under the MAX_TIMES limit. Next, we find out where we inserted the time, so we can return it and eventually display it to the user. Finally, we save the times back to persistent storage, and return the spot, if any, at which the new time was inserted.

End Game

Now that we can determine when the player finishes a level, the time he took during the level, and how that time fits in against existing best times, we can make a nice display when the level is finished. We want to display a "level complete" message like we did in the 2D game, and additionally display the player's Best Time rank. The end game methods will look a lot like they did in the 2D game:

```
//RingsState.h
@interface RingsState : GLESGameState3D <UIAccelerometerDelegate> {

// code snipped

}

- (void) renderEndgame;
- (void) updateEndgame:(float)time;
- (void) touchEndgame;

@end
```

Since the end game graphics are in 2D, we want to call renderEndgame near our other 2D code used for the throttle graphics:

```
//RingsState.mm
- (void) Render {
// code snipped
    //draw the slider knob at the proper position
    [[g_ResManager getTexture:@"knob.png"]
        drawAtPoint:CGPointMake(xmin+speed_knob*slide_groove, ycenter)
        withRotation:90 withScale:1];
    [self renderEndgame];
    //end drawing 2d stuff
```

We need to link in touches, so the player can continue back to the Main menu:

```
-(void)touchesBegan:(NSSet*)touches withEvent:(UIEvent*)event
{
    [self touchSpeedKnob:[touches anyObject]];
    [self touchEndgame];
}
```

And also update, for animation:

```
- (void) Update {
// code snipped
    [self updateEndgame:time];
}
```

The renderEndgame function has a bit more complexity than the one used in the 2D example. In addition to the Level Complete and Tap to Continue messages, we want to display the player's rank in the Best Times screen. We also have to rotate the messages so that they display in landscape mode:

```
- (void) renderEndgame{
    if(endgame_state != 0){
        //xoff is used to lay items out in a vertical flow, from top of screen:
        int xoff = self.frame.size.width-32;
        //center items in middle of screen:
        int yoff = self.frame.size.height/2;
        if(endgame_state == WINNING) {
            [[g_ResManager getTexture:@"levelcomplete.png"]
            drawAtPoint:CGPointMake(xoff, yoff)
            withRotation:min(endgame_complete_time, 0.25f)*4*2*180 -90
            withScale:min(endgame_complete_time, 0.25f)*4];
        }
        if(newbest != -1){
            //special message for when player gets a new best time
            xoff -= 64;
            if(endgame_complete_time > 1.0f){
                //draw "new best time" prompt
                [[g_ResManager getTexture:@"newbest.png"]
                drawAtPoint:CGPointMake(xoff, yoff)
                withRotation:-90 //landscape mode
                withScale:1
                ];
                xoff -= 64;
                //draw which rank they got
                glPushMatrix();
                    //font class can't rotate by itself, unfortunately
                    glRotatef(90, 0, 0, -1);
                    [[g_ResManager defaultFont]
                    drawString:[NSString
                        stringWithFormat:@"Rank %d", newbest+1]
                    atPoint:CGPointMake(-yoff, xoff)
                    withAnchor:GRAPHICS_HCENTER | GRAPHICS_VCENTER];
                glPopMatrix();
            }
        }
        xoff -= 64;
        //draw tap to continue prompt after 2 seconds
        if(endgame_complete_time > 2.0f){
            [[g_ResManager getTexture:@"taptocontinue.png"]
            drawAtPoint:CGPointMake(xoff, yoff)
            withRotation:-90
            withScale:1
            ];
        }
    }
}
```

The updateEndgame function is the same as in the 2D version; we just need to update the time to make animation sequences work:

```
- (void) updateEndgame:(float) time{
    if(endgame_state != 0){
        endgame_complete_time += time;
    }
}
```

The touchEndgame function is mostly the same, except that we need to release the accelerometer before switching back to the Main menu:

```
- (void) touchEndgame{
    if(endgame_complete_time > 2.0f){
        //will crash if you don't reset the accelerometer delegate before
        //freeing this game state.
        [[UIAccelerometer sharedAccelerometer] setDelegate:nil];
        [m_pManager doStateChange:[gsMainMenu class]];
    }
}
```

Conclusion

We have only scratched the surface of 3D game programming, but you now know more than enough to begin your own project. Modify the current engine to add lighting, meshes with bone animation, or fire projectiles, or create a new engine.

As long as you keep in mind the special considerations of the iPhone input, there is a lot of room to do things that have never been done on a mobile platform. Now is the time to show the world what you can do.

CHAPTER 6

Considerations for Game Design

In the preceding five chapters, we covered the basics of 2D and 3D game programming for the iPhone. But we have only scratched the surface and you've nearly reached the end of the book. You may be asking yourself, "What is the next step?"

Depending on your interests, there are many possibilities. You could modify the current engine to fit your own needs, or you could create a new one. Every game design poses a unique problem; your game code is the solution. Different types of game engines represent different methods of solving those problems.

A first-person shooter (FPS) type game requires 3D graphics that respond quickly to user input along with accurate rendering and physics detection. A real-time strategy (RTS) game, however, focuses more on being able to render many entities with lower detail, and it requires a user interface that can organize and manage many actions at once.

It follows, then, that a game engine created to handle FPS games is not well suited to RTS games. Learning how to solve the unique problems of your game design with efficient trade-offs is what game programming is all about.

Resource Management

Our example games were very simple in their use of resources. However, more complicated games will have more art and sound assets that can be loaded into the device's memory at one time.

A good resource manager will always be able to find space in memory for the required resources by unloading resources that are less important. But knowing what is and isn't important can be hard to determine from the engine's perspective, since the value of resources in memory changes when the game states change. When you're in the Main menu screen, you want the menu images and a background sound; but when you're playing the game, none of those has value...unless you're about to switch back out to the menu again!

We can give the resource manager a hint about what resources will be used in each state by listing the required resources, preloading them at each state transition, and unloading any resources that aren't needed. However, this becomes tedious (especially during development when assets are constantly being added or removed). Furthermore, this also causes us to unload and reload assets when switching back and forth between two states with different resource needs.

A smarter resource manager will cache resources, unloading assets only when there isn't enough memory. By keeping a timestamp on each resource in memory, the resource manager can search through its list and unload the Least Recently Used (LRU) resource.

Statistically, this will ensure that resources that are frequently called on will stay in memory even across state changes, instead of wasting time loading and unloading them repeatedly.

User Input Design

The biggest challenge to creating compelling iPhone games is implementing a good user input design.

As we discussed before, the conflict between using the screen as input versus output is the driving problem, but you also have to deal with the inaccuracy of touch input and the conflict between a comfortable holding angle and using the accelerometer for input.

A good game design will consider these factors when deciding exactly what the goal of game play is and how the user must interact with the device to accomplish that goal.

For instance, although an FPS game on the PC may use the pinpoint accuracy of the mouse and keyboard to its advantage, porting to the iPhone would require a change in design. Rather than expecting accurate aiming from the player, it should focus more on rewarding the player for being in the right place at the right time—perhaps by automatically correcting the player's aim within the current view angle.

EA's SimCity for the iPhone is an excellent example of adapting a complicated user input design to the iPhone. The original game requires a keyboard and mouse, expecting pinpoint selection of squares on a grid, as well as click-dragging for multiple selections. There is also a heads-up display (HUD) with a slew of buttons for various macro-management features.

In the SimCity port to the iPhone, the designers increased the size of all HUD elements so they are touchable. They simplified submenus and split them into multiple pages to account for the new larger buttons. With the understanding that the player's interaction with the touch screen can sometimes be inaccurate, they split click and drag operations into multiple steps with confirmation screens to make sure the player intended the exact input that was given.

Due to the specific challenges of input on the iPhone, games should try to simplify the interaction with the player and limit the penalty for erroneous input.

Networking

One of the most exciting aspects of the iPhone as a mobile platform is the ability to network from anywhere. Most people think of networked games as real-time multiplayer, but they can also take the form of a turn-based multiplayer, interactive community (think leader boards and achievements), or downloadable content.

Those familiar with network programming will be interested to know that both UDP/IP and TCP/IP are available. In addition, the 3.0 SDK, which Apple released in June 2009, now has the ability to use Bluetooth to automatically discover and network with other iPhone users in the area. See the Game Kit Programming Guide on the Apple developer website for more information.

Apple has also added an API to allow publishers to use the App Store to charge players for downloadable content natively within the game, thereby increasing the life span of your game and the value you can provide to customers.

Third-Party Code

By now, it should be painfully apparent how much hard work and expertise go into making even small games. It's almost overwhelming, but fear not! You don't have to reinvent the wheel; no matter what type of game you are creating, reusable bodies of code are available that can supplement many parts of your game engine. They come in the form of libraries, middleware, and even fully fledged open source games.

Libraries

The iPhone SDK makes available many low-level Apple APIs (such as Core Graphics and Core Audio) and mid-level APIs (such as `NSUserDefaults`, `NSImage`, `NSSound`, and `NSNetService`). But you are not limited to these alone; many other libraries are available, and some even come with the SDK (such as OpenGL and OpenAL).

Libraries exist to help you with sound, networking, and many other tasks that you might find too low level.

Perhaps you want to store and organize large amounts of data; SQLite provides database functionality on the iPhone. Most likely you don't want to write volumes of linear algebra code for your 3D physics; that's OK—Newton, Open Dynamics Engine, and Bullet have beat you to the punch. For a really cool 2D rigid body physics library, you should check out Box2D.

The iPhone is a relatively new platform and new libraries are still being made available. Fortunately, the iPhone shares a lot of code with the OS X platform, so many libraries that work for the Mac can be used for the iPhone with a little tweaking.

Middleware

If your goal is simply to make a game in the easiest way possible, gluing together a game engine of your own from scratch (even with the help of libraries) might not be the right choice for you. Fortunately, a number of middleware solutions are available for the iPhone.

Think of middleware as a game engine (with all of the graphics, audio, and input components you would expect), but without a game sitting on top of it. All you have to do is write your game logic and add the art resources: middleware gives you a huge jump-start toward a finalized game.

Packages vary in quality and price, from hobbyist and research projects to open source projects such as cocos2D and the Oolong Game Engine (which are both freely available) to proven cross-platform commercial products such as Torque 3D and the Unity engine.

Our favorite open source middleware project, IrrLicht, has been ported by the community, can boast of several successfully published iPhone apps, and will soon have a fully supported release.

Open Source Games

Another direction to consider is to modify an existing game. Just as there are open source libraries and middleware, there are open source games.

Some of the games built off the open source middleware engines listed earlier are also open source. In addition, others have also released their game code to the public.

Tris is a *Tetris* clone that was originally released on the App Store, but was later removed by request of The Tetris Company.

id Software (maker of *Doom*, *Quake*, and many other FPS games) has a policy of releasing its code under the GNU Public License (GPL) once some time has passed and a game has become unprofitable.

For example, a fan of the game Quake3 ported its open source PC project to the iPhone. Because the source is GPL'd, the results also must be under the GPL and are therefore freely available to the public.

In fact, John Carmack (the head graphics programming guru of id Software) is involved in iPhone development. The company recently released *Wolfenstein 3D*, and Carmack ported an open source project named Wolf3D Redux on SourceForge, itself based on the open source version of *Wolfenstein 3D* originally released by id Software. Naturally, Wolfenstein 3D for the iPhone was also released to the public.

Even if you don't intend to modify and rerelease an open source game, simply browsing through the source can provide unique insight into the ways others have solved the problems of game development.

App Store

Once you have completed your game, you will want to make it available on the App Store for others to play. The web interface Apple has set up for this (*http://itunesconnect .apple.com*) is very easy to use, but you will have to prepare a few things first.

You will be creating either a Paid Application Contract or a Free Application Contract with Apple (depending on whether you are charging for your app or releasing it for free). If your app is not free, you will need to provide Apple with financial information such as a bank account number and tax ID (such as an Employee Identification Number for a company or a Social Security number for an individual), as well as fill out all contact information fields on the form.

Regardless of whether you plan to charge for your application, you need to provide:

- One or more screenshots of your game.
- An application description that will show up on the App Store page for your game.
- A product web page containing your screenshot(s), your application description, an icon, and a link to the game in the App Store when it has been made available.
- A support web page and email address. The support web page may be a forum or a contact form.
- A 512 × 512 version of the application icon, which should match the app icon's appearance. It will be shown in the App Store page for your game.

Once you have submitted your game for approval, it might not pass on the first try. For instance, if your game connects to the Internet but does not handle a loss of service, it will be rejected. At that point, you may create a new build of your application that fixes this problem, and resubmit it.

Once your game has been approved, it will be available on the App Store! However, this initially covers only the U.S. market. To support markets worldwide, you will need to create additional application contracts as necessary. For instance, the Japanese market entails a large amount of additional tax requirements and information, and it may take a larger portion of your earnings compared to most countries.

As time marches on, you may wish to update your application with new features or bug fixes (some applications broke when the iPhone SDK 3.0 was released and it was forced to release updated builds to work again). You can do this easily on the same Apple website you used to submit the application.

Conclusion

We hope that this book has given you the desire, knowledge, and inspiration to begin creating your first iPhone game.

The iPhone represents a world of opportunity for creativity and innovation. Now that world is open to you: go for it!

References

Throughout this book, we mentioned useful documentation, libraries, and software products that you might want to check out during your game development work—this appendix lists those resources.

Code Reference

Game Kit Programming Guide: *http://developer.apple.com/iphone/library/documenta tion/NetworkingInternet/Conceptual/GameKit_Guide/Introduction/Introduction.html*

Physics Libraries

SQLite (SQL database): *http://www.sqlite.org/*

Bullet (3D physics): *http://www.bulletphysics.com/*

Open Dynamics Engine (3D physics): *http://www.ode.org/*

Newton (3D physics): *http://newtondynamics.com/*

Box2D (2D physics): *http://www.box2d.org/*

Middleware

Cocos2D: *http://code.google.com/p/cocos2d-iphone/*

Oolong: *http://oolongengine.com/*

Torque 3D: *http://www.garagegames.com/products/torque-3D*

Unity: *http://unity3d.com/*

IrrLicht Engine: *http://irrlicht.sourceforge.net*

Open Source Games

Tris (Tetris clone): *http://code.google.com/p/tris/*

Wolfenstein 3D (by John Carmack)—*ftp://ftp.idsoftware.com/idstuff/wolf3d/wolf3d _iphone_v1.0_src.zip*

iPhone *Quake 3 Arena* (port of the PC original): *http://code.google.com/p/quake3 -iphone/*

Index

Symbols
: (colon), 31
; (semicolon), 27

A
AAC format, 57
accelerometer
    player input and, 190, 197
    3D game design, 186
accessor functions, 32
afconvert tool, 78
AI (artificial intelligence) agents, 38, 63
Alpha value (pixels)
    defined, 43
    texture blending, 44
ambient sound, 57
animation
    animation controllers, 48
    culling, 49
    level-of-detail technique, 50
    particle systems, 48
    resource management, 50
    skeletal, 48
    texture files, 49
    texture sorting, 49
    3D games, 46, 47
    2D games, 46, 110–121
Animation class
    animation sequences, 113–119
    drawAtPoint function, 121
    functionality, 111
    Level 2 implementation, 150
    property list, 111–113
animation controllers, 48

animation sequences, 113–119, 157
AnimationSequence class
    functionality, 113–119, 121
    Level 2 implementation, 146
App ID (Application Identifier), 23
App Store, 227, 229
AppDelegate class
    calculating fps, 75
    creating, 71
    inheritance, 73
    overview, 73–76
Apple developer accounts
    paid version, 2
    Program Portal, 22
    registering, 1
Apple Program Portal, 22
application bundles
    defined, 2
    typical iPhone structure, 3
application framework (game engines)
    AppDelegate class, 73–76
    data store, 89–93
    event handling, 76
    game state management, 70–73
    implementing, 71–73
    main loop, 36
    overview, 35
    removing status bar, 73
    render engine, 80–86
    Resource Manager, 78
    skeleton application, 93
    sound engine, 87–89
Application Identifier (App ID), 23
artificial intelligence (AI) agents, 38, 63
audio engine

We'd like to hear your suggestions for improving our indexes. Send email to *index@oreilly.com*.

About the Authors

Paul Zirkle has five years of mobile game programming experience and is currently a lead mobile programmer at Konami Digital Entertainment. He has worked on the porting, rewriting, and full development of more than 40 titles. Occasionally, Paul is called upon to give lectures on game development at the University of Southern California.

Joe Hogue has five years of mobile game programming experience. He worked with Paul at Konami and currently works for Electronic Arts as a mobile programmer. Joe has also worked on the porting, rewriting, and full development of over 40 titles. Joe has written an iPhone game that is currently available on the iTunes AppStore.

Colophon

The animal on the cover of *iPhone Game Development* is a greater roadrunner (*Geococcyx californianus*), a long-legged bird belonging to the cuckoo family. It is the largest North American cuckoo at approximately 22 inches long, and it weighs about 10 ounces. It has a dark head and back, an oversized beak, a long tail, a pale belly, and four toes on each foot.

It is found in the Mojave, Sonoran, and Chihuahuan deserts as well as in other parts of the southwestern U.S. It is well adapted to desert life for a number of reasons, including the fact that it reabsorbs water from its feces before excretion; it is quiet during midday, which is the hottest time in the desert; and it is very fast and can catch prey while it is in mid-air. Although it can fly, it would rather sprint and can run as fast as 20 miles per hour.

The roadrunner's diet primarily consists of insects, small reptiles, rodents, small birds, fruit, and seeds. Its incredible speed enables it to also prey on rattlesnakes. It grabs a coiled rattlesnake by the tail and slams the snake's head against the ground until it dies. The roadrunner then consumes the snake whole, but oftentimes can't eat it all in one sitting, so the bird will go about its day with the remaining snake hanging out of its mouth until what it has previously eaten has digested and it is ready to consume more.

The cover image is by Lorrie LeJeune. The cover font is Adobe ITC Garamond. The text font is Linotype Birka; the heading font is Adobe Myriad Condensed; and the code font is LucasFont's TheSansMonoCondensed.

Get even more for your money.

Join the O'Reilly Community, and register the O'Reilly books you own. It's free, and you'll get:

- $4.99 ebook upgrade offer
- 40% upgrade offer on O'Reilly print books
- Membership discounts on books and events
- Free lifetime updates to ebooks and videos
- Multiple ebook formats, DRM FREE
- Participation in the O'Reilly community
- Newsletters
- Account management
- 100% Satisfaction Guarantee

Signing up is easy:

1. Go to: oreilly.com/go/register
2. Create an O'Reilly login.
3. Provide your address.
4. Register your books.

Note: English-language books only

To order books online:
oreilly.com/store

For questions about products or an order:
orders@oreilly.com

To sign up to get topic-specific email announcements and/or news about upcoming books, conferences, special offers, and new technologies:
elists@oreilly.com

For technical questions about book content:
booktech@oreilly.com

To submit new book proposals to our editors:
proposals@oreilly.com

O'Reilly books are available in multiple DRM-free ebook formats. For more information:
oreilly.com/ebooks

O'REILLY®

Spreading the knowledge of innovators   oreilly.com

Have it your way.

Lightning Source UK Ltd.
Milton Keynes UK
UKHW030625130819
347844UK00009BA/673/P